P9-DZM-691

OUR EARTH

5000 MILLION YEARS AGO 4990 4980 4970 4960 49

← - - - - - - - - - - Formation of the sun (over 5 000 000 000 years ago)

This is a time scale. See page 14 for explanation.

Copyright © 1982 Huck Scarry
Copyright © 1982 Arnoldo Mondadori Editore, S.p.A., Milan
All rights reserved including the right of
reproduction in whole or in part in any form
Published by WANDERER BOOKS, A Division of Simon & Schuster, Inc.
Simon & Schuster Building
1230 Avenue of the Americas, New York, New York 10020

WANDERER and colophon are registered trademarks of Simon & Schuster, Inc.
Also available in Julian Messner Library edition.
Originally published in Italian under the title LA NOSTRA TERRA
Published simultaneously in Great Britain by Hodder & Stoughton
First American Edition 1984

Manufactured in Spain by Artes Graficas, Toledo
10 9 8 7 6 5 4 3 2 1

Library of Congress Cataloging in Publication Data

Scarry, Huck.
Our earth.

Translation of: Nostra terra.
Bibliography: p.
Includes index.
1. Civilization—History—Juvenile literature.
2. Evolution—Juvenile literature. I. Title.
CB94.S2913 1984 909 83-17033
ISBN 0-671-49846-0
0-671-50016-3 (lib bdg.)
D. L. TO: 1312 -1983

This is a distance scale. See page 14 for explanation.

0 KM 10 MILLION KM 20 30 40 5

Sun (1 392 000 km diameter)

4940
4930
4920
4910 MILLION YEARS AGO
4900
HUCK SCARRY
OUR EARTH
I live in the city of Geneva, Switzerland, home of many international organizations like the United Nations and the Red Cross. Geneva is "home" for people of many lands, and from my window, under one of the old city gates, I see the whole world go by!
WANDERER BOOKS
Published by Simon & Schuster, Inc., New York
60
70
80
90 MILLION KM
100
Mercury
(58 000 000 km from the sun)

Preface

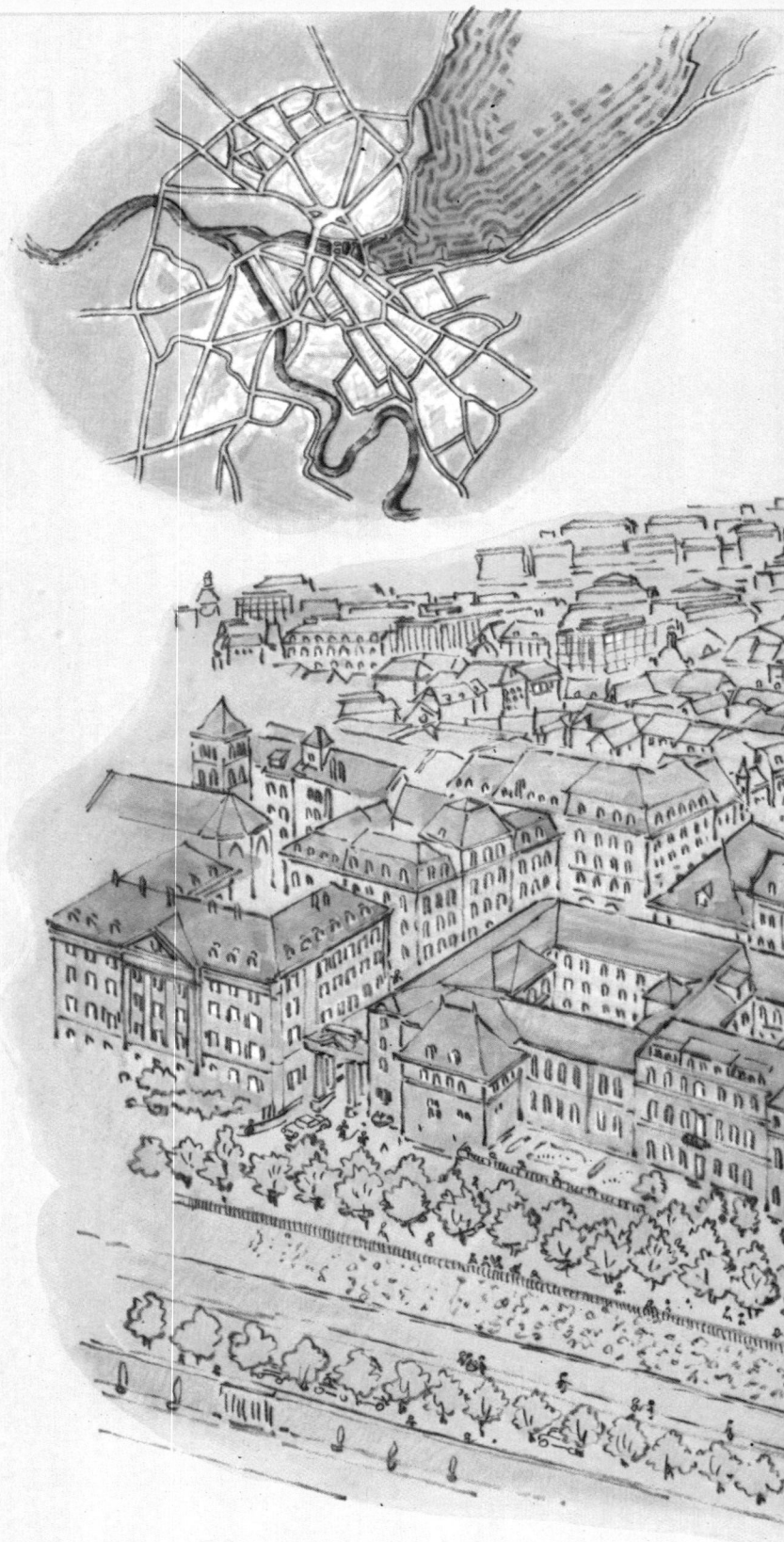

In a way, each one of us is like a star. Each of us is aglow with his own life. We all have a family, and perhaps pets, which are close and dear to us, and who go through life beside us, like planets. Each one of us is the center of his own personal universe.

From my own window I can see on the street below many other "stars." I don't know them by name; they are all distant and unfamiliar to me. Yet each star is important – immensely important to itself, and very dear to its own set of planets; the center of its own universe.

There are over four and a half billion such "stars" living on our planet today, each one a bit different, but essentially all alike. We are all like leaves on the trees, budding and maturing, and when it is time wrinkling up and falling, leaving our place for other young leaves to bud. In living we are all alike, and in living we are like everything else within our earth and without. A living thing. A changing thing.

The soil beneath our feet is living. The air we breathe is living. Even the light from the sun, which is energy, is living, too. The earth, the sun, and all the stars in the universe are living. They were once born, and they will once die, and others will be born to replace them.

This book is a story of life: about the life of the stars and of our own earth, and also about human life as well.

For all of us, in spite of our similarities, are each a bit different from the rest. We come from different parts of the earth, and we have different ways of life, to suit where and how we live. Ultimately, we each have different thoughts.

Too often, we tend to see the world from just our own point of view: from the center of our own personal universe. It is a limited place, compared with the real one we all live

The view I have of the world from my own window seems tiny indeed! My window is one among millions of others in the city. From the air the world looks much different from on the ground. From space, the world looks different still. The whole city is but a dot in the country; the country just a smudge on a continent; the continent . . .

. . . only a patch on the globe!

Geneva, Switzerland

in! I hope that by getting to know about our earth, its place in the vast heavens and our place on its tiny, brittle surface, we can put aside our own personal universe, and understand better the universe of others. It would make it a better place to live . . . in the world around us!

Contents

8 Preface
12 Man's View of the Earth
14 Time Is Distance, Distance Is Time
16 What Is the Universe?
18 Of Atoms and Elements
20 The Life of the Stars
22 The Vital Sun
24 Earth's Neighborhood, the Solar System
the Solar System
26 The Moon
28 Heavenly Clockwork:
the Earth–Moon–Sun System
30 Meet Planet Earth!
32 Forces That Build Up
34 Forces That Break Down
36 Earth's Changing Face
38 Our Planet's Portrait
40 Earth's Protective Overcoat
42 Planet Ocean
44 The Bricks of Life
46 The Family Tree of Life
48 From the Roots of Life . . .
50 . . . To the Uppermost Branches
52 Man the Maker
54 Man the Thinker

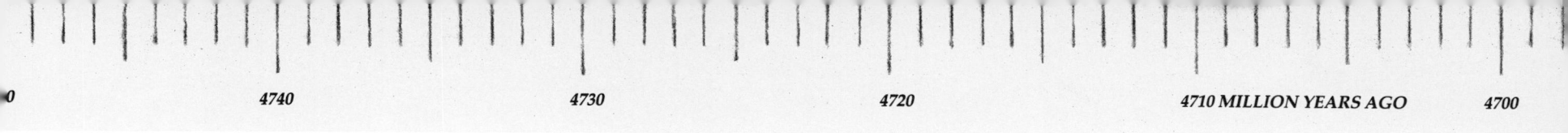

56 Man the Inquirer
58 Man the Speaker
60 From Hunter to Herder
62 Of Herders and Harvesters
64 Something Borrowed, Something New
66 Reading, Writing and 'Rithmetic
68 Enter Civilization!
70 Of Business and Bondage
72 Keeping Time with the Sky
74 Brilliance from Dark Ages
76 Conquest and Exploration
78 Variety and Acceptance
80 Function and Expression
82 Rhythm and Punctuation
84 God and Religion
86 Mores and Culture
88 Power and Administration
90 Fear and Aggression
92 Resources and Conservation
94 From Cotton to Computers
96 Inquiry and Investigation
98 Conclusion
100 Index
103 Bibliography
104 The Last Million Years

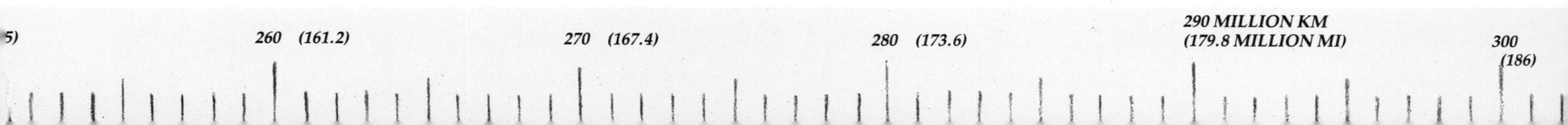

Man's View of the Earth

You have probably seen photos of the earth taken from outer space. From them you can see that the earth is like a sphere, and you can probably name the different continents on it. But these photos are very new, and until only a short time ago no one had ever seen what the earth really looked like.

Fixed with their feet on the ground, people could only see the world immediately around them, and for the rest they relied on information brought to them by others. Although man had never seen the earth from the air, his scientific mind discovered that the earth was round. He was even able to measure its size, and its distance from the sun and other planets.

Ancient Egyptian view of the heavens.

Ancient people believed the earth was flat and the sky was a star-studded dome. Until fairly recently people thought that the earth was the center of the universe and that it didn't move.

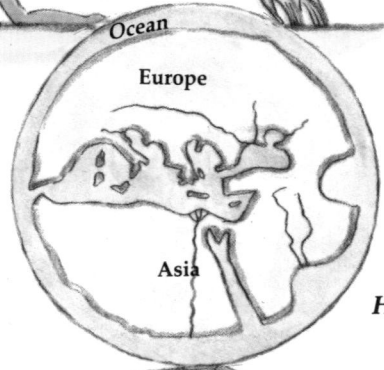

A world map, based on writings of the Greek, Hecataeus, 500 BC

The Ptolemaic System

Planets were placed in epicycles, or orbits within their orbit, to account for periodic reverse movements.

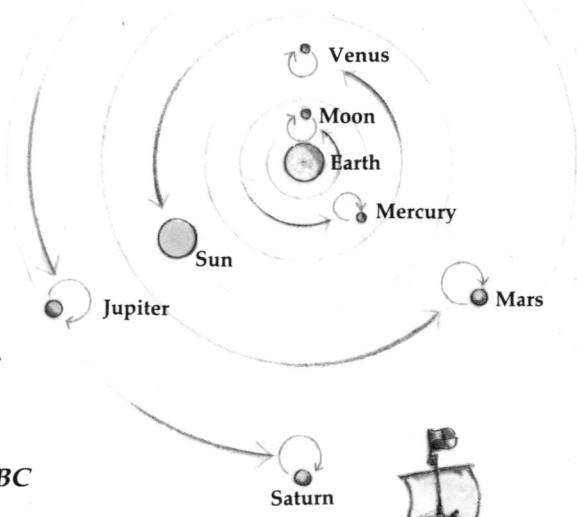

To a famous Greek astronomer named Ptolemy this made sense. It was only logical to assume that the sun and planets moved around the earth, as they appear to do from its surface. Ptolemy did an experiment to prove that the earth didn't move: he showed that an object thrown in the air falls straight back to earth. If the earth had moved, he argued, the object would have landed some distance behind!

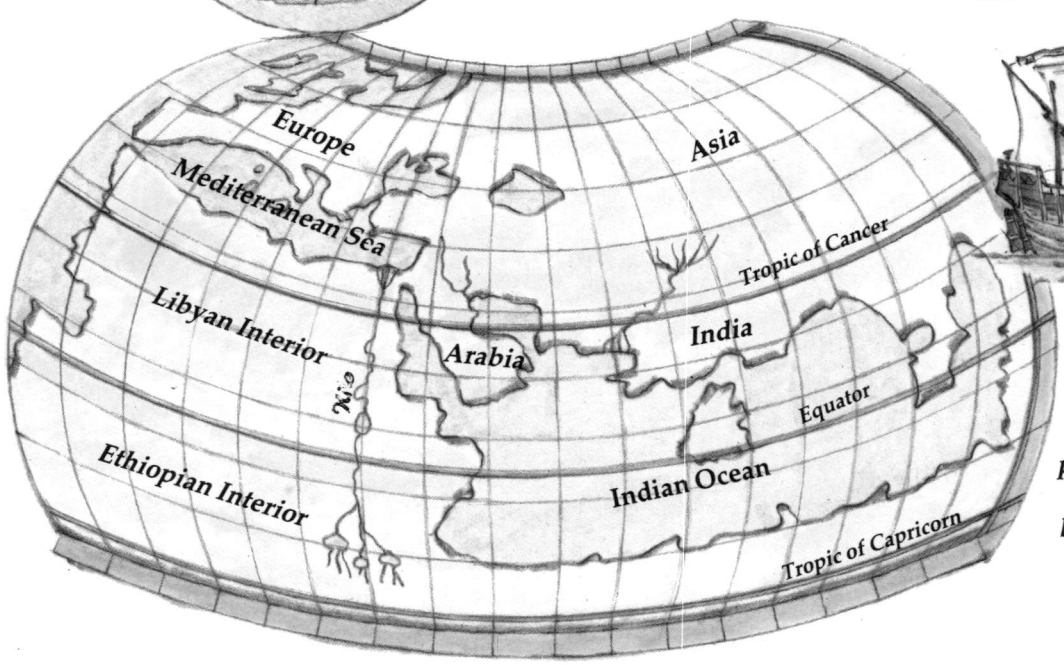

The Santa Maria of Christopher Columbus.

Ptolemaic world map, printed in Ulm, Germany, in 1482, only ten years before Columbus' famous voyage!

With every new discovery, our image of the earth changes, giving a truer picture of the planet we live on. Every advancement in our knowledge of the universe rewards us with an ever smaller and seemingly insignificant place in it.

It seems an unjust reward for our curiosity!

An ancient Greek mathematician called Eratosthenes, who lived in Alexandria, Egypt, came across a bit of information in the Alexandrian Library. The paper mentioned the town of Syene, 500mi (800km) southward, where, on the longest day of the year, the summer solstice, at noon, all shadows disappear. At the bottom of a deep well one could see the sun's reflection, which was directly overhead.

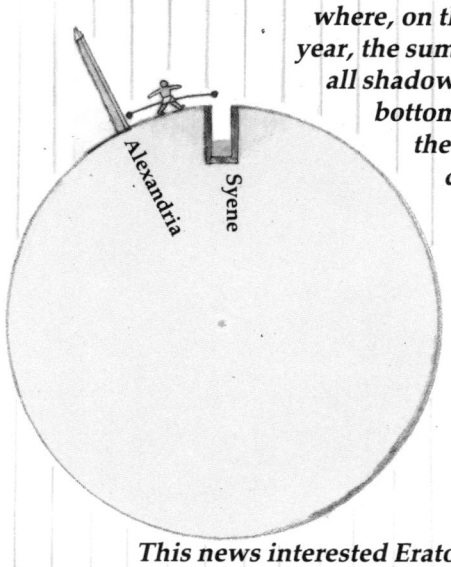

This news interested Eratosthenes, who, at the next summer solstice, made a little experiment.

He erected an upright pole, but noticed, at noon, that there nonetheless was still a shadow. He concluded, since the sun's rays fall parallel to each other, that the earth must be curved . . . even round. Measuring the angle of the shadow, which was one-fiftieth of a circle, he multiplied 50 by the 500mi (800km) separating Alexandria from Syene. He arrived at 24,800mi (40,000km), very nearly the actual circumference of the earth!

The Copernican System

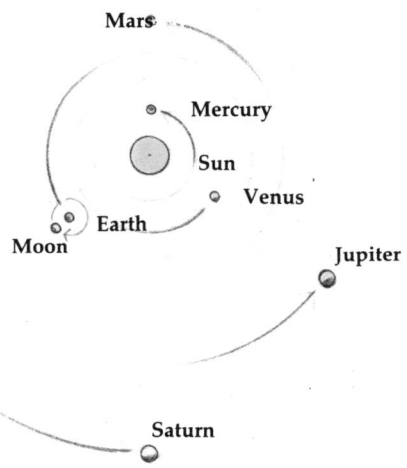

The Church believed that a divinely created world should naturally sit at the center of the universe. However, as men studied the sky more carefully during the Renaissance, the Ptolemaic system showed some shortcomings. Nicholas Copernicus, for one, was disturbed by the fact that the planets appeared to stop and move backwards before resuming their paths across the night sky. Could it not be, he asked, that the earth, too, was moving, modifying our point of view? Copernicus was led to believe, after long hesitation, that this might indeed be true, and he designed a planetary chart of his own. We call it the solar system!

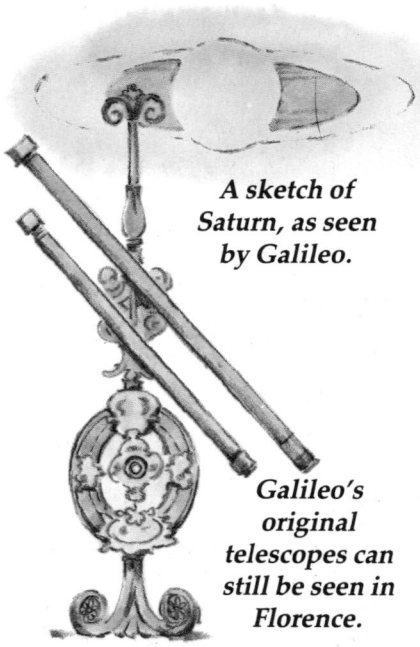

A sketch of Saturn, as seen by Galileo.

Galileo's original telescopes can still be seen in Florence.

Columbus was not the first man to believe that the earth was round. Ancient Greek thinkers had already observed how sailing ships gradually disappeared over the horizon, concluding, in fact, that the earth must be round. The idea was confirmed by Eratosthenes' experiment.

The lifespan of some of the people mentioned on these pages can be seen on pages 96–7.

Time Is Distance, Distance Is Time

We are accustomed to speed limit signs on roads. This one means that drivers must not travel faster than 45. Nature also has speed limits. The ultimate speed is the speed of light. There is nothing that can go faster. That is the law of nature. Light travels at 186,000mi (300,000km) per second! That seems a terrifically fast speed on earth, but it can be extremely slow in the vast distances of outer space.

We measure our lives in bits of time called years. Although a year is always the same length, it can seem quite different to two different people. To a five-year-old boy, a year seems endless – it is, after all, one-fifth of his life. But to a fifty-year-old man, it is only one-fiftieth of his life!

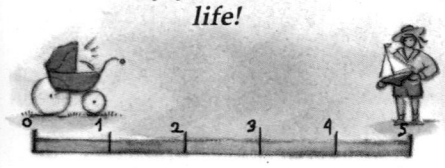

To our old, old earth, a year is very short indeed. If its age were compressed into the life-span of a hundred-year-old man, then a year would only represent six-tenths of a second in all his life!

Before going further into this book, I think it is important to stop for a moment to study the subject of time and distance.

If I asked you "How far is your school from home?" you might not know the answer. You would probably know how long it takes to get there though, and you might answer "Ten minutes away." Although minutes do not measure distance we can picture how far we will have travelled in ten minutes' time. So we *can* measure distance by time.

Speed is measured by combining distance and time. We know, for instance, that we are driving at sixty miles (100km) per hour, if we can travel sixty miles (100km) in the space of one hour. So time is very closely related to distance. We could even say that time *is* distance, and that distance is time!

At the top of this page, and running right through the book, I have drawn a time scale. It is like a giant ruler, measuring not inches, but years. Each notch on the scale represents not one year, nor one hundred, nor a thousand . . . but *one million years*! With this scale you can see just how long it took for living things to appear, and when human life began.

Similarly, at the bottom of the page and all

When we look up at the night sky, we see millions of stars. They are all extremely far from earth – so far that it takes starlight, which travels at 186,000mi (300,000km) per second, millions of years to reach us! The light we see from a star may have left that star well before dinosaurs roamed the earth. When we look into the night sky, we look at the past. The farther away the star we see, the farther back in time we go!

What does that mean? When we see two stars in the night sky, they look as though they are shining at the same time. However, the farther of the two may, in fact, be no longer shining, although its light still reaches us. What we see is only what appears to be! Similarly, to three boys on a football field, a kicked ball travels in different directions to each of the boys. To one, the ball is going away; to another, it is approaching; to the third, it is passing him by! What each boy sees depends on from where he sees it, or his relation to the moving ball.

ONE	1	10^0
TEN	10	10^1
ONE HUNDRED	100	10^2
ONE THOUSAND	1000	10^3
TEN THOUSAND	10 000	10^4
ONE HUNDRED THOUSAND	100 000	10^5
ONE MILLION	1 000 000	10^6
TEN MILLION	10 000 000	10^7
ONE HUNDRED MILLION	100 000 000	10^8
ONE BILLION	1 000 000 000	10^9

This little table may help you get accustomed to the great numbers used throughout this book, which deals with vast distances, both in space and in time! The last column shows the powers of 10. ($10^2=10\times10=100$; $10^3=10\times10\times10=1000$; and so on.)

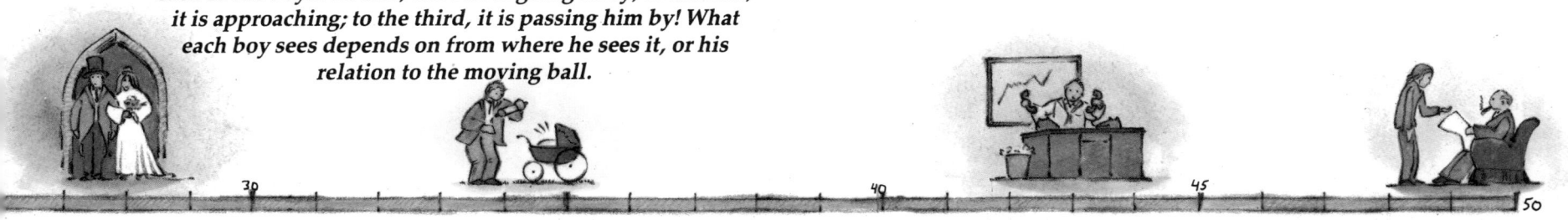

through the book there is a distance scale. It doesn't measure either inches or even simple miles. Each notch represents *one million miles*! I have drawn the sun to the correct scale at the start, on page 6, and as you go through the pages, along the ruler, you can find the place of each of the tiny, tiny planets in our solar system . . . out as far as Neptune. (I ran out of pages for Pluto!)

Seeing the distances to be covered between one place and another in space, it becomes immediately apparent that measuring in miles or kilometers is of little use. Instead, astronomers use a much larger unit of measure, called a light-year. It is the distance light can travel in one year. (Light travels through space at 186,000 miles [300,000km] per second.) In one year, it goes about5,878,000,000,000mi(9,460,800,000,000 km). That's far!

Our sun is about eight light-minutes away, and the moon a little less than a light-second. The next closest star is four light-years away. Our galaxy measures about 100,000 light-years across. The visible universe measures about 8,000,000,000 light-years from earth. Can you picture just how far *that* is?

What Is the Universe?

Perhaps the most difficult question astronomers still have to answer is "How old, and how large is the universe?" If neither the earth, nor the sun, nor even our galaxy is the center of the universe, then where is it?

Looking out at the stars, farther and farther into space (and back into time!), one asks, "How far can one go?" Does the universe spread out in every direction forever? Or does it finally stop somewhere? But if it stops, then what comes after it?

Optical telescopes can see only a limited portion of the universe, for very distant stars become too faint. Modern radio telescopes can "see" somewhat farther, but they can only pick up radio waves out to about 8 billion light-years. Beyond that is a mystery.

Today astronomers believe that distant galaxies may be moving away from our own. The farther they are, the faster they recede. At some point their speed may reach the speed of light! If this is true, then we will never know. We will never see them if their light rays never have a chance to reach us!

The theory of an expanding universe is not just a fancy, but based on careful study of the stars. The nature of different stars was studied on a spectroscope, which breaks up their light into a wide band of colors of the rainbow, called a spectrum. Those moving towards the earth showed a dominance of blue in their spectrum, while those moving away showed more red. It was found that all the distant galaxies had a dominant red spectrum, and this phenomenon, sometimes called "the red shift," led scientists to believe that these distant stars are receding, and that the universe is indeed expanding.

This theory, if correct, poses a host of new and equally difficult questions. Where is the universe expanding from? When did it start to expand? Some scientists propose that the whole universe at zero time was a tiny, dense ball of matter, which exploded in a big bang and has been growing ever since. But if there was a zero time, then what came before?

Our earth rotates around the sun, one star among 400 billion others in the Milky Way galaxy, 100,000 light-years from end to end.

It used to be thought that you could count back to the creation of the earth, following the generations listed in the Old Testament of the Bible. Our earth was thought to be about 4000 years old!

Sun

The apparent size of the universe has been gradually widening as astronomers looked farther and farther into it with more powerful telescopes. There is still no end in sight!

Isaac Newton's seventeenth century reflecting telescope

A radio telescope and what it "sees"

It reads like a contour map, the tightest rings indicating a radio source: a star or galaxy.

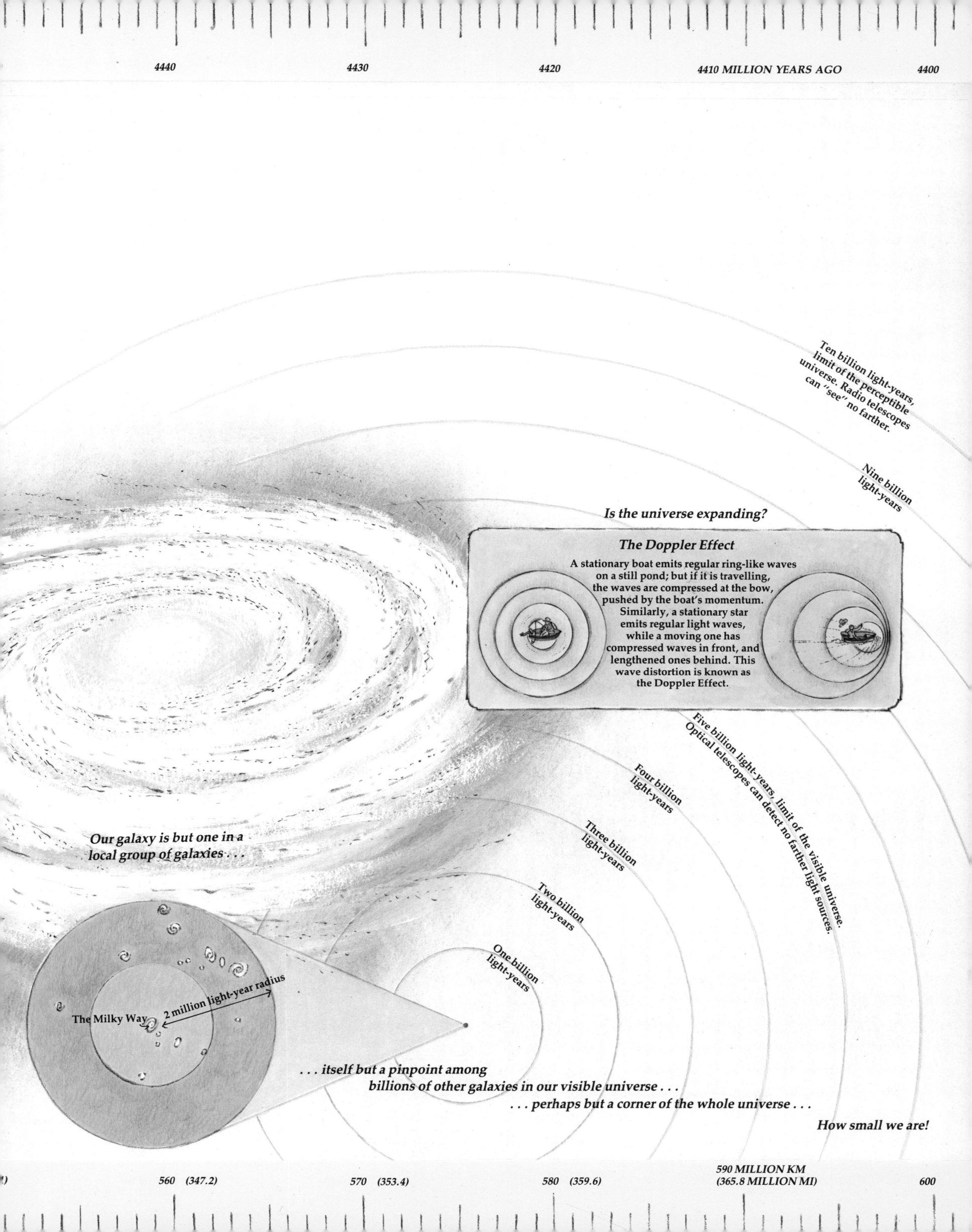
4440
4430
4420
4410 MILLION YEARS AGO
4400
Ten billion light-years, limit of the perceptible universe. Radio telescopes can "see" no farther.
Nine billion light-years
Is the universe expanding?
The Doppler Effect
A stationary boat emits regular ring-like waves on a still pond; but if it is travelling, the waves are compressed at the bow, pushed by the boat's momentum. Similarly, a stationary star emits regular light waves, while a moving one has compressed waves in front, and lengthened ones behind. This wave distortion is known as the Doppler Effect.
Five billion light-years, limit of the visible universe. Optical telescopes can detect no farther light sources.
Four billion light-years
Three billion light-years
Two billion light-years
One billion light-years
Our galaxy is but one in a local group of galaxies . . .
The Milky Way
2 million light-year radius
. . . itself but a pinpoint among billions of other galaxies in our visible universe . . .
. . . perhaps but a corner of the whole universe . . .
How small we are!
560 (347.2)
570 (353.4)
580 (359.6)
590 MILLION KM (365.8 MILLION MI)
600

Of Atoms and Elements

Around 400 BC , a Greek philosopher called Democritus thought that if you cut something in two, and then in two again, again and again, you would eventually come to a particle so small that it could not be cut any further. Democritus called this particle an atom (*atomos*), meaning "indivisible."

Today we know that virtually everything, from the largest stars to the tiniest microbes, is made up of billions of atoms. Atoms are the smallest components of nature. Ten million of them side by side would measure only 0.04 inch (1mm)! Yet, like outer space, they are mostly emptiness!

There are 103 different atoms. The number of protons in an atom makes it different from the others. Each different atom is a piece of a different element, or basic substance, from

This is the simplest, and lightest atom: hydrogen. It has just one proton and one electron. The proton is 2000 times heavier than the electron!

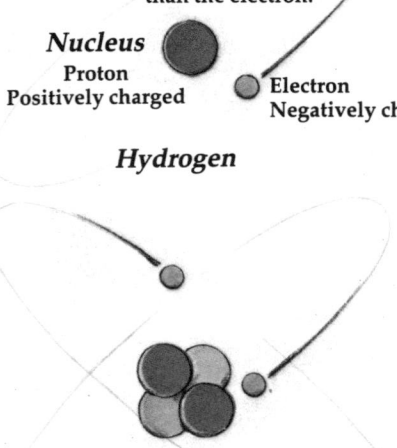

Hydrogen

Helium

Atoms themselves are made of still smaller neutrons, protons and orbiting electrons. Recently it has been discovered that these are made of even smaller and more numerous particles.
Matter consists of molecules made up of atoms.
Two atoms of the same element can join to make a molecule of an element. Two atoms of different elements can join to make a molecule of a compound.

The nucleus of an atom is made of protons and neutrons. Neutrons bind the positively charged protons together, but have no charge themselves. Atoms usually have an equal number of protons and electrons, but those which have had some electrons added are known as ions. Those with extra neutrons are called isotopes.

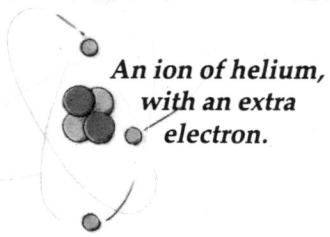

An ion of helium, with an extra electron.

An isotope of hydrogen, with an extra neutron. This hydrogen atom is called deuterium, or heavy hydrogen.

The number of protons and equal number of electrons makes each atom—and thus each element—different from another. By counting the number of protons you can find an atom's "atomic number." This ranges from (1) for hydrogen, the lightest element, to the most complex atoms, or heaviest elements, found in nature, like uranium (92).

Scientists have recently discovered that the sub-atomic particles are themselves made up of numerous tinier bits known as quarks. These, in their turn, may be made up of even smaller pieces. The universe within seems as limitless as the universe without!

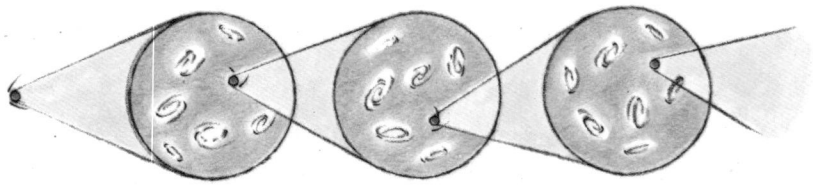

Lithium

Indeed, there is a theory that the sub-atomic particles, which make up the entirety of our universe, may in fact be other universes on a different scale. Our universe would then be but a particle of some other universe on a greater scale!

There is an idea to chew on!

An atom is almost all empty space. The distance between the nucleus and the revolving electrons is about 10,000 times the diameter of the atom's nucleus. If we imagine the atom nucleus as 0.04inch (1mm) wide, then its electrons revolve eleven yards (10m) away!

which everything is made. Most elements are natural, but man has recently modified some atoms by changing the number of protons in them, thus creating new elements.

The same elements found on earth, and within ourselves, can be found in distant stars throughout the universe. Where do atoms come from? Ultimately, all atoms come from the stars. The formation of the earth is related to that of the sun. The sun is a star, composed of gases left by earlier, exploded stars.

You and I are made up of atoms, the same ones found in the stars. In this way we are actually children of the stars, and the atoms are our link to the universe.

Isn't that wonderful?

What is the earth made of? The chart on the right shows the make-up of our earth's crust, divided into elements. Eighty percent of the crust is divided between only three elements, while ninety-four others make up only 20 percent. The most dominant element is oxygen . . .

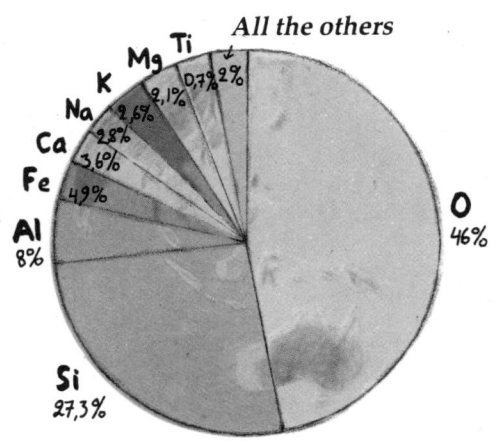

. . . which we think of as a gas, but which can also be found in a liquid or solid state. Oxygen atoms serve as a skeleton in the earth. Between the bones are sandwiched all the other elements, in different quantities, that make up the earth!

This is a table of elements. The combinations of different atoms and elements make up the enormous number of compounds found in nature.

1 H Hydrogen																	2 He Helium
3 Li Lithium	4 Be Beryllium											5 B Boron	6 C Carbon	7 N Nitrogen	8 O Oxygen	9 F Fluorine	10 Ne Neon
11 Na Sodium	12 Mg Magnesium											13 Al Aluminium	14 Si Silicon	15 P Phosphorus	16 S Sulphur	17 Cl Chlorine	18 Ar Argon
19 K Potassium	20 Ca Calcium	21 Sc Scandium	22 Ti Titanium	23 V Vanadium	24 Cr Chromium	25 Mn Manganese	26 Fe Iron	27 Co Cobalt	28 Ni Nickel	29 Cu Copper	30 Zn Zinc	31 Ga Gallium	32 Ge Germanium	33 As Arsenic	34 Se Selenium	35 Br Bromine	36 Kr Krypton
37 Rb Rubidium	38 Sr Strontium	39 Y Yttrium	40 Zr Zirconium	41 Nb Niobium	42 Mo Molybdenum	43 Tc Technetium	44 Ru Ruthenium	45 Rh Rhodium	46 Pd Palladium	47 Ag Silver	48 Cd Cadmium	49 In Indium	50 Sn Tin	51 Sb Antimony	52 Te Tellurium	53 I Iodine	54 Xe Xenon
55 Cs Caesium	56 Ba Barium	57 La Lanthanum	72 Hf Hafnium	73 Ta Tantalum	74 W Tungsten	75 Re Rhenium	76 Os Osmium	77 Ir Iridium	78 Pt Platinum	79 Au Gold	80 Hg Mercury	81 Tl Thallium	82 Pb Lead	83 Bi Bismuth	84 Po Polonium	85 At Astatine	86 Rn Radon
87 Fr Francium	88 Ra Radium	89 Ac Actinium															
			Lanthanides	58 Ce Cerium	59 Pr Praseodymium	60 Nd Neodymium	61 Pm Promethium	62 Sm Samarium	63 Eu Europium	64 Gd Gadolinium	65 Tb Terbium	66 Dy Dysprosium	67 Ho Holmium	68 Er Erbium	69 Tm Thulium	70 Yb Ytterbium	71 Lu Lutetium
			Actinides	90 Th Thorium	91 Pa Protactinum	92 U Uranium	93 Np Neptunium	94 Pu Plutonium	95 Am Americium	96 Cm Curium	97 Bk Berkelium	98 Cf Californium	99 Es Einsteinium	100 Fm Fermium	101 Md Mendelevium	102 No Nobelium	103 Lr Lawrencium

Reactive metals
Transition metals
Non-metals
Noble (inert) gases
Lanthanide series
Actinide series

How far to the electron's orbit? (Go to page 56!)

The Life of the Stars

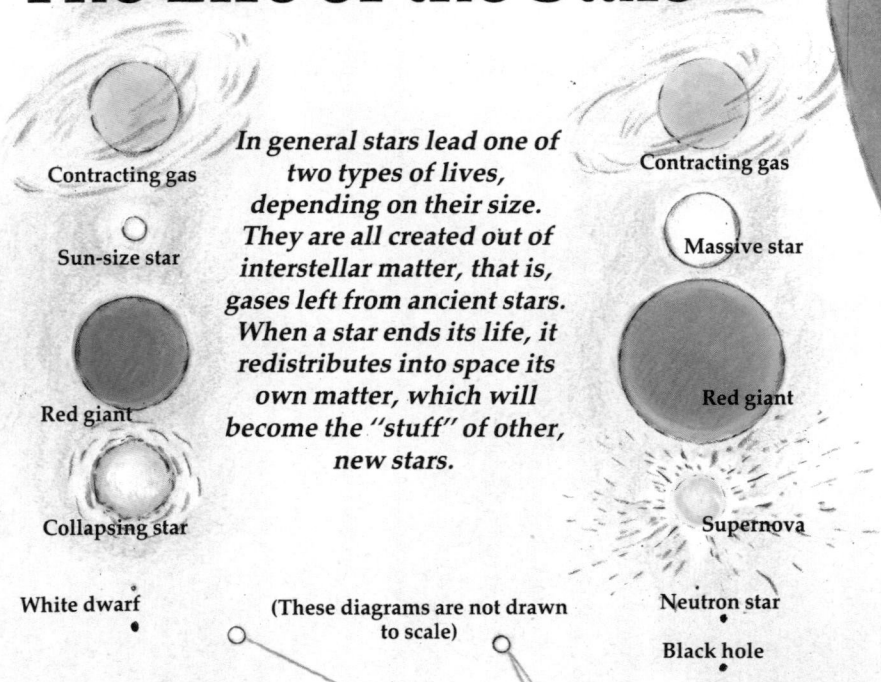

In general stars lead one of two types of lives, depending on their size. They are all created out of interstellar matter, that is, gases left from ancient stars. When a star ends its life, it redistributes into space its own matter, which will become the "stuff" of other, new stars.

(These diagrams are not drawn to scale)

Many stars live in couples, and are called binary stars. Others pulsate, becoming brighter and dimmer as they let off more or less energy.

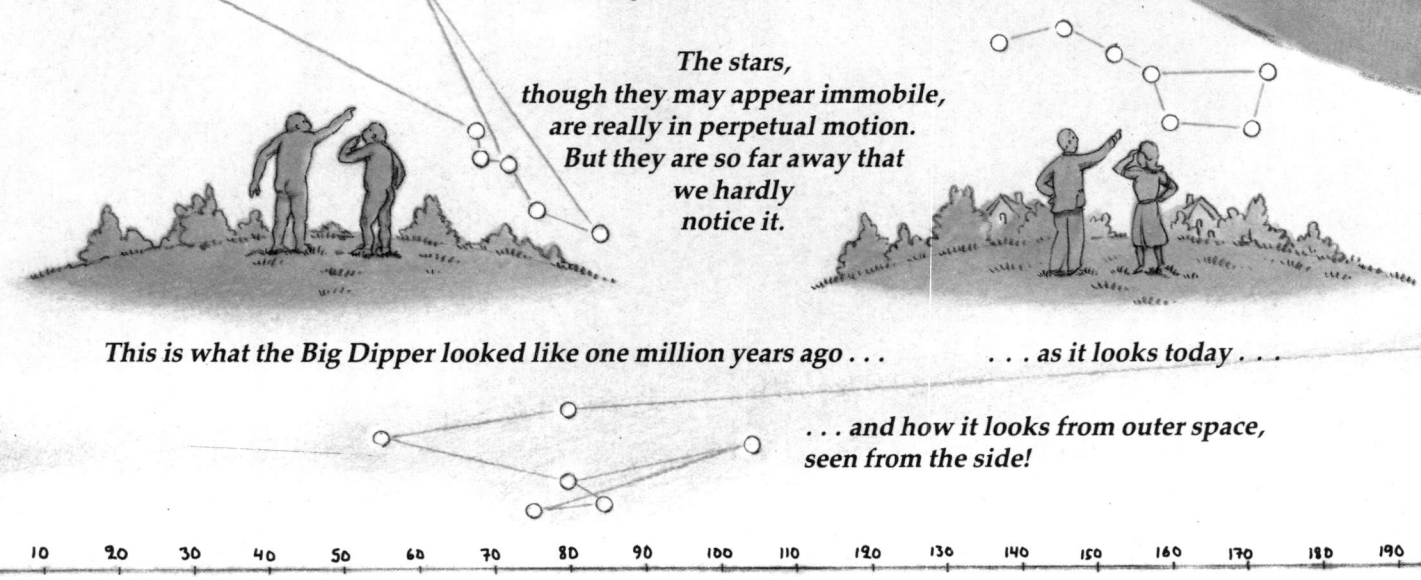

The stars, though they may appear immobile, are really in perpetual motion. But they are so far away that we hardly notice it.

This is what the Big Dipper looked like one million years ago . . .

. . . as it looks today . . .

. . . and how it looks from outer space, seen from the side!

Stars have long been thought of as eternal. Indeed from earth they seem immovable and unchanging, and for centuries they have been reliable markers for mariners navigating the seas. Yet, just like you and me, the stars are alive and changing.

How are stars born? Floating around in the universe are great clouds of dust and gas, the remains of ancient stars. Over millions of years a cloud may condense. As it packs together, the molecules may be pressed so tightly that they collide with one another, and generate heat.

If it gets hot enough then the hydrogen atoms in the gas fuse, in a nuclear reaction, into helium. The change in structure emits huge energy, which we see as light. A star is born!

An average star, like our sun, may burn its hydrogen for as long as ten billion years. But

Here, drawn to scale, are the comparative sizes of a red giant and our sun (250:1).

Sun: 100 times larger than . . .

White dwarf: 700 times larger than . . .

Neutron star: 3 times larger than . . .

Black hole

The Milky Way is a spiral galaxy.

Spiral galaxies

Elliptical galaxies

Barred galaxies

Stars are usually born in groups and live in great families of about 100 billion members, called galaxies. Galaxies are in constant motion, spinning on their own axes, while they move as a pack through space. Our sun, and we with it, makes one full turn through our galaxy every 250 million years! There are many different types of galaxies, which have been classed in groups. We do not know if one type evolves into another.

The gravity of a black hole is so great that it could suck in the matter of even the most massive stars!

at some point the fuel runs low. When this happens the star cools, shedding its outer layers, and bloating into a red giant.

Medium-sized stars like the sun then become unstable, eject their matter into space, and finish their days as a tiny, pale white dwarf.

Bigger stars experience a more violent end. After their red giant stage, they explode as a supernova, and the leftovers contract into dense neutron stars, measuring only a few miles across! They are so dense that a handful may weigh many tons. Their gravity may be so great that *nothing* can escape them, not even light. Virtually invisible, they are called black holes and in spite of their small size, they are frighteningly powerful, for their gravity can suck up anything that crosses their path . . . even other stars!

The Vital Sun

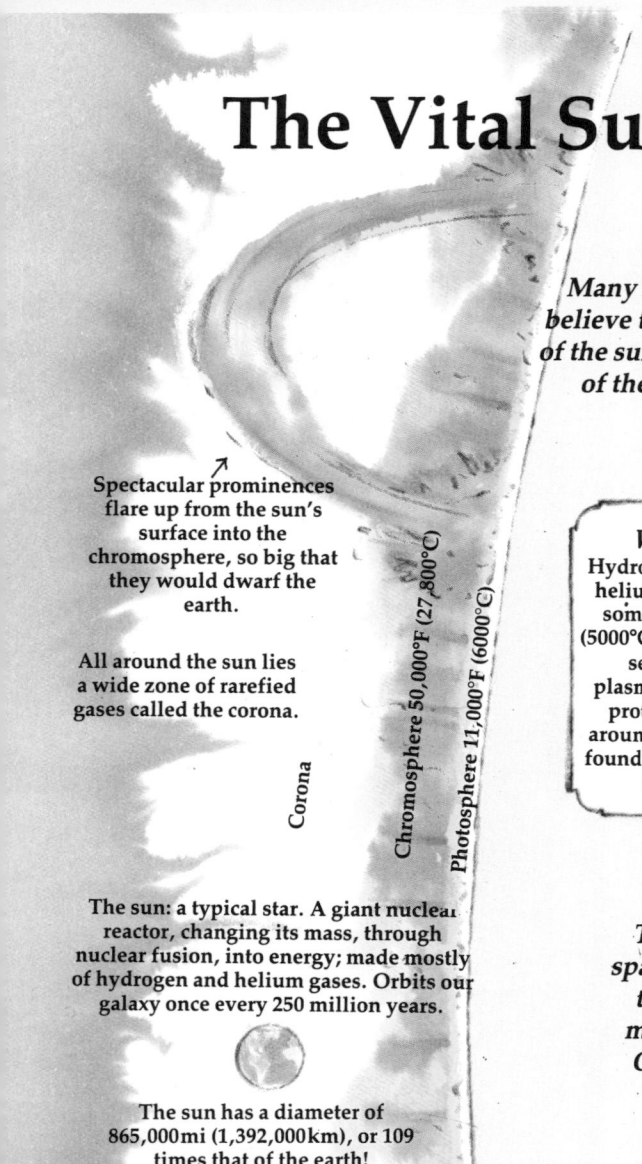

Many scientists today believe that the evolution of the sun is related to that of the solar system.

Interstellar gas cloud

Gas cloud starts condensing, forming denser clumps and a nucleus.

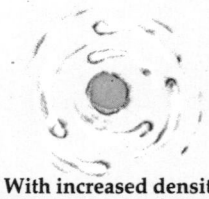
With increased density, heat rises enough in the nucleus to create nuclear fusion, and the sun begins to shine.

Orbiting clumps pull in the remaining cloud with their gravity. The sun's heat increases.

What makes the sun shine?

Hydrogen, in the process of changing into helium through nuclear fusion, converts some of its mass into energy. At 9000°F (5000°C) atoms are destroyed. The electrons separate from their nucleus and a plasma – a kind of soup of disconnected protons and electrons – is created. At around 27 million degrees, a temperature found in the sun, the protons (nuclei) fuse together in a nuclear reaction.

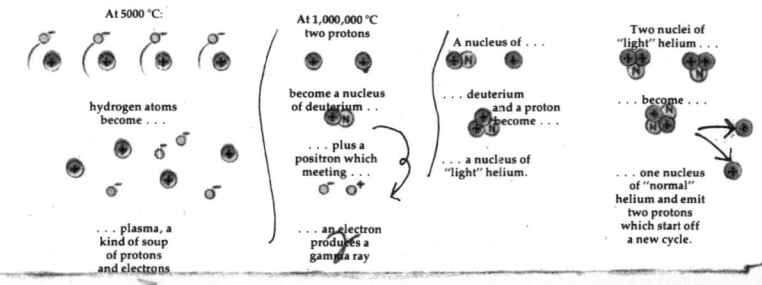

The sun ejects charged protons into space in a solar wind! Some particles of this wind get trapped in the earth's magnetic field in the Van Allen Belt. Others fall through the polar sky as aurorae.

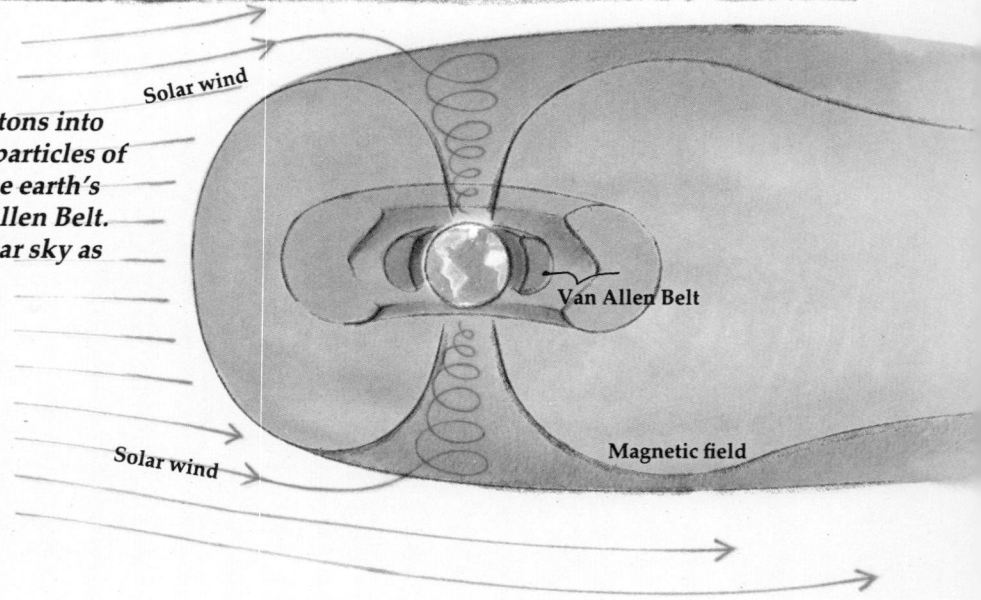

Doubtless you have heard that the three vital necessities for man are food, clothing, and shelter. But have you ever thought how you could live without the sun? The sun is *the* vital necessity, not only for man, but also for every plant and every animal.

Imagine a morning that the sun didn't rise. The day would be absolutely dark. Even if there was a full moon we wouldn't see it, for it would reflect no sunlight. Without sunlight plants could not grow, and without plants, which carry out a process called photosynthesis, we would run out of air to breathe.

But alas, even before we had time to worry about our plants, death would already be at our doorstep! Even though we could keep on our electric lights, we'd notice the earth quickly growing colder and colder, deprived of the sun's warming rays. In no time everything would freeze. Lakes, rivers, even the oceans would turn as hard as ice. So would

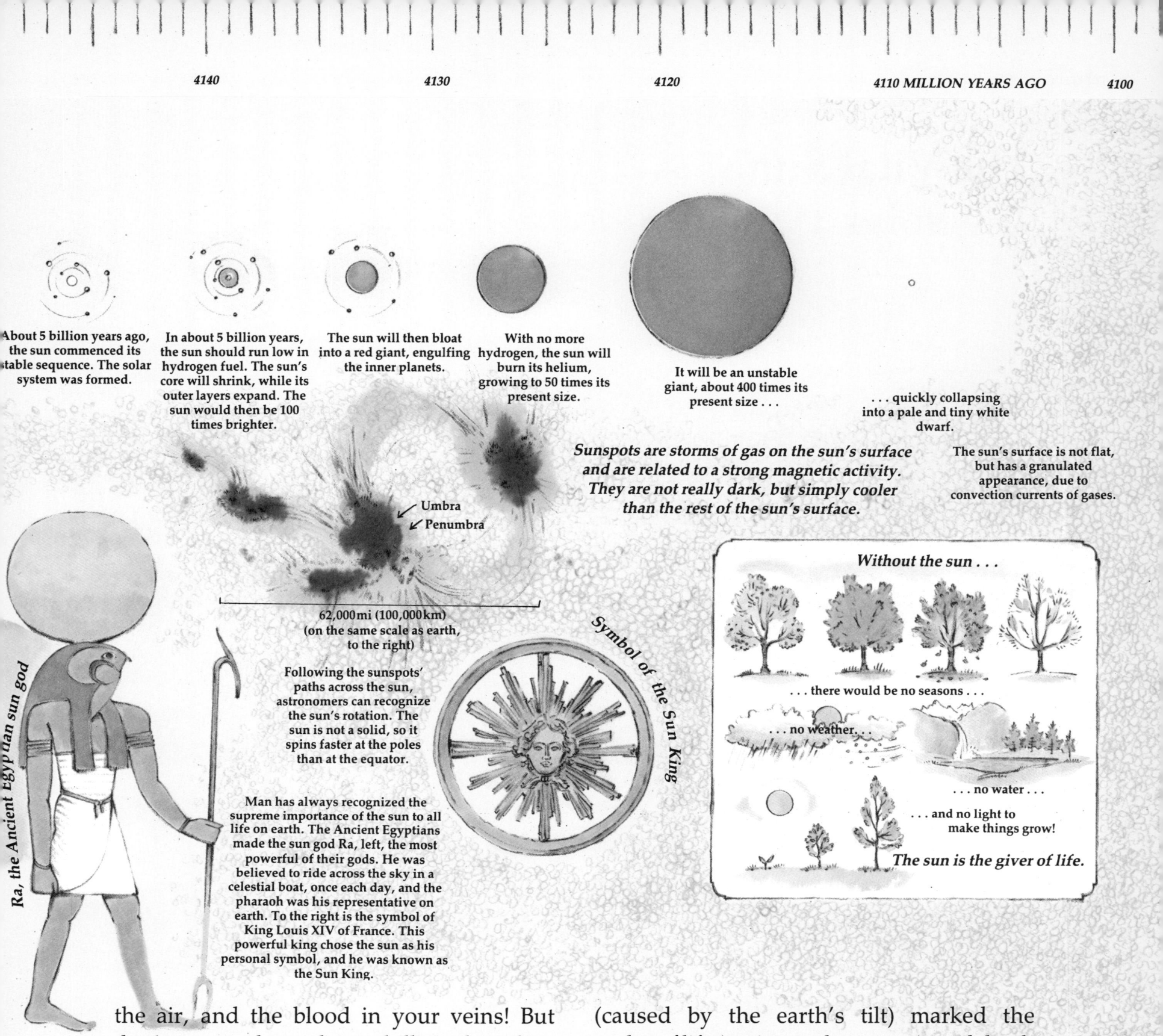

the air, and the blood in your veins! But don't worry about these chilling thoughts. The sun should keep rising each morning for at least another five billion years.

It is not surprising that ancient and primitive civilizations worshipped a sun god. They fully recognized our dependency on this great giver of life. Dates of the year which pass scarcely noticed today were an occasion for great celebration in the past. The shortest and longest days of the year (caused by the earth's tilt) marked the cycles of life (spring and summer), and death (autumn and winter).

It is interesting to note that even our Christmas, celebrating the birth of Christ, falls within a few days of the winter solstice (December 22nd), the shortest day of the year . . . and the celebration of the rebirth of the sun, with the progressive growing and warming of each new day.

Earth's Neighborhood, the Solar System

In ancient times the night sky was believed to be a giant canopy of fixed stars which revolved around the earth. The Ancient Greeks enjoyed studying the stars, and on the canopy they joined groups of stars with lines to form pictures. These pictures we call constellations.

However, they noticed that some of the brightest stars moved a bit each night, crossing from one constellation to another. The Greeks called these stars *planetes,* which meant "wanderers." They could see five wanderers in the sky, without telescopes, and they were named: Mercury, Venus, Mars, Jupiter, and Saturn.

Until the sixteenth century people believed that the planets revolved around the earth. Then a Polish astronomer called Copernicus discovered that all the planets, including our own earth, revolve around the sun. A new name was needed to describe this. We call it the solar system.

We know now that there are more than five planets in the solar system. A full count of the sun's family would run like this:

Planets	Nine
Moons (planetary satellites)	Thirty-three at least
Asteroids	Several thousand
Comets	Several dozen
Meteorites and meteors	Millions

Although it may look like a crowded family the solar system is mostly empty space. The sun alone accounts for about 99 percent of its total mass!

Many planets have orbiting moons. Some of Jupiter's moons are bigger than the planet Mercury, while other moons may measure only some 60mi (100km) wide. We now believe that the whole solar system was created at roughly the same time.

Only our own planet earth is suitable for us to live on. The other planets are either too cold, or too hot, have not enough air or water, or too much gravity. But some have numerous similarities with our own. It is quite possible that other planets, even if no life is found there today, may have once been home for some other form of life. It may also be possible that primitive life is burgeoning on another planet in our system right now! But no other planet, from space, shows such richness, variety and beauty as our own.

Explanatory note: Figures for gravity are based upon earth's gravity=1. Figures for density are based on water=1.

The solar system, as far out as Neptune, is drawn to scale all along the bottom of the pages of this book. Isn't it a big and empty place?

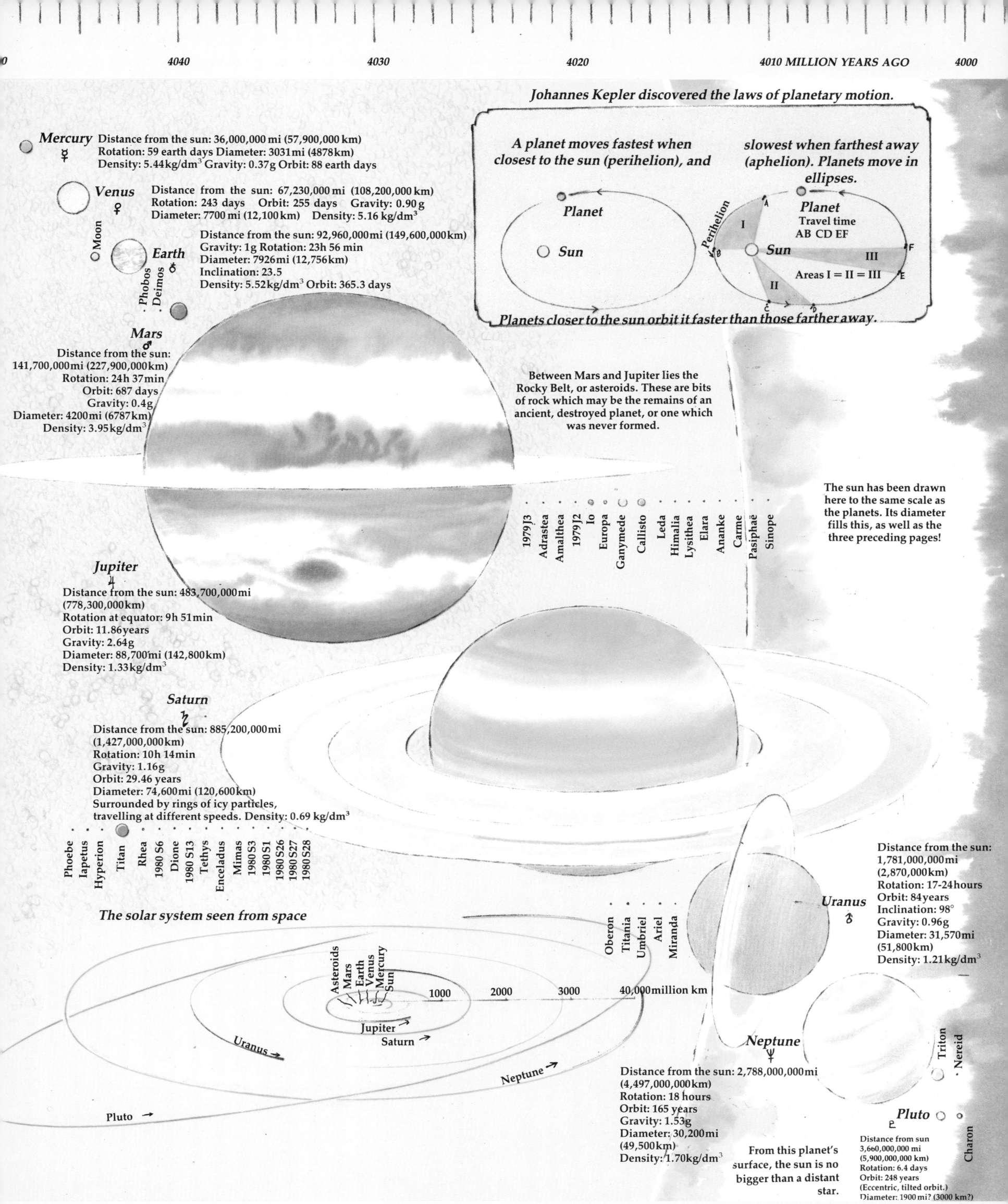
4040
4030
4020
4010 MILLION YEARS AGO
4000
Johannes Kepler discovered the laws of planetary motion.
A planet moves fastest when closest to the sun (perihelion), and slowest when farthest away (aphelion). Planets move in ellipses.
Planet
Sun
Perihelion
Planet
Travel time
AB CD EF
Sun
Areas I = II = III
Planets closer to the sun orbit it faster than those farther away.
Mercury
Distance from the sun: 36,000,000 mi (57,900,000 km)
Rotation: 59 earth days Diameter: 3031mi (4878km)
Density: 5.44kg/dm³ Gravity: 0.37g Orbit: 88 earth days
Venus
Distance from the sun: 67,230,000 mi (108,200,000 km)
Rotation: 243 days Orbit: 255 days Gravity: 0.90 g
Diameter: 7700 mi (12,100 km) Density: 5.16 kg/dm³
Moon
Earth
Distance from the sun: 92,960,000mi (149,600,000km)
Gravity: 1g Rotation: 23h 56 min
Diameter: 7926mi (12,756km)
Inclination: 23.5
Density: 5.52kg/dm³ Orbit: 365.3 days
Phobos
Deimos
Mars
Distance from the sun: 141,700,000mi (227,900,000km)
Rotation: 24h 37min
Orbit: 687 days
Gravity: 0.4g
Diameter: 4200mi (6787km)
Density: 3.95kg/dm³
Between Mars and Jupiter lies the Rocky Belt, or asteroids. These are bits of rock which may be the remains of an ancient, destroyed planet, or one which was never formed.
1979J3
Adrastea
Amalthea
1979J2
Io
Europa
Ganymede
Callisto
Leda
Himalia
Lysithea
Elara
Ananke
Carme
Pasiphaë
Sinope
The sun has been drawn here to the same scale as the planets. Its diameter fills this, as well as the three preceding pages!
Jupiter
Distance from the sun: 483,700,000mi (778,300,000km)
Rotation at equator: 9h 51min
Orbit: 11.86years
Gravity: 2.64g
Diameter: 88,700mi (142,800km)
Density: 1.33kg/dm³
Saturn
Distance from the sun: 885,200,000mi (1,427,000,000km)
Rotation: 10h 14min
Gravity: 1.16g
Orbit: 29.46 years
Diameter: 74,600mi (120,600km)
Surrounded by rings of icy particles, travelling at different speeds. Density: 0.69 kg/dm³
Phoebe
Iapetus
Hyperion
Titan
Rhea
1980 S6
Dione
1980 S13
Tethys
Enceladus
Mimas
1980 S3
1980 S1
1980 S26
1980 S27
1980 S28
The solar system seen from space
Asteroids
Mars
Earth
Venus
Mercury
Sun
1000
2000
3000
40,000million km
Jupiter
Saturn
Uranus
Neptune
Pluto
Oberon
Titania
Umbriel
Ariel
Miranda
Uranus
Distance from the sun: 1,781,000,000mi (2,870,000km)
Rotation: 17-24hours
Orbit: 84years
Inclination: 98°
Gravity: 0.96g
Diameter: 31,570mi (51,800km)
Density: 1.21kg/dm³
Neptune
Distance from the sun: 2,788,000,000mi (4,497,000,000km)
Rotation: 18 hours
Orbit: 165 years
Gravity: 1.53g
Diameter: 30,200mi (49,500km)
Density: 1.70kg/dm³
Triton
Nereid
Pluto
Charon
Distance from sun 3,660,000,000 mi (5,900,000,000 km)
Rotation: 6.4 days
Orbit: 248 years
(Eccentric, tilted orbit.)
Diameter: 1900 mi? (3000 km?)
From this planet's surface, the sun is no bigger than a distant star.
960 (595.2)
970 (601.4)
980 (607.6)
990 MILLION KM
(613.8 MILLION MI)
1000

The Moon

The silvery moon is earth's closest relative in the solar system. On first sight there is little their two faces have in common, but the moon influences so much of what happens here on earth that we might call it earth's little brother.

We know that the moon orbits the earth, held by the earth's gravity. But the moon's gravity is also tugging on earth, and in fact both bodies revolve around a barycenter, or an in-between point between their axes. The moon's gravity tugs at the water in our oceans, and as it and the earth revolve, creates the tides.

The regular waning and waxing of the moon enabled ancient peoples to measure weeks and months. (The word "month" comes from "moon.") Although the moon's radius is only a quarter that of the earth's, it is proportionately much larger than the

If we were to take a long cord and pull the moon alongside our planet, like a dinghy to a ship, here is how big our nearest neighbor in space would look!

Earth's diameter, for comparison: 7927mi (12,756km)

The Moon

Distance from the earth: 238,900mi (384,000km)
Diameter: 2160mi (3476km)
Day temperature: 214°F to 266°F (101° to 130°C)
By night – 307°F (–153°C)

The great, flat, circular maria, or seas, may have been created by the impact of a large, massive body, or meteorite, which dug so deep that lava welled up from within and filled up its own crater.

There are mountain ranges on the moon as lofty as those found on earth. Those in the Apennines rise to more than 21,300ft (6500m).

Craters are formed either by striking objects or by volcanoes.

On a clear night, take a pair of binoculars and look at the moon. It is a fascinating sight!

moons' of any of the other planets. Since it exerts so much influence on earth, some scientists consider the earth and moon as a binary planet system.

Scientists believe that the moon was formed in a similar manner to the other planets of the solar system, from bits of condensing matter pulled together by gravity. The moon's gravity is only about one-sixth that on earth, too little to hold down an atmosphere. There is no air and no water there.

The most striking feature of the moon is its craters. Where do they come from? Many craters are made by the impact of meteorites or other bodies crashing on its surface. Probably if the earth had no atmosphere in which falling meteors can burn up by friction it would have a rather similar pockmarked surface! Other craters are the remnants of extinct moon volcanoes, and these can be recognized in chains on moon maps. There are also wide, calm, flat regions, which our ancestors called seas. These were probably once lowlands which were filled with inner, molten lava at some early time in the moon's life that has since solidified.

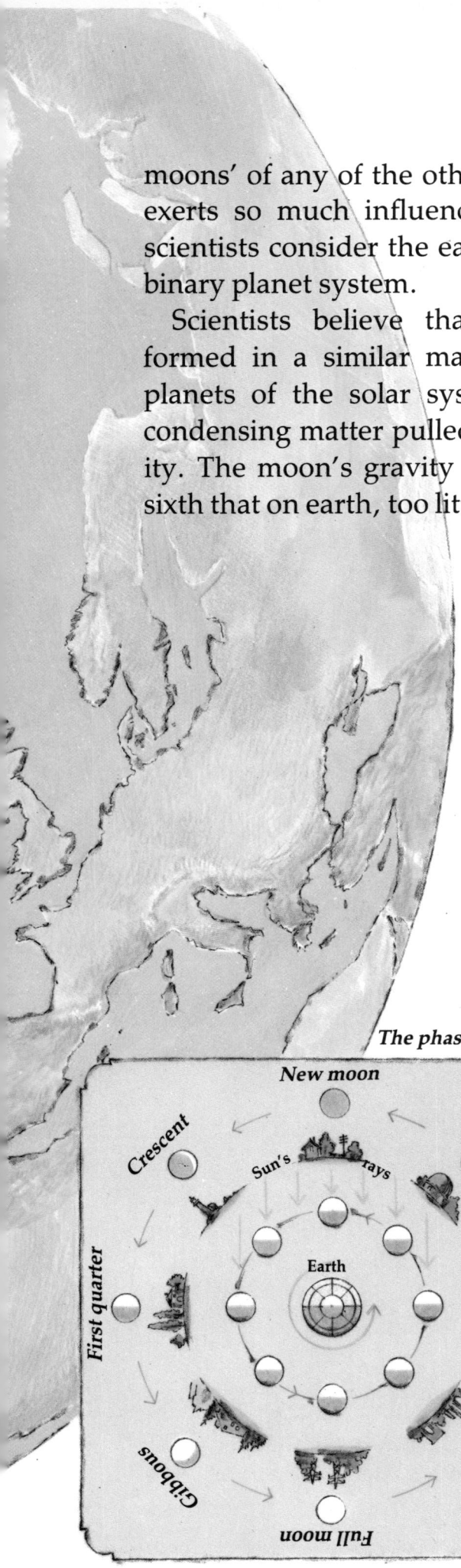

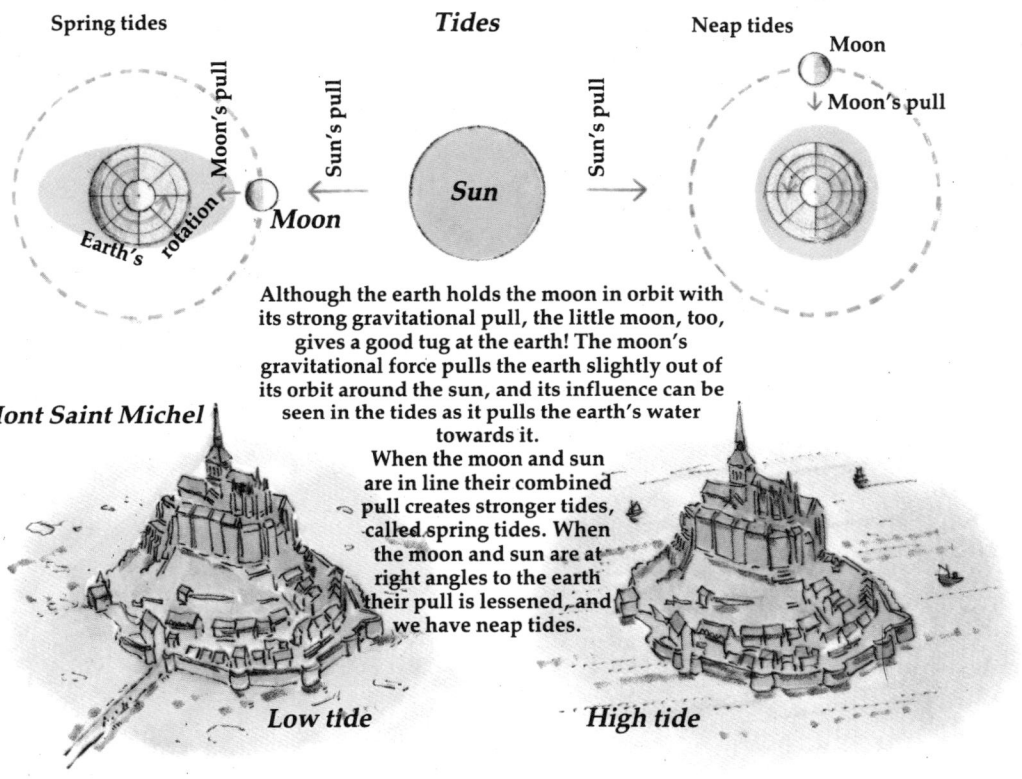

Although the earth holds the moon in orbit with its strong gravitational pull, the little moon, too, gives a good tug at the earth! The moon's gravitational force pulls the earth slightly out of its orbit around the sun, and its influence can be seen in the tides as it pulls the earth's water towards it.

When the moon and sun are in line their combined pull creates stronger tides, called spring tides. When the moon and sun are at right angles to the earth their pull is lessened, and we have neap tides.

Heavenly Clockwork: the Earth-Moon-Sun System

Every day throughout the year we ride on the hands of a giant celestial clock. This clock tells us when it is day, when it is night, when the tide is high, and what season we're in. It has only three gears . . . the sun, the moon and the earth.

How does it work? The clock runs on two natural forces: gravity and centrifugal force. The sun's gravity pulls on the earth, but the earth propels itself through space and the momentum pulls it away from the sun's gravity. The two forces are just strong enough to equalize each other: the sun keeping the earth from flying away, and the earth's momentum keeping it from falling into the sun. The earth is held, then, in orbit.

The moon orbits the earth in just the same way. One orbit of the earth around the sun makes one year, and one orbit of the moon around the earth makes one lunar month.

While the earth and moon are in their orbits they are spinning like tops on an axis. One spin around is called a rotation. The earth makes one rotation in about twenty-four hours, making one day, while the moon takes twenty-seven earth days to make just one rotation.

The earth's axis of rotation is not perpendicular to its orbit around the sun. If it were, then every day of the year would receive the same amount of sunlight. Instead the earth rides its orbit (called the ecliptic) with a tilt, so that the length of days throughout the year are never equal. This tilt gives us the seasons.

Before the recent age of mechanical clocks and watches, the only way to tell time or know the date was to read the celestial clock. People counted the time from one full moon to the next and sometimes built in their temples a marker which the sun might light only once a year.

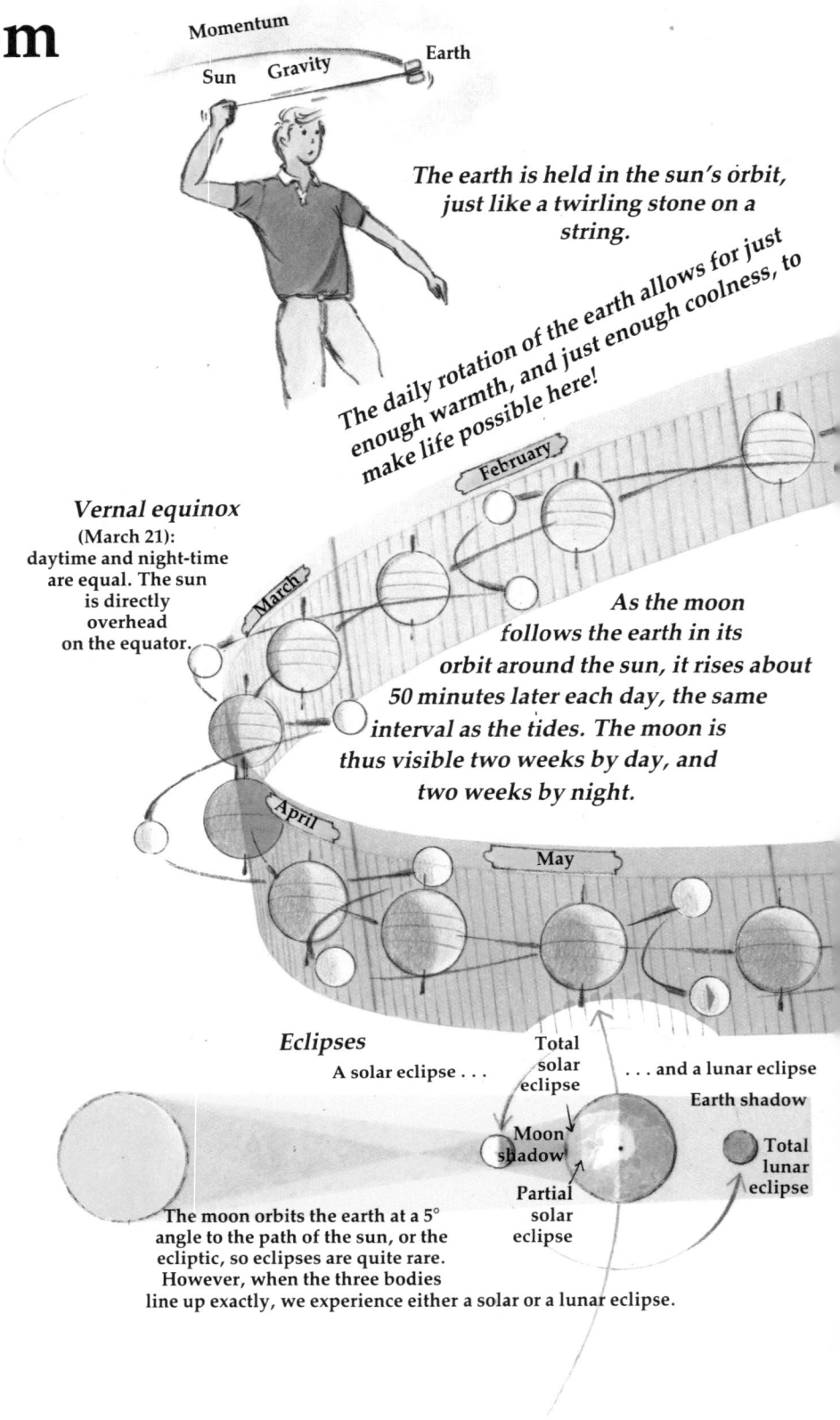

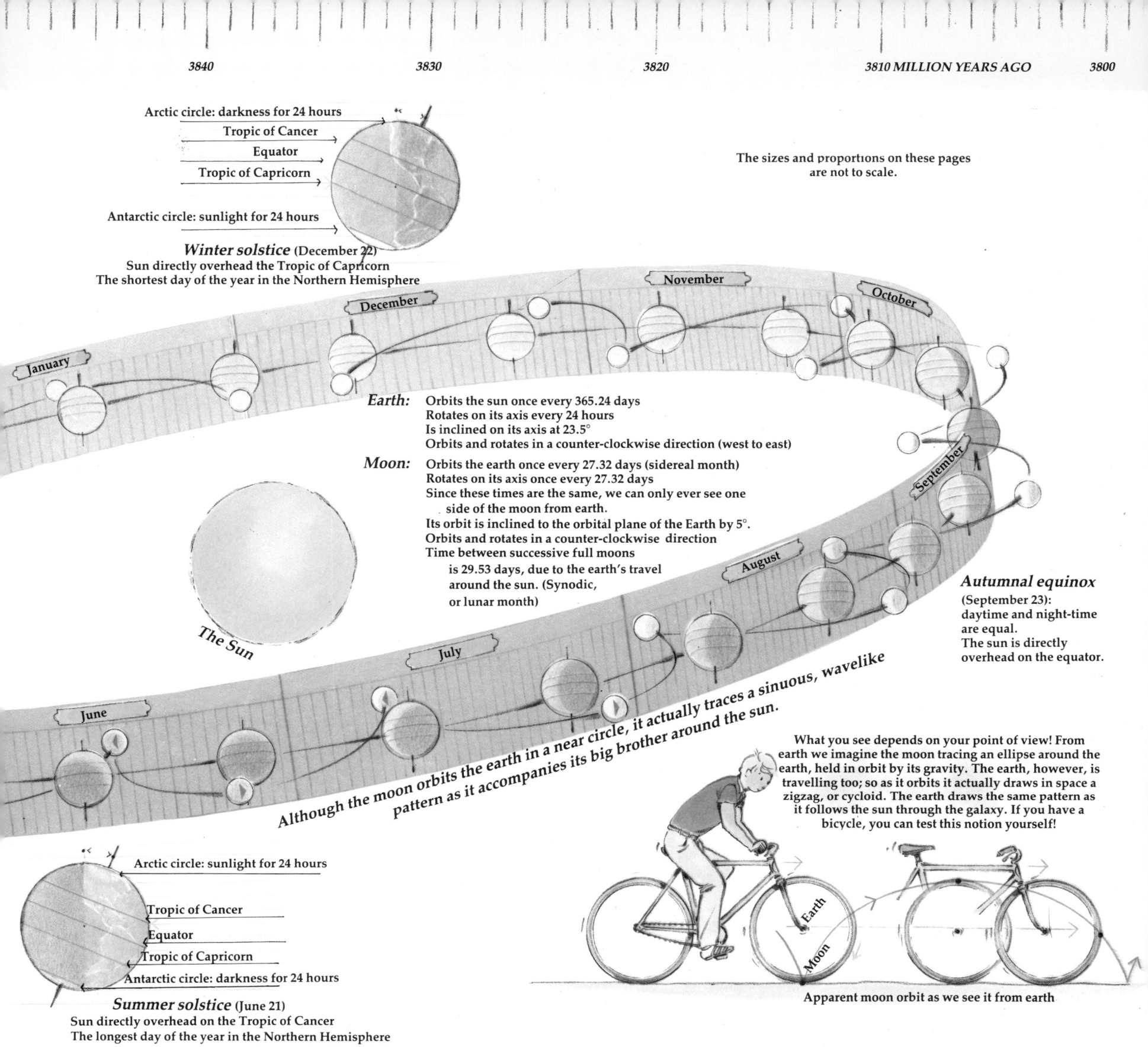

Although the ancients needed no clocks to catch a train, they depended on exact knowledge of the march of the seasons. Knowing just when to plant and when to harvest might be an affair of life or death! By keeping careful track of the year the Ancient Egyptians, for instance, knew when the Nile River would flood, so they could open their irrigation sluice gates to feed their crops with water.

Meet Planet Earth!

We are very lucky to live on earth. It is certainly the most unusual and most beautiful planet in the solar system. If a space traveller ever came close enough to our sun to distinguish the planets, there is little doubt that he would be intrigued enough to take a closer look at the brilliant blue sapphire, veiled in swirling cotton clouds, which is our planet.

What makes our planet unique among others is that it is the only place we know of where life exists. There are other planets with an atmosphere, and with water locked up as ice, but none has just the right combination of oxygen, water and sunshine to make life as we know it possible.

If the earth rotated just a bit slower, the days would be intolerably hot and life might not be possible. If the earth orbited the sun a bit closer to Mars, it would be impossibly cold! If the earth had been bigger, more massive, its gravity might have held down hydrogen gas, rendering our atmosphere poisonous. Had the earth been smaller, its gravity might not have held any atmosphere at all, and our planet might have looked like the pockmarked moon!

The earth is a very small and rare place, and we can only exist on the thin film of its surface. Such a unique planet merits our respect, and care for its preservation.

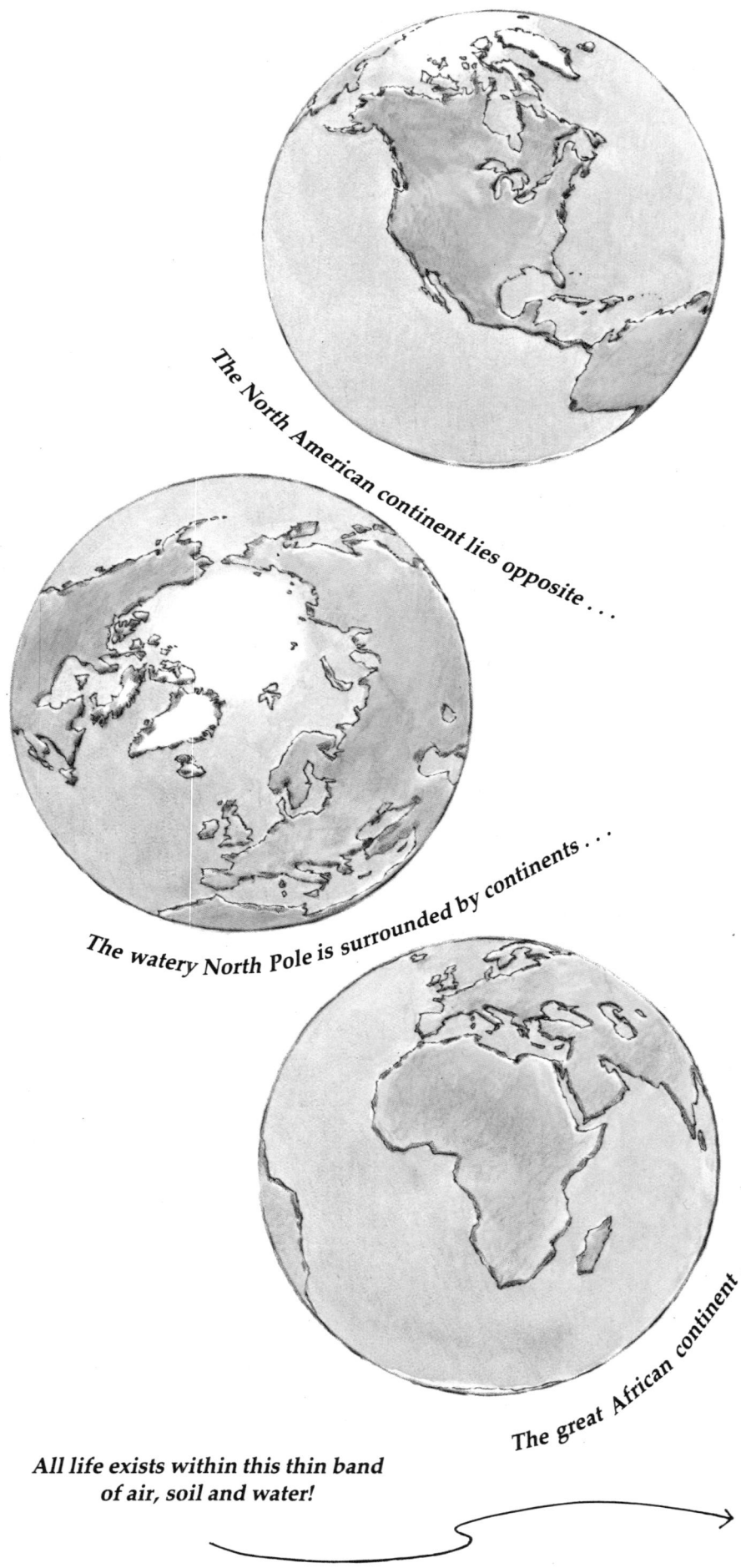

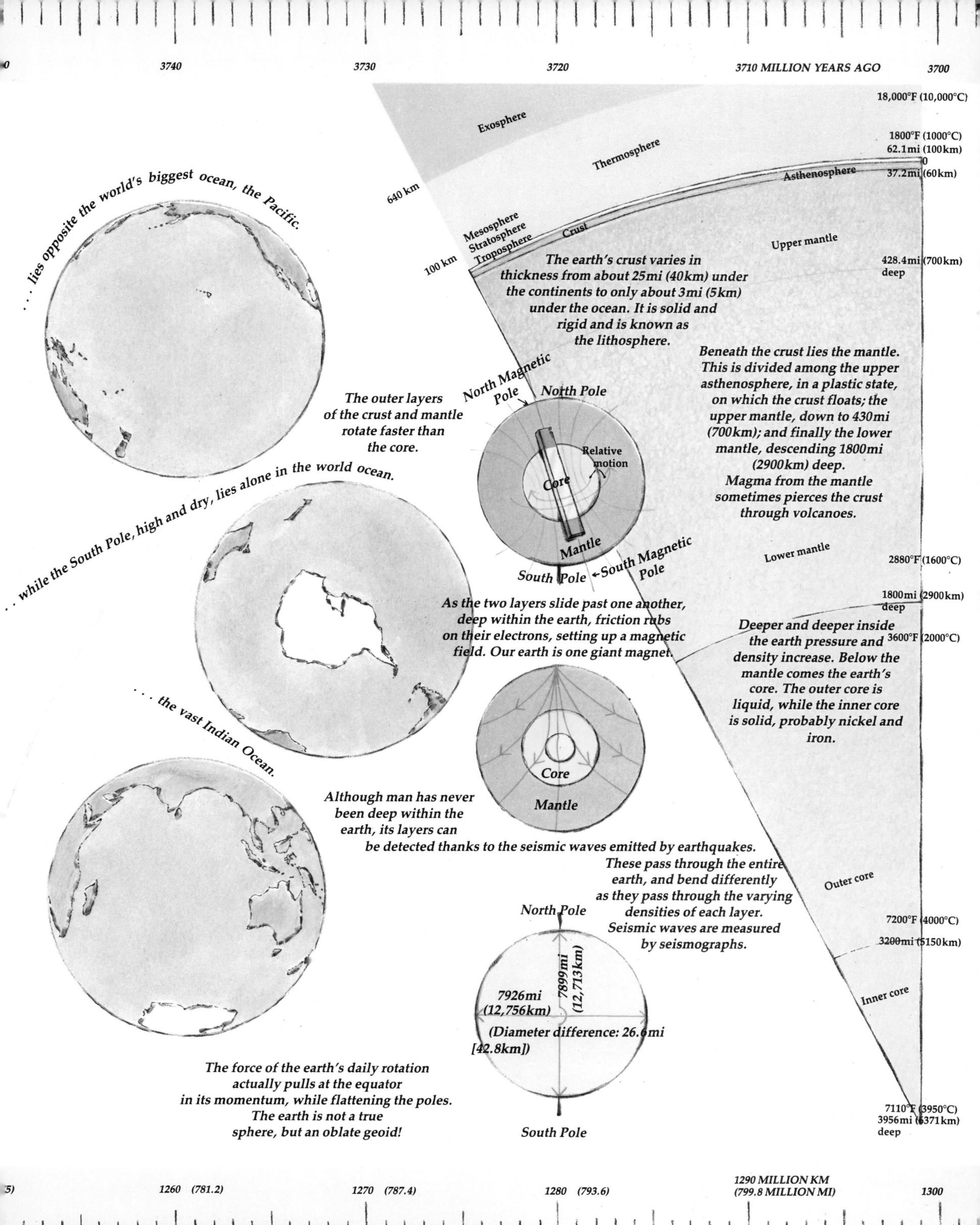
3740
3730
3720
3710 MILLION YEARS AGO
3700
18,000°F (10,000°C)
Exosphere
1800°F (1000°C)
62.1mi (100km)
0
Thermosphere
Asthenosphere
37.2mi (60km)
640 km
Mesosphere
Stratosphere
Troposphere
Crust
100 km
Upper mantle
428.4mi (700km) deep
. . . lies opposite the world's biggest ocean, the Pacific.
The earth's crust varies in thickness from about 25mi (40km) under the continents to only about 3mi (5km) under the ocean. It is solid and rigid and is known as the lithosphere.
Beneath the crust lies the mantle. This is divided among the upper asthenosphere, in a plastic state, on which the crust floats; the upper mantle, down to 430mi (700km); and finally the lower mantle, descending 1800mi (2900km) deep.
Magma from the mantle sometimes pierces the crust through volcanoes.
North Magnetic Pole
North Pole
The outer layers of the crust and mantle rotate faster than the core.
Relative motion
Core
Mantle
South Pole
South Magnetic Pole
Lower mantle
2880°F (1600°C)
. . . while the South Pole, high and dry, lies alone in the world ocean.
1800mi (2900km) deep
As the two layers slide past one another, deep within the earth, friction rubs on their electrons, setting up a magnetic field. Our earth is one giant magnet.
Deeper and deeper inside the earth pressure and density increase. Below the mantle comes the earth's core. The outer core is liquid, while the inner core is solid, probably nickel and iron.
3600°F (2000°C)
. . . the vast Indian Ocean.
Core
Mantle
Although man has never been deep within the earth, its layers can be detected thanks to the seismic waves emitted by earthquakes.
These pass through the entire earth, and bend differently as they pass through the varying densities of each layer.
Seismic waves are measured by seismographs.
Outer core
North Pole
7200°F (4000°C)
3200mi (5150km)
7899mi (12,713km)
7926mi (12,756km)
Inner core
(Diameter difference: 26.6mi [42.8km])
The force of the earth's daily rotation actually pulls at the equator in its momentum, while flattening the poles.
The earth is not a true sphere, but an oblate geoid!
7110°F (3950°C)
3956mi (6371km) deep
South Pole
1260 (781.2)
1270 (787.4)
1280 (793.6)
1290 MILLION KM (799.8 MILLION MI)
1300

Forces That Build Up

From space the earth's rough surface of mountains and valleys, cliffs and canyons, cannot be seen at all. If a giant could hold the earth in his hand, it would feel as smooth as a glass marble, covered with a thin, damp film . . . the oceans!

Yet tiny as we are on the earth's surface, we are surrounded by a variety of terrain, ranging from mirror-smooth plains to rolling hills and jagged peaks. How did they get there?

There are two distinct forces constantly at work, molding and sculpting the landscape. The first, the mountain-building force, is set to work by the intense heat generated deep within the earth's mantle. This heat wells upward in convection currents, pressing against the fragile crust. The molten magma may force its way up through a crack and reach the surface as a volcano which, as it cools, adds new rock to the earth's surface.

The earth's crust is made up of rock, which over millions of years regenerates itself in a rock cycle. Rocks exposed on the earth's surface are weathered; broken down into small particles by the constant friction of wind and water. These particles are carried by rivers to the sea, where they get deposited as sedimentation. As layers of sediment build up, the lower levels are compressed into sedimentary rock. Sometimes this is pushed by the plates that make up the crust into deep trenches where it melts into molten magma. New surface rock is made from cooling lava ejected from volcanoes.

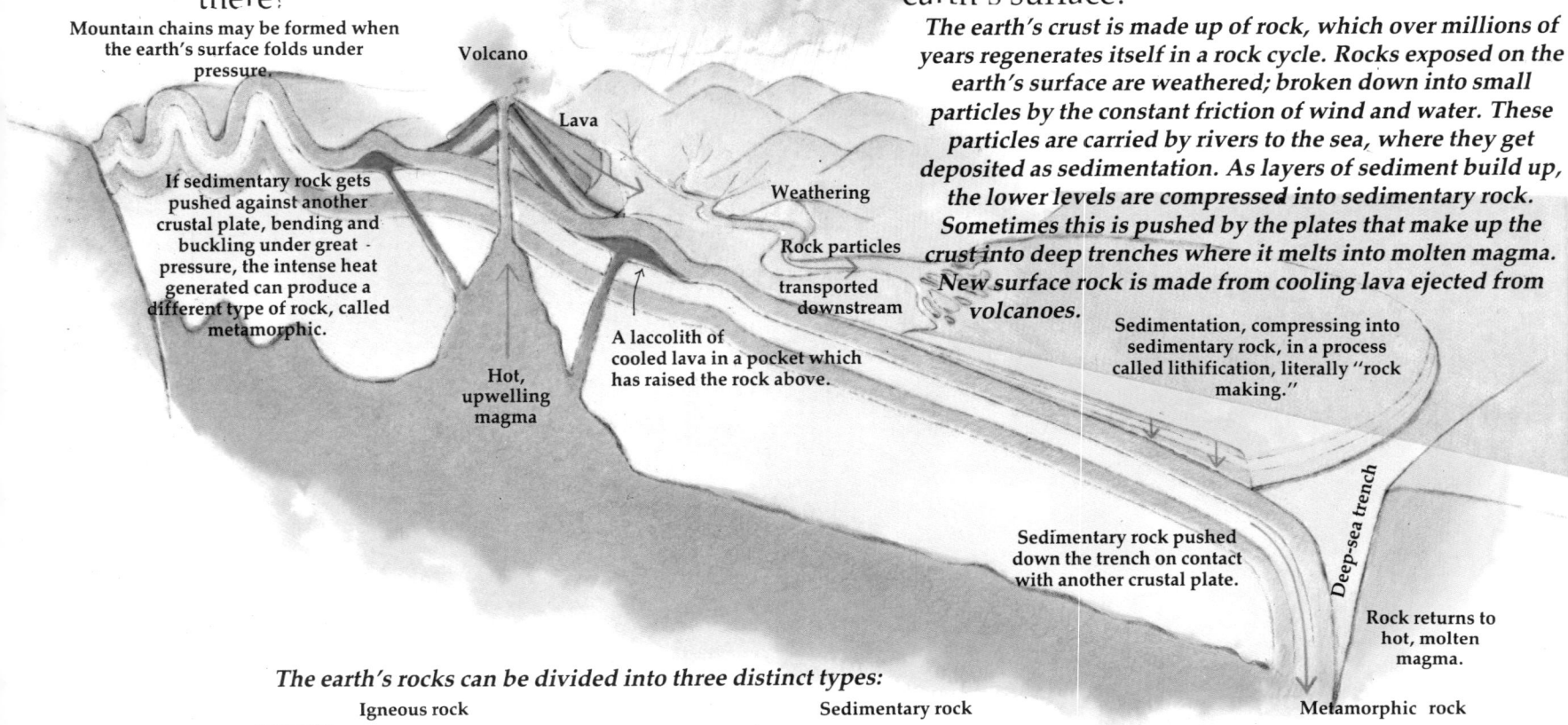

The earth's rocks can be divided into three distinct types:

Igneous rock

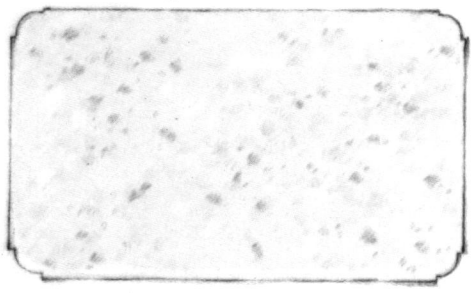

Igneous rock gets its name from the Latin word *ignis*, meaning "fire." Igneous rocks come from molten magma deep within the earth. They surface either by means of volcanoes (extrusive); or through erosion of other overlying rocks (intrusive). Igneous rocks make up about four-fifths of the earth's crust, and they produce excellent agricultural soil. Obsidian, pumice, basalt and granite are some typical igneous rocks.

Sedimentary rock

Sedimentary rock is made up of accumulated material, usually bits of stone, mud and shells, carried by water and deposited on the bottom of lakes and seas in layers. When many layers have accumulated, the bottom ones are pressed together so hard that they cement to become sedimentary rock. This process is called lithification. These rocks form just a thin layer on the earth's surface, but are filled with clues to the earth's past history.

Places where sedimentary rock is found were once underwater, and ancient fossils can be found in them. Sedimentary rocks also hold the world's reserves of gas, oil, coal, salt and groundwater. Shale, clay, sandstone and limestone are examples of sedimentary rock.

Metamorphic rock

Metamorphic rock gets its name from the Greek words meaning "change of form," which is just what happens to igneous or sedimentary rocks which have undergone intense heat and pressure. They turn into metamorphic rock. Two crustal plates pressing on one another may bend sedimentary rocks into new forms. Intense heat may alter the crystal structure of igneous rocks. Metamorphic rocks are found where fold mountains were once built. Some typical examples are gneiss, marble, quartzite and slate.

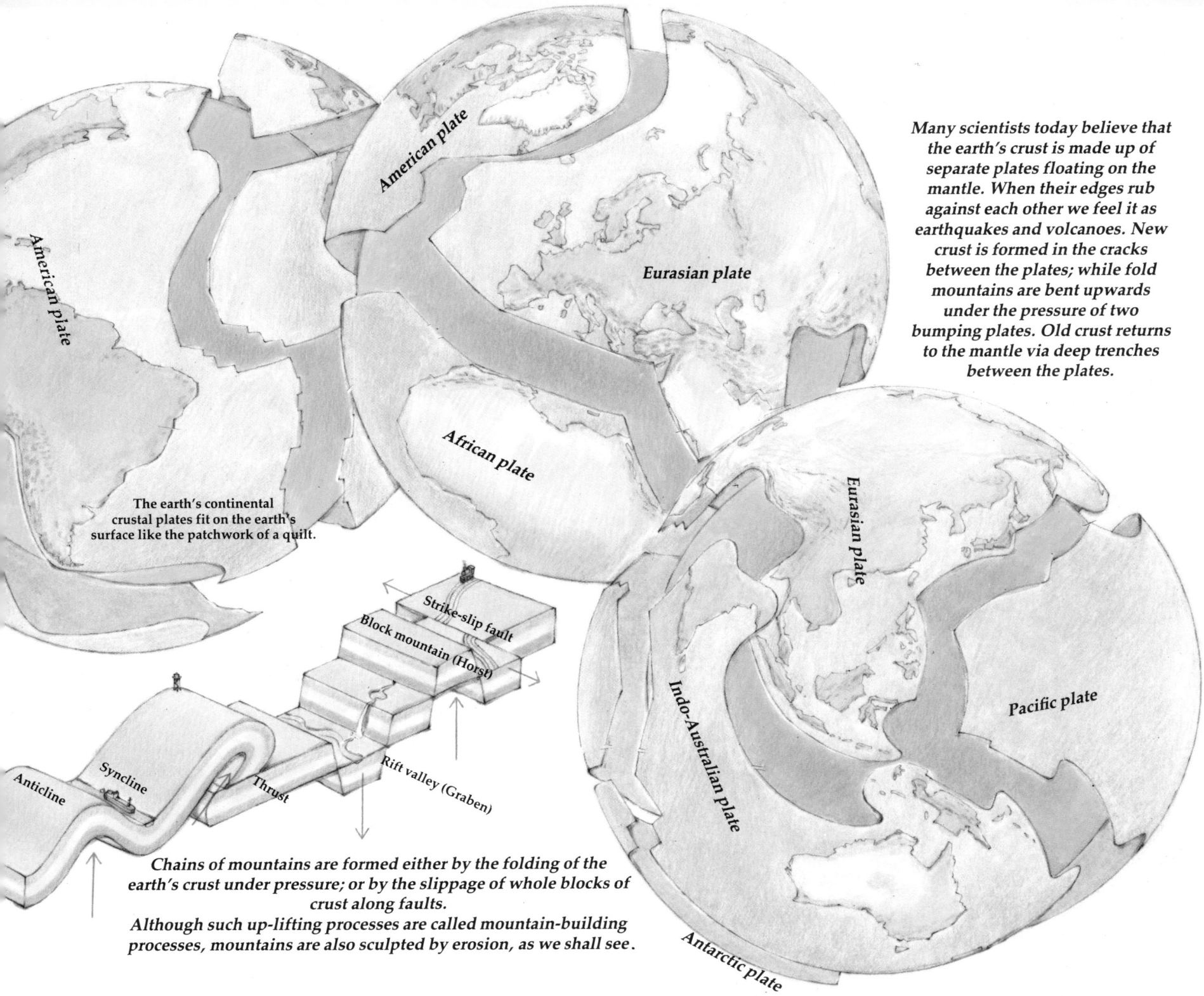

Many scientists today believe that the earth's crust is made up of separate plates floating on the mantle. When their edges rub against each other we feel it as earthquakes and volcanoes. New crust is formed in the cracks between the plates; while fold mountains are bent upwards under the pressure of two bumping plates. Old crust returns to the mantle via deep trenches between the plates.

The earth's continental crustal plates fit on the earth's surface like the patchwork of a quilt.

Chains of mountains are formed either by the folding of the earth's crust under pressure; or by the slippage of whole blocks of crust along faults.
Although such up-lifting processes are called mountain-building processes, mountains are also sculpted by erosion, as we shall see.

The earth's crust is actually believed to float on the denser, but molten, mantle like a scum of cream on the surface of a bowl of milk. The crust is broken into several pieces, or plates, which we also call continents. A plate of crust may be pushed aside by welling-up magma, or by friction against another plate, causing an earthquake. Over longer periods of time, the magma may bend and buckle the plate skywards to form mountain ranges.

Were this mountain-building force to go unchecked, the earth's surface might resemble that of the moon. But all the time the earth is building itself up, another force is busily breaking it down! We call this force the weathering force or, more simply, erosion.

Forces That Break Down

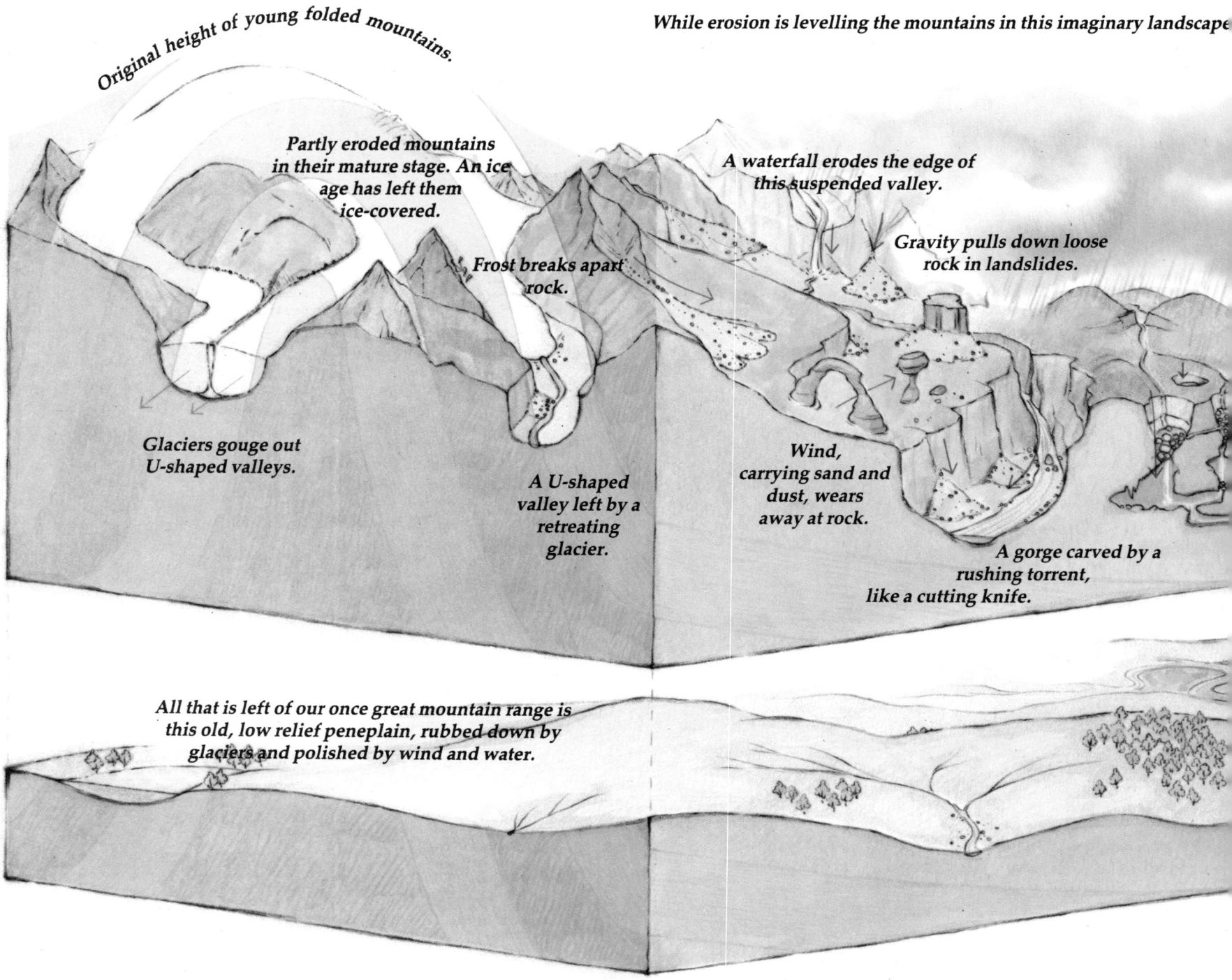

During a cold, icy winter, you have perhaps seen the roads' surface crack and break. In summer, by the sea, standing barefoot by the wet shore, you may have noticed how the waves pull the sand from beneath your feet. You have probably seen old paint flake off housefronts; or how cars, or wood, when left in the rain, will rust or rot. You are witnessing the weathering force!

The earth is one of the few planets in the solar system with an atmosphere, and perhaps the only one with water. A planet like the moon has little or no weathering, or erosion, since there is no wind or water to wear things down. Planet earth, however, because of its atmosphere, its tilt (varying seasons), and its frequent day and night cycle (heat and frost), has wind and weather to rub and grind down the surface.

Because the earth has vast reserves of

the mountain-building process is busy making new ones elsewhere!

In this imaginary landscape we can see how the weathering force is always changing the look of the land.

Blowhole
Arch
Stack
A rushing river eats away at the riverbed, creating a canyon.
Rainwater flows down hillsides as rushing streams . . .
Crumbling cliff
Sea waves, generated by wind, eat away at the coastline.
. . . carrying earth and pebbles with them.
Tree roots dig into the soil, often breaking up rocks near the surface.
A spring
Water filtering through limestone rocks creates holes and caverns.
A slow, wide, meandering river.
All the material that rivers and streams have carried downhill has been built up into new land by the sea.

The principal motor that drives the weathering force is the water cycle, running on sunlight (causing evaporation) and gravity.

water and a good gravity force there is rain and snow. The water provides rushing streams and waterfalls to cut out valleys and canyons, and rivers to carry the gouged stone and mud elsewhere.

The forces of erosion work like a great polishing stone, wearing the planet's face smooth. Why, if erosion had all its own way, it would level the earth's surface absolutely flat!

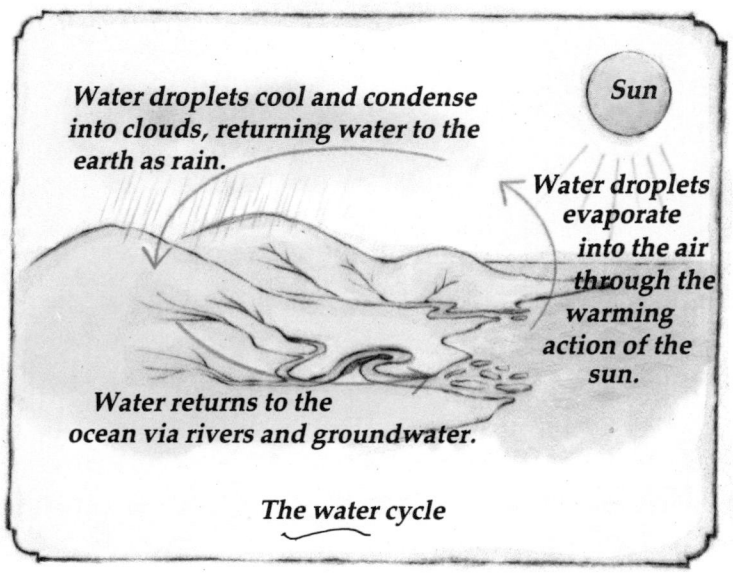

The water cycle

Earth's Changing Face

It is fun to look at old photos. You probably have some pictures of yourself when you were a baby. It's hard to believe that the baby is really you, the face looks so different! How will it compare with a picture of you in sixty years, all gray hair and wrinkles? It is hard to believe that the different faces belong to the same person.

Just as people's faces change with age, so does the earth's. If we had a photo of our planet several million years old, we would have a hard time recognizing where we live. The continents would have unfamiliar shapes, the oceans would be in different places and some of the great mountain chains might not appear at all! Similarly, a photo of our planet in the future would be equally surprising, for the mountains we ski on today will have been eroded flat, and the continents will have moved to new positions. For as we have seen, the earth is in a constant state of change from the two great forces that are right now building it up, and breaking it down.

As we go through life we are constantly changing. Our cells regenerate and our bone structure develops continuously. The change is relatively slow so that we don't see the changes from day to day, but only after several years.

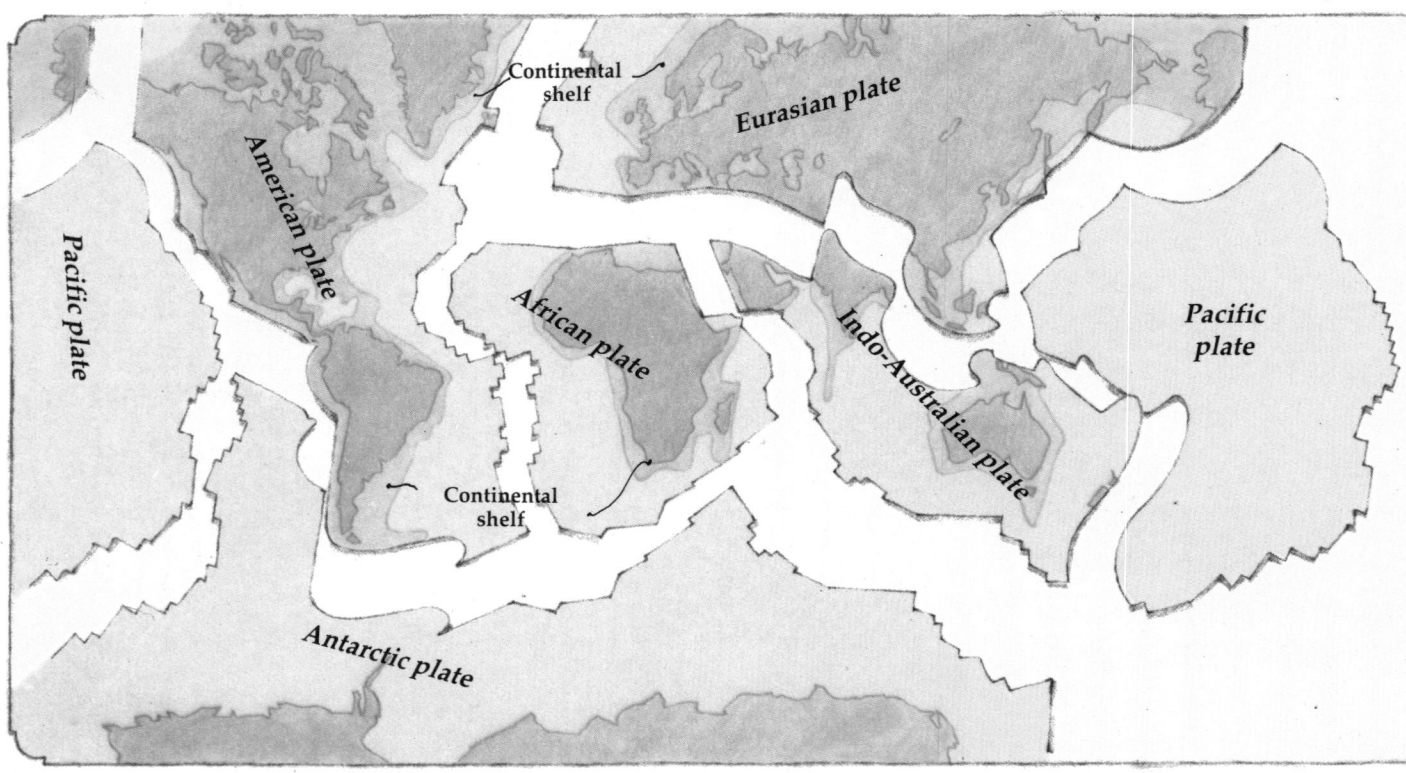

The earth's structure is also changing, but its life is so much longer that we can see the differences only after thousands of years. The earth's crust is made up of a number of plates which are floating on the molten mantle beneath, like blocks of ice on water.

Convection currents in the mantle may force the plates to shift on the earth's surface, moving the continents with them. The earth's face is constantly changing (over great spans of time), through this process called continental drift.

Coastlines do not form the real edges of the continents, any more than a waterline shows the bottom of a boat: their real bottom is under water! Continents have their true edges on their continental shelves, often many miles out to sea.

Recent exploration of the oceans has shown that the sea floor is much thinner and much newer than the rock beneath the continents. Great chains of active volcanoes have also been found running along the ocean floors. Many scientists now believe that new crust is being created by these submerged volcanoes, and that they are actually pushing apart the existing crustal plates, in a process called sea-floor spreading. As the crustal plates move apart, the continents move too, floating on an ocean of magma beneath. This idea of moving continents is known as the theory of continental drift.

If new crust is being formed beneath the sea, and the crustal plates are spreading, then what is happening at their opposite edges? The opposite edges quite simply bump together, folding the crust up into mountains, or folding it down to return to the molten mantle. However, sometimes the strain on a plate will become so great that it breaks violently, and then we feel an earthquake.

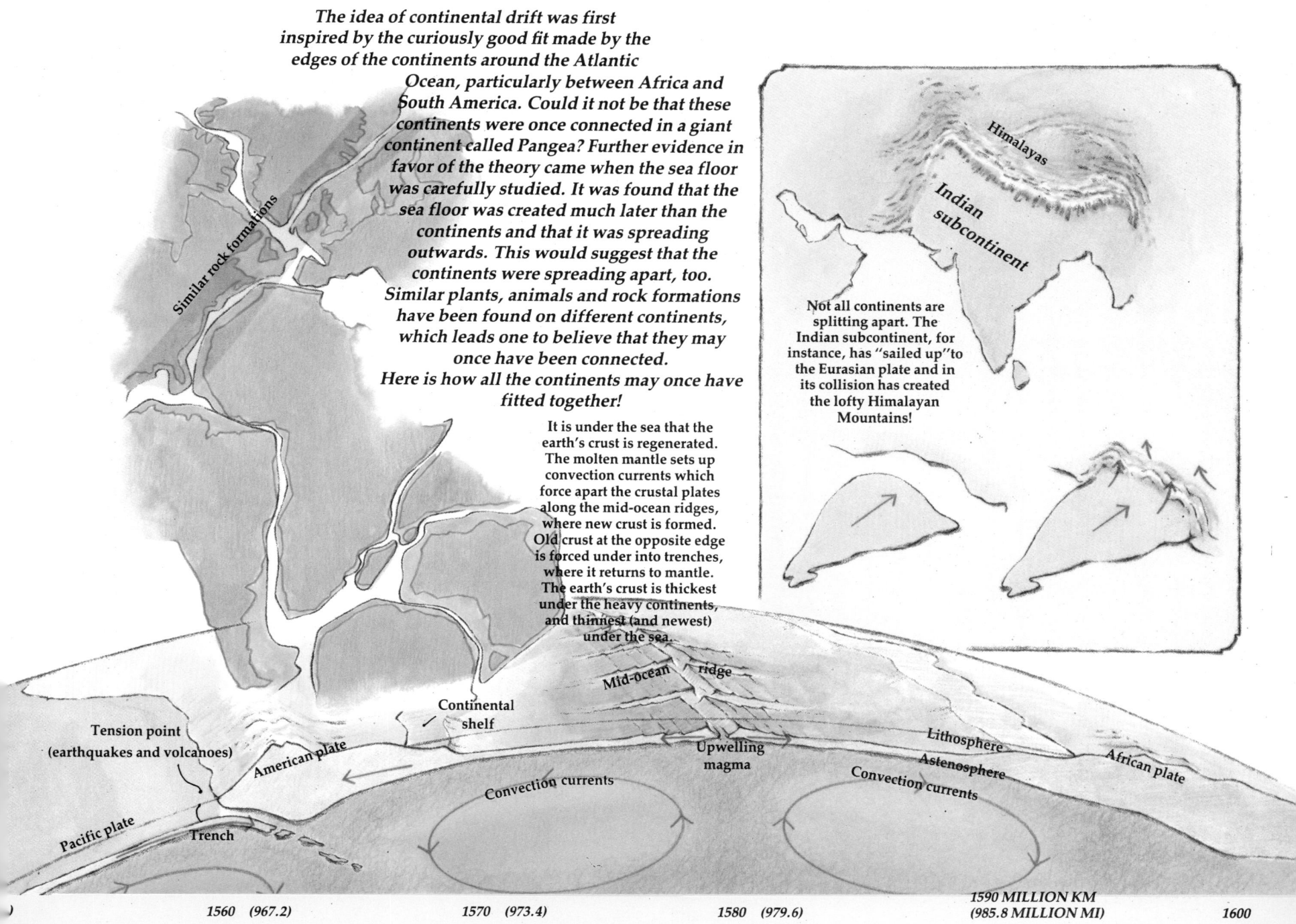

The idea of continental drift was first inspired by the curiously good fit made by the edges of the continents around the Atlantic Ocean, particularly between Africa and South America. Could it not be that these continents were once connected in a giant continent called Pangea? Further evidence in favor of the theory came when the sea floor was carefully studied. It was found that the sea floor was created much later than the continents and that it was spreading outwards. This would suggest that the continents were spreading apart, too. Similar plants, animals and rock formations have been found on different continents, which leads one to believe that they may once have been connected. Here is how all the continents may once have fitted together!

It is under the sea that the earth's crust is regenerated. The molten mantle sets up convection currents which force apart the crustal plates along the mid-ocean ridges, where new crust is formed. Old crust at the opposite edge is forced under into trenches, where it returns to mantle. The earth's crust is thickest under the heavy continents, and thinnest (and newest) under the sea.

Not all continents are splitting apart. The Indian subcontinent, for instance, has "sailed up" to the Eurasian plate and in its collision has created the lofty Himalayan Mountains!

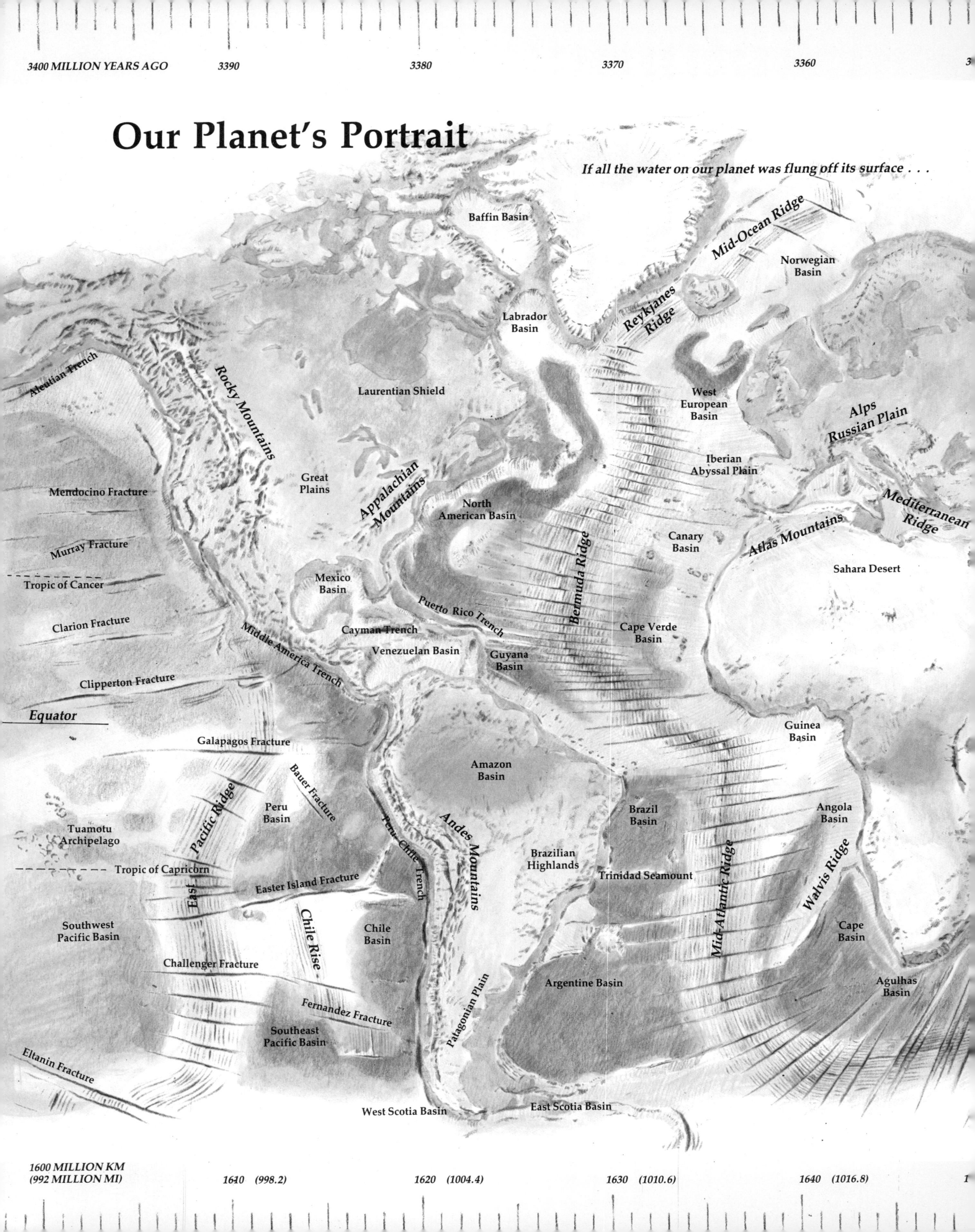
3400 MILLION YEARS AGO
3390
3380
3370
3360
Our Planet's Portrait
If all the water on our planet was flung off its surface . . .
Baffin Basin
Mid-Ocean Ridge
Norwegian Basin
Labrador Basin
Reykjanes Ridge
Aleutian Trench
Rocky Mountains
Laurentian Shield
West European Basin
Alps
Russian Plain
Iberian Abyssal Plain
Great Plains
Appalachian Mountains
Mendocino Fracture
North American Basin
Mediterranean Ridge
Canary Basin
Atlas Mountains
Murray Fracture
Bermuda Ridge
Sahara Desert
Tropic of Cancer
Mexico Basin
Puerto Rico Trench
Clarion Fracture
Cayman Trench
Cape Verde Basin
Middle America Trench
Venezuelan Basin
Guyana Basin
Clipperton Fracture
Equator
Guinea Basin
Galapagos Fracture
Amazon Basin
Bauer Fracture
Pacific Ridge
Peru Basin
Brazil Basin
Angola Basin
Tuamotu Archipelago
Peru-Chile Trench
Andes Mountains
Brazilian Highlands
Tropic of Capricorn
Trinidad Seamount
Mid-Atlantic Ridge
Walvis Ridge
East
Easter Island Fracture
Chile Rise
Chile Basin
Cape Basin
Southwest Pacific Basin
Challenger Fracture
Argentine Basin
Agulhas Basin
Fernandez Fracture
Patagonian Plain
Southeast Pacific Basin
Eltanin Fracture
West Scotia Basin
East Scotia Basin
1600 MILLION KM
(992 MILLION MI)
1610 (998.2)
1620 (1004.4)
1630 (1010.6)
1640 (1016.8)

. . . here is what we'd see! Compare this "earth-scape" with that of the moon on page 26.

Earth's Protective Overcoat

Our existence on earth is rather like living at the bottom of a big ocean. We crawl about on its floor like little crabs, and airplanes and birds dart through it like fish in water. We scarcely feel this "ocean's" presence, and rarely even see it, but without it we could not live. We call it the atmosphere.

The atmosphere is made up of a mixture of gases. Several other planets also have an atmosphere, but only earth's has just the right gases to permit life: oxygen, nitrogen, carbon dioxide and water vapor.

Like real oceans, the atmosphere has weight and pressure. Held down by the earth's gravity, it is densest at the bottom . . . the earth's surface.

Our atmosphere also acts as a protective shield, filtering out many harmful light rays from the sun. And, like a duck's eiderdown, it helps retain the sun's warmth during the hours of night. The atmosphere also protects the earth's surface from being hit by interplanetary matter, for friction against it burns up any such matter.

The mixture of gases in the atmosphere, which we call air, carries dust and water droplets. These, in the form of clouds, carry water all over the earth's surface, allowing plants to grow.

When the earth was newly formed the atmosphere around it condensed, forming water. Centuries of rain filled most of the planet's surface and gave us the deep, blue seas which became the cradle of life on earth.

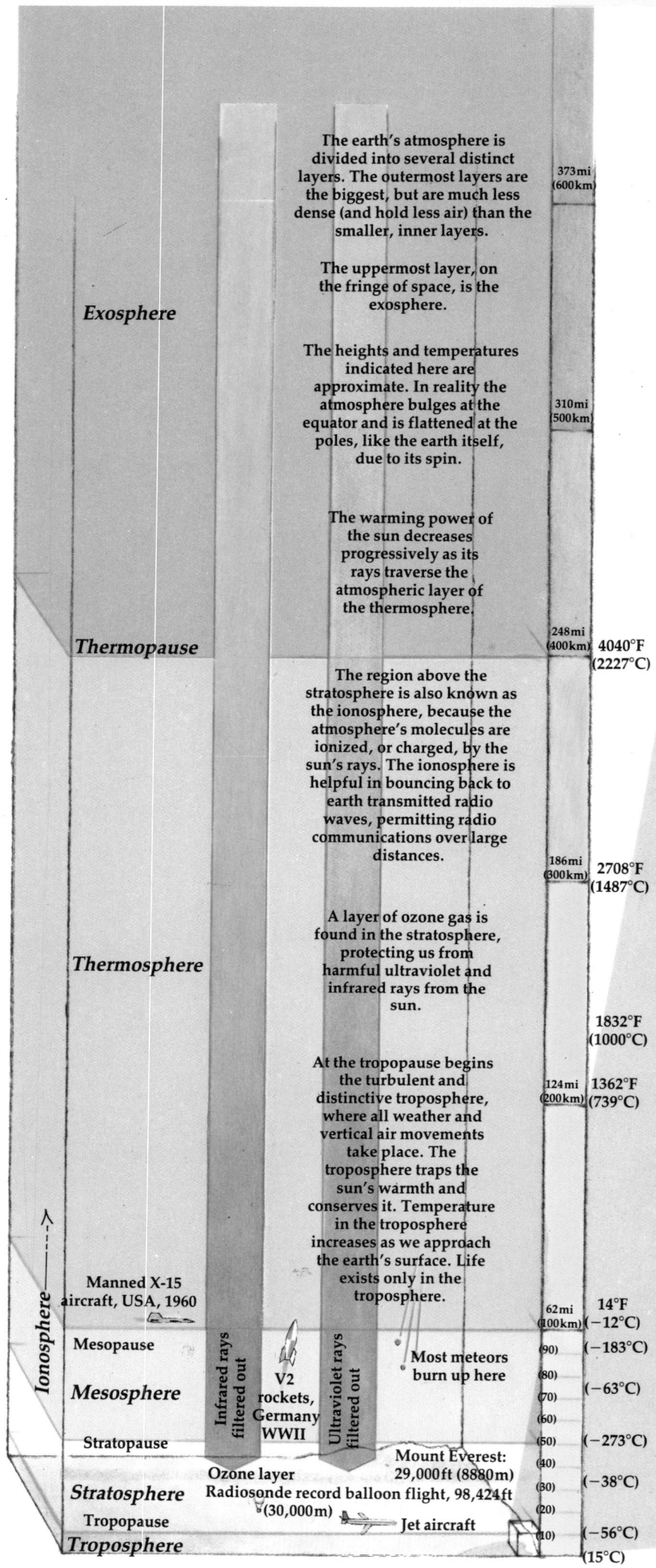

Why is the sky blue?

Light emitted from the sun is white, comprising all the colors of the spectrum. As the sunlight meets the molecules of air in the atmosphere, the bluish rays become scattered and so the sky appears blue. At sunset the sun's rays must pass through more atmosphere and more rays are filtered out, letting mostly red rays pass through. The sky appears red.

The winds

Sun

Horse latitudes

Equator

Doldrums

The sun's warming rays turn the troposphere into a giant, circulating radiator! Air heated at the equator rises skyward and cooler air moves in to replace it. This makes wind.

Where air rises or descends there is little or no wind on the earth's surface. Such regions are known as the doldrums and horse latitudes. However, the earth's tilt, the seasons, land and water masses, make the atmosphere a constantly changing and unpredictable place. The earth's spin deflects all surface winds in what is known as the coriolis effect. Winds in the north veer to the right, while those to the south veer left.

Earth's rotation

Clouds are formed by condensing water droplets in the troposphere. Here are some of them:

Cirrus

Cirrocumulus

Cirrostratus

Altocumulus

Altostratus

Cumulonimbus

Nimbostratus

Cumulus

Stratus

The ocean of air moves much like the oceans of water. Currents of cold air chase movements of warm air, setting up winds, changes in temperature and the weather. Places where warm and cold air masses meet are known as fronts. Cold fronts move under warm air masses, while warm fronts move over cold masses. Both movements can bring clouds and precipitation.

Gliders use the upward currents of warmed air masses to stay aloft.

Warm air

Cold air

Warm air

Cold air

Wind provides power for sailing ships . . .
. . . and for windmills.

996
Low pressure
1004
1012
1016
1020
1024
High pressure

Cold front

Warm front

A hydrogen balloon stays aloft because it is filled with a gas whose weight is less than that of the surrounding air. It floats through the ocean of air like an air bubble in the sea.

Because air has density, it causes friction against things moving through it. A parachute makes a slow and gentle descent thanks to the air's density. An airplane stays aloft due to differing air densities on each side of its wings.

6.2mi (10km)
5.5mi (9km)
4.9mi (8km)
4.3mi (7km)
3.7mi (6km)
3.1mi (5km)
2.4mi (4km)
1.8mi (3km)
1.2mi (2km)
0.6mi (1km)
0 Sea level

(This diagram is not drawn to scale)

Air pressure, or the density of air, also varies from place to place. As you rise in altitude, air pressure decreases. But air pressure can also vary over large surfaces on the earth, and these, in constant movement, affect the weather. Generally places of high pressure cause clouds to evaporate, while low pressure zones accumulate clouds and suffer from rainy weather.

Planet Ocean

For most of us, in our minds, the earth is land. Many of us have never seen the ocean, and most have only seen its shore. From land our view of the earth is far from complete. Indeed, from space we can see that the continents are but islands floating on a planet of water. In fact the oceans, or more correctly *the* world ocean, covers a good 70 percent of our planet. We might be tempted to rename our planet earth, planet ocean!

The ocean has always been a mysterious place. Even today more is probably known about the surface of the moon than the depths of our own planet.

In the past the ocean was seen by man as a terrifying barrier, blocking his route to distant shores. Fishing its waters was a perilous business reserved only for the brave or foolhardy.

Today we are just beginning to change that idea. The vast ocean, rich in life and resources, may be man's only salvation to continue living on an overcrowded earth.

In its infant years the earth bore little resemblance to the one we know today. The atmosphere was a poisonous gas, and the unfiltered sunrays made life intolerable on the earth's surface. It was under the protective blanket of water that the first micro-organisms flourished. Feeding on water and sunlight, through a process called photosynthesis, these micro-plants emitted oxygen into the atmosphere. After millions of years the atmosphere took on a more familiar composition, and the first plants were able to poke their heads above water and eventually take root on land.

Animals, which had developed exclusively in the sea, followed. Perhaps the first animals to put their nose on a beach did so to lay their eggs there, safe from predators. With food available on land, in the form of plants, animals adapted to spend more and more time out of their original element, the sea.

We, as human beings, the last link in the chain of evolution, have lost all contact with the sea. For generations we have dumped our waste there and have been fishing its inhabitants to extinction. Yet the sea is our birthplace, and it is fitting that in this era of dwindling land resources man is seeking his future in the sea.

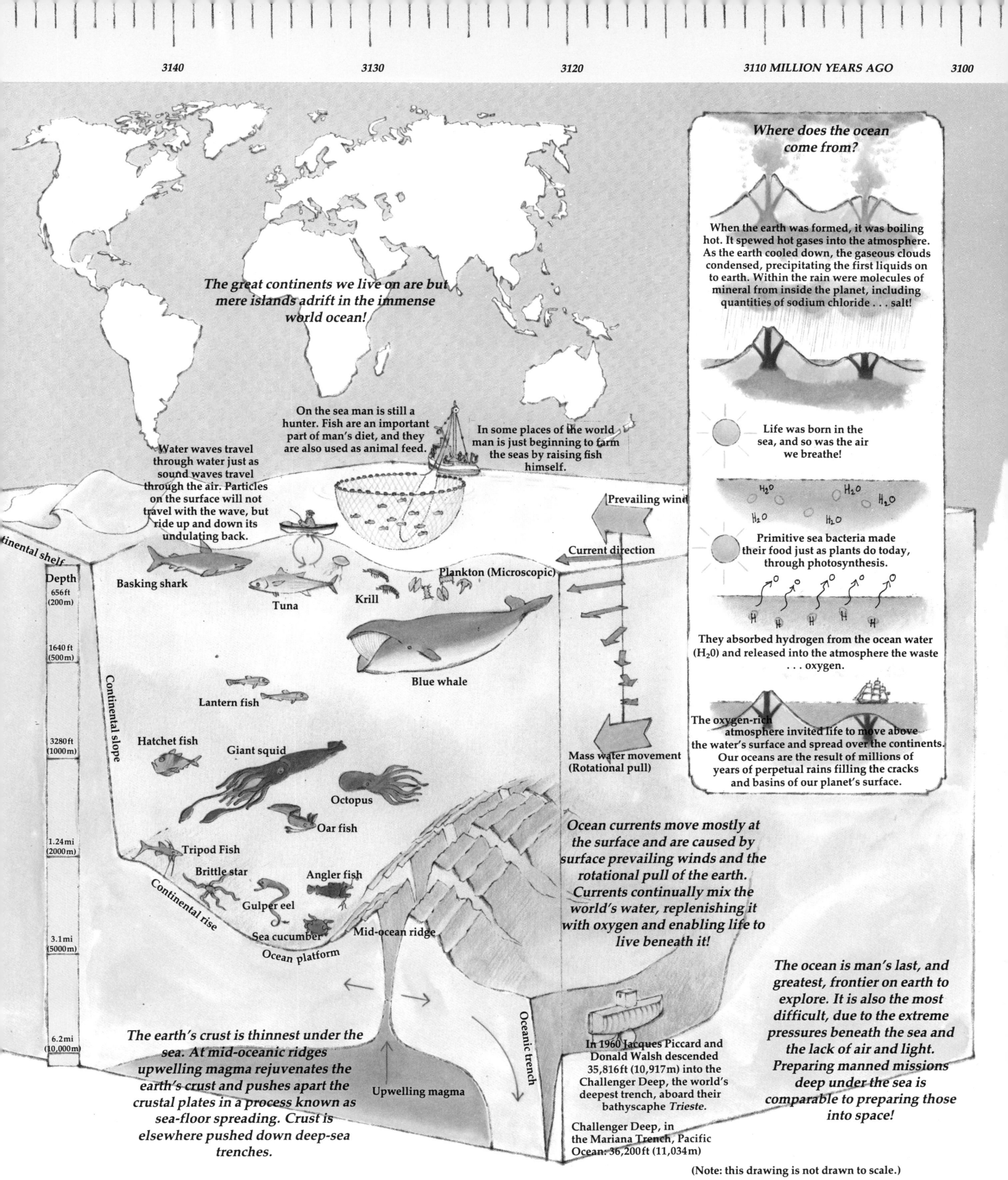
3140
3130
3120
3110 MILLION YEARS AGO
3100
The great continents we live on are but mere islands adrift in the immense world ocean!
On the sea man is still a hunter. Fish are an important part of man's diet, and they are also used as animal feed.
In some places of the world man is just beginning to farm the seas by raising fish himself.
Water waves travel through water just as sound waves travel through the air. Particles on the surface will not travel with the wave, but ride up and down its undulating back.
Prevailing wind
Current direction
Basking shark
Tuna
Krill
Plankton (Microscopic)
Blue whale
Lantern fish
Hatchet fish
Giant squid
Octopus
Oar fish
Tripod Fish
Brittle star
Angler fish
Gulper eel
Sea cucumber
Mid-ocean ridge
Ocean platform
Continental slope
Continental rise
Oceanic trench
Upwelling magma
Mass water movement (Rotational pull)
Depth
656 ft (200m)
1640 ft (500m)
3280 ft (1000m)
1.24 mi (2000m)
3.1 mi (5000m)
6.2 mi (10,000m)
Where does the ocean come from?
When the earth was formed, it was boiling hot. It spewed hot gases into the atmosphere. As the earth cooled down, the gaseous clouds condensed, precipitating the first liquids on to earth. Within the rain were molecules of mineral from inside the planet, including quantities of sodium chloride . . . salt!
Life was born in the sea, and so was the air we breathe!
H_2O
Primitive sea bacteria made their food just as plants do today, through photosynthesis.
They absorbed hydrogen from the ocean water (H_2O) and released into the atmosphere the waste . . . oxygen.
The oxygen-rich atmosphere invited life to move above the water's surface and spread over the continents. Our oceans are the result of millions of years of perpetual rains filling the cracks and basins of our planet's surface.
Ocean currents move mostly at the surface and are caused by surface prevailing winds and the rotational pull of the earth. Currents continually mix the world's water, replenishing it with oxygen and enabling life to live beneath it!
The ocean is man's last, and greatest, frontier on earth to explore. It is also the most difficult, due to the extreme pressures beneath the sea and the lack of air and light. Preparing manned missions deep under the sea is comparable to preparing those into space!
The earth's crust is thinnest under the sea. At mid-oceanic ridges upwelling magma rejuvenates the earth's crust and pushes apart the crustal plates in a process known as sea-floor spreading. Crust is elsewhere pushed down deep-sea trenches.
In 1960 Jacques Piccard and Donald Walsh descended 35,816 ft (10,917m) into the Challenger Deep, the world's deepest trench, aboard their bathyscaphe Trieste.
Challenger Deep, in the Mariana Trench, Pacific Ocean: 36,200 ft (11,034m)
(Note: this drawing is not drawn to scale.)
1860 (1153.2)
1870 (1159.4)
1880 (1165.6)
1890 MILLION KM (1171.8 MILLION MI)
1900

The Bricks of Life

If you were asked "Just *what* is a living thing?" would you know the answer? You might say that a living thing breathes. Yes, but so does a bellows, and that is not alive. Living things move, but so do non-living things, like cars. Living things grow, but crystals, non-living, can grow too, adding new layers to themselves. There is just one thing that non-living things cannot do, and that is to reproduce. Everything that is alive, be it you, your dog, a flower or a tree, has the ability to make replicas of itself, or offspring.

Everything alive is made up of millions upon millions of tiny, living cells. Cells are the bricks, or building-blocks, of living things. Cells can reproduce too, by splitting themselves in two. If you stumble and scrape your knee, your skin cells will get to work to reproduce the damaged skin and repair the wound.

You may wonder, as scientists have wondered for years, who tells the cells when and what to do? Scientists have recently discovered a marvelous microscopic molecule, located deep within the cells. These molecules, called DNA, are made like long,

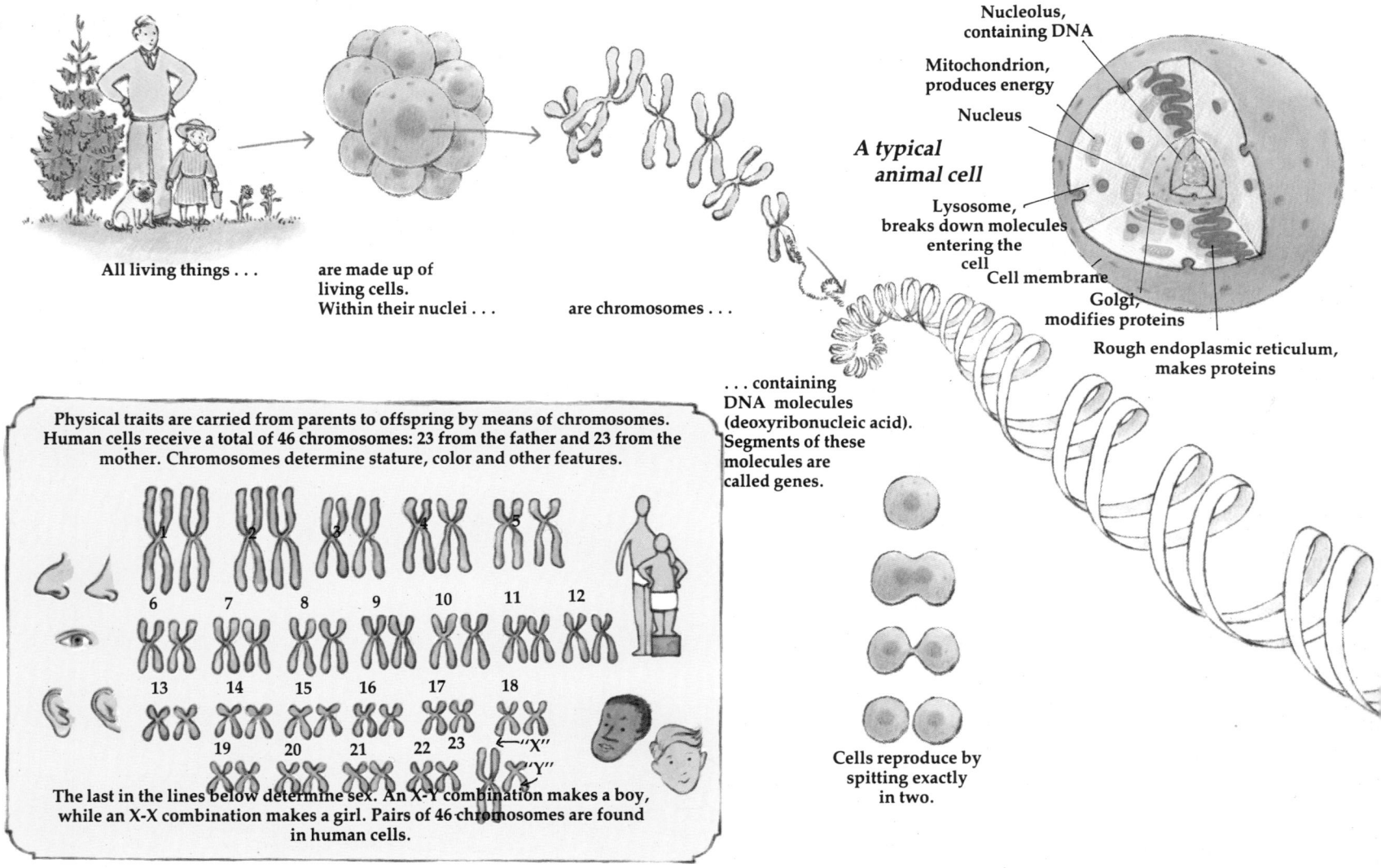

From giant whales to minute insects, and shady trees to perfumed

twisted ladders, and on each rung are the instructions for the cell to follow. Scientists are fascinated with DNA molecules because they are the ultimate "grains of life," and control of them might heal man's illnesses.

When the cells of a living thing split, to produce offspring, they usually reproduce exact copies of themselves. Sometimes, however, they might accidentally make offspring not quite faithful to the original. The offspring might have a deficiency – lacking a finger, for instance. But sometimes, very rarely, it might make the offspring even better suited for life. Such modifications in offspring are called mutations.

As the earth itself has changed through the ages, so have living things adapted to those changes. The changes have been gradual, over many generations. We are the result of innumerable mutations, stemming from apes, which permit us to live in almost any part of the globe. Through mutations in offspring nature selects those best suited for life. Thus, as the earth has evolved, so have the living things. That is the story of evolution through natural selection.

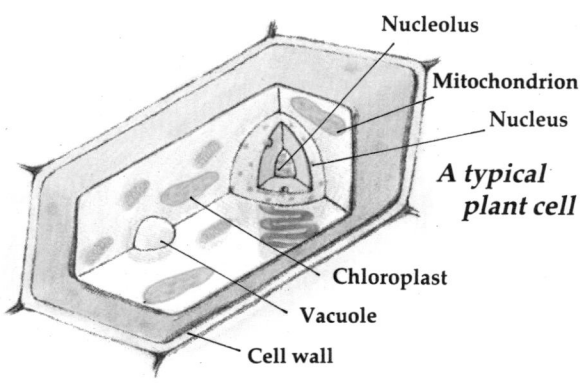

A typical plant cell

Deep within the nucleus of the cell are long molecules strung like curly party-streamers. These molecules, called DNA, hold all the instructions for the living cell to perform its tasks. The structure of DNA is one of a spiral ladder. The twisted legs hold the ladder rungs. The rungs may be one of four nucleic acid bases: adenine (A); thymine (T); cytosine (C); or guanine (G). The sequence of these acids along the ladder provides the recipe of tasks for the cell to follow.

DNA molecules reproduce during cell division by splitting neatly down their middle and entwining new ladder legs with the old. Since A can only match T, and C can only match G, the molecule easily makes replicas of itself.

Should it accidentally make a mistake in copying, the mistake will affect the nature of the gene. A mutation will occur in the offspring.

lowers, we are each made of the same "bricks" of life. . . .

We are all members of one family of life on earth!

The Family Tree of Life

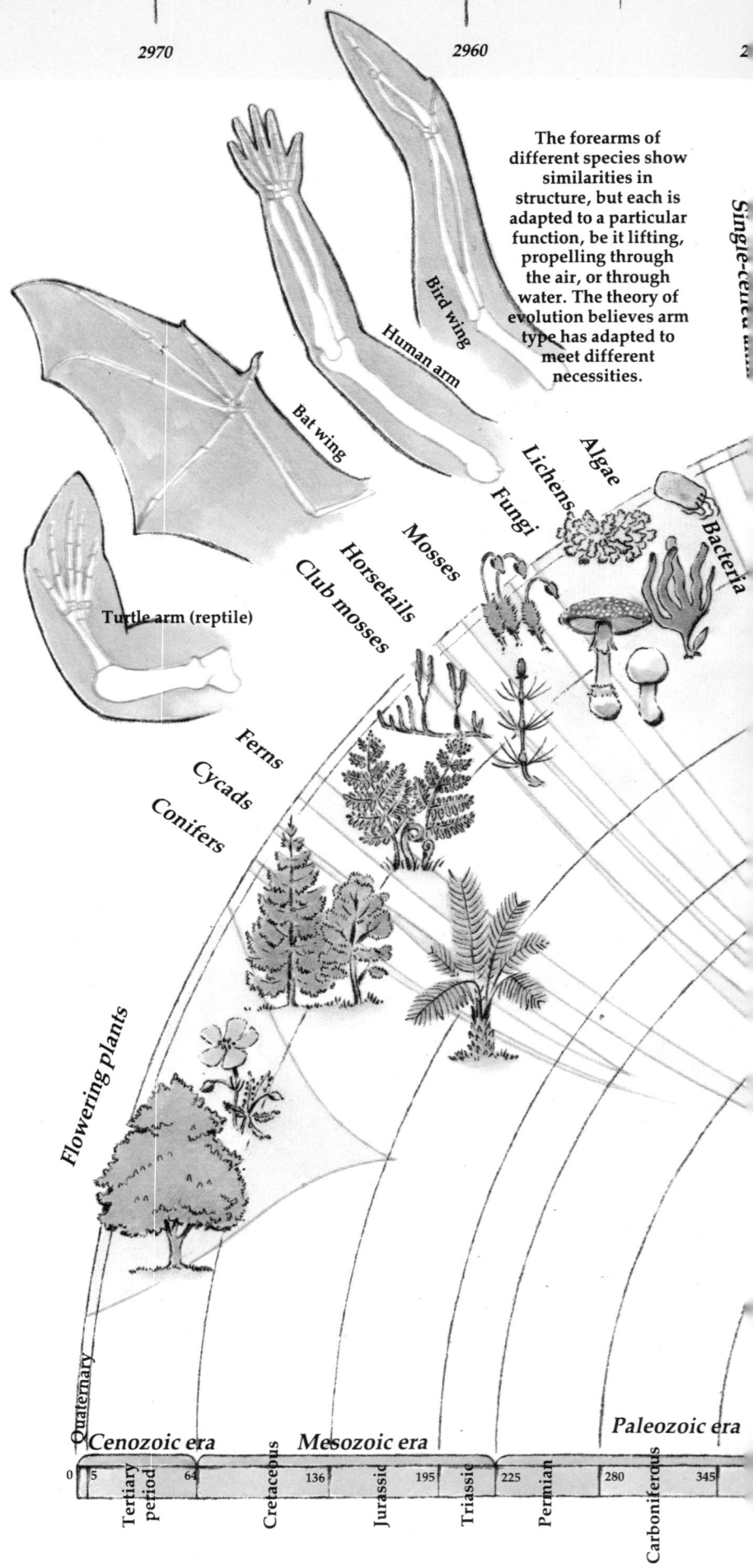

The Old Testament of the Bible states that God created the earth in just six days. He made the oceans one day, the mountains on another, all the plants and animals, and on the sixth day man himself. After all that work, he took the seventh day to rest. For hundreds of years people believed this was how the earth was made, and all its inhabitants created.

We know now that the earth has been going through perpetual change. Its once poisonous atmosphere became a supporter of life; its continents shifted, tore apart, or bumped together. It has gone through periods of intense cold, when the oceans became locked in ice. No animals on earth today could have endured such drastic changes in climate, so could it not be that animals changed, or adapted themselves to suit the changes of the earth? This is the question that a young English naturalist aboard a sailing ship in the tropical seas asked himself. His name was Charles Darwin.

Coming from the temperate climate of England, Darwin was impressed by the profusion of life forms in the tropics. He found dozens of varieties of the same type of animal: tortoises with slightly different shells; or birds with slightly different beaks, depending on where they lived and what they found to eat. Would God have made so many endless varieties of animal to inhabit the earth? Could it be that nature had adapted the animals over generations to survive where they lived?

After returning to England, and after

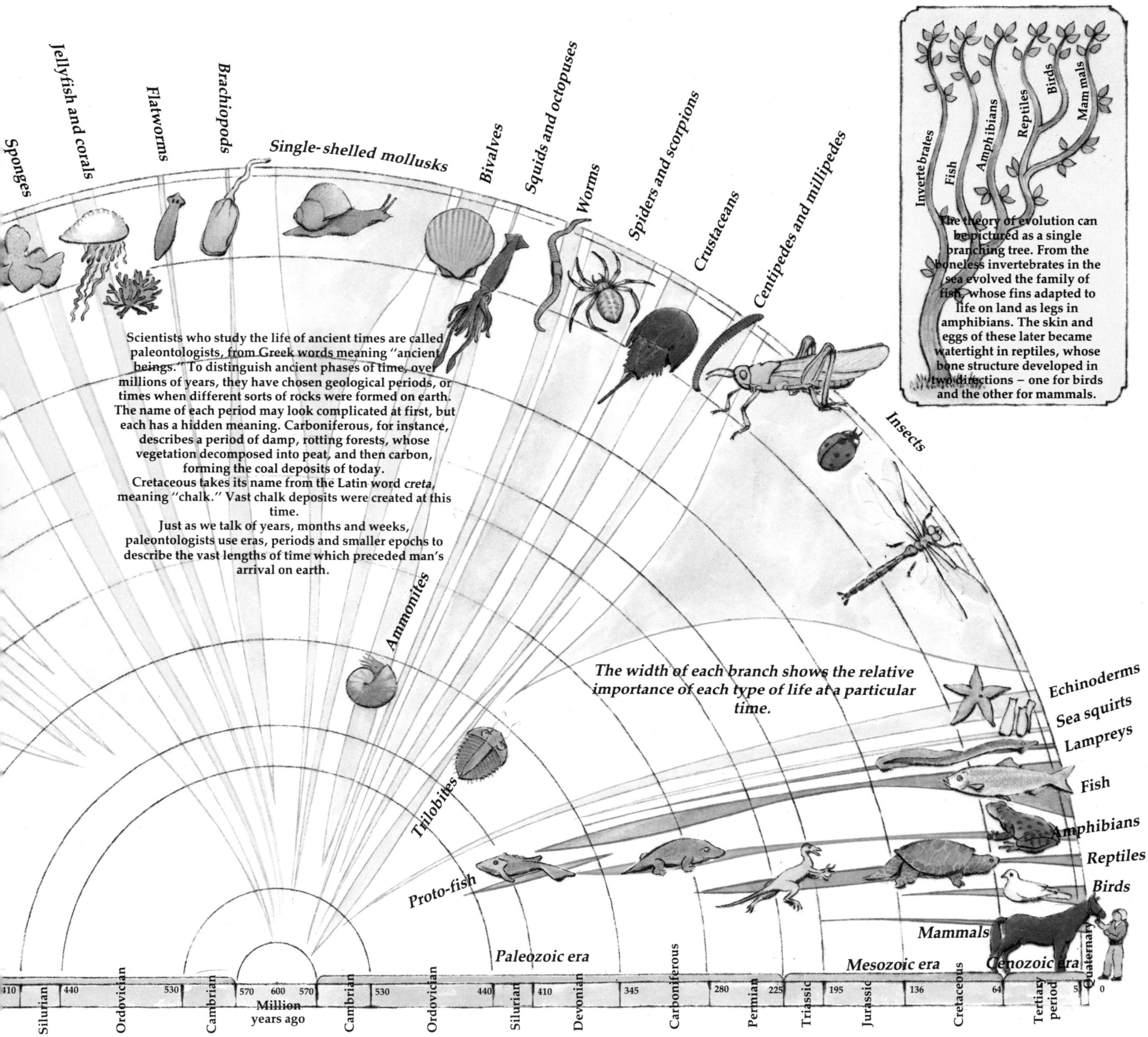

years of hesitation, Darwin published his ideas on evolution. Everyone ridiculed his theories, which related man himself to the apes!

Since then we have learned that the variety of life, from microbes to plants, through fish, reptiles, birds and mammals, is a chain of innumerable mutations in heredity to enable life to cope with the ever-changing earth.

From the Roots of Life . . .

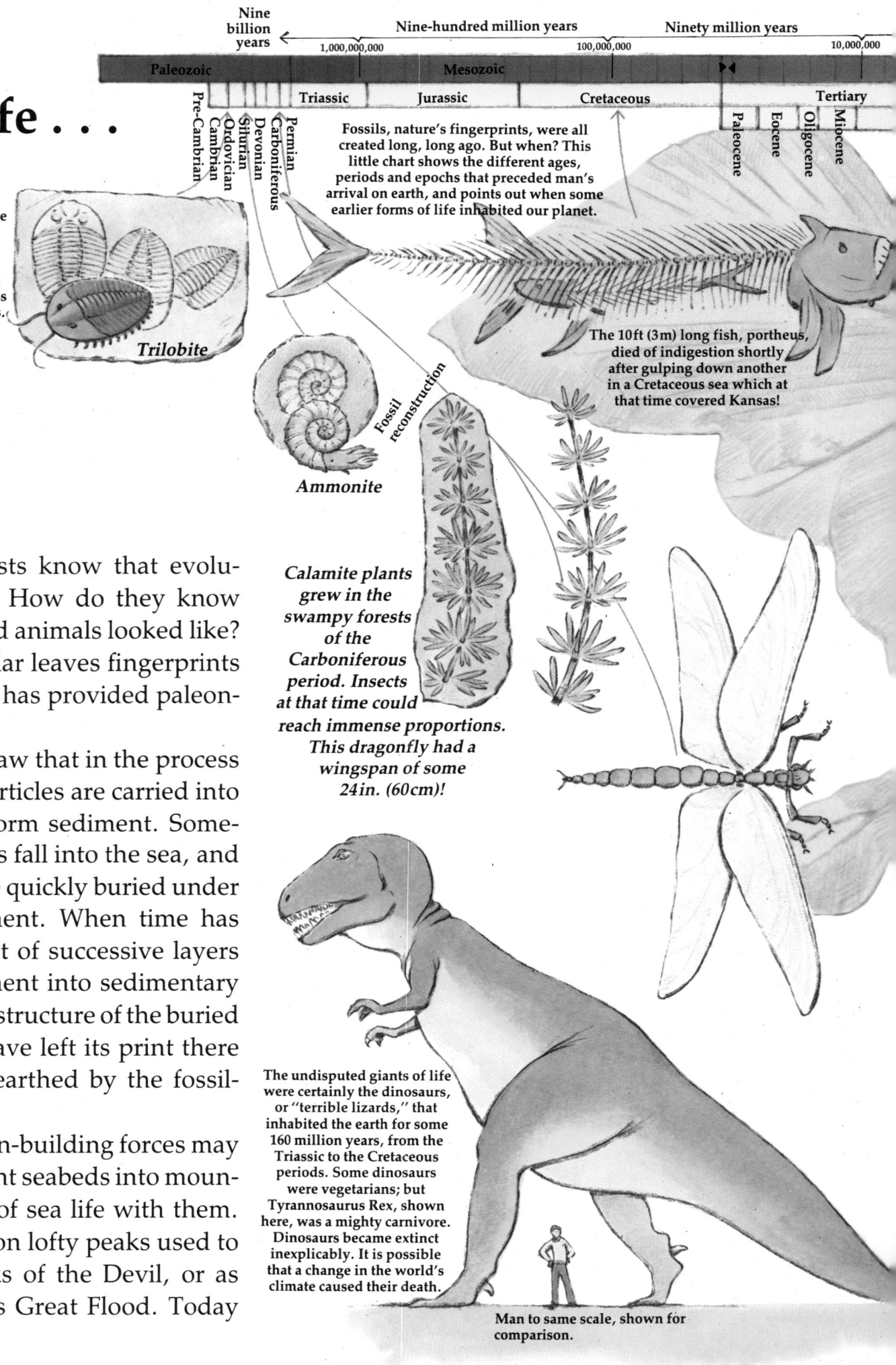

How do paleontologists know that evolution has taken place? How do they know what extinct plants and animals looked like? Just as a careless burglar leaves fingerprints for a detective, nature has provided paleontologists with fossils.

On pages 34–5 we saw that in the process of erosion fine rock particles are carried into the sea, where they form sediment. Sometimes plants or animals fall into the sea, and just rarely they may be quickly buried under a layer of new sediment. When time has passed and the weight of successive layers has pressed the sediment into sedimentary rock, the hard or bony structure of the buried plant or animal will have left its print there . . . waiting to be unearthed by the fossil-hunter's hammer!

The earth's mountain-building forces may bend and buckle ancient seabeds into mountains, carrying fossils of sea life with them. Fossils of sea animals on lofty peaks used to be thought of as tricks of the Devil, or as evidence of the Bible's Great Flood. Today

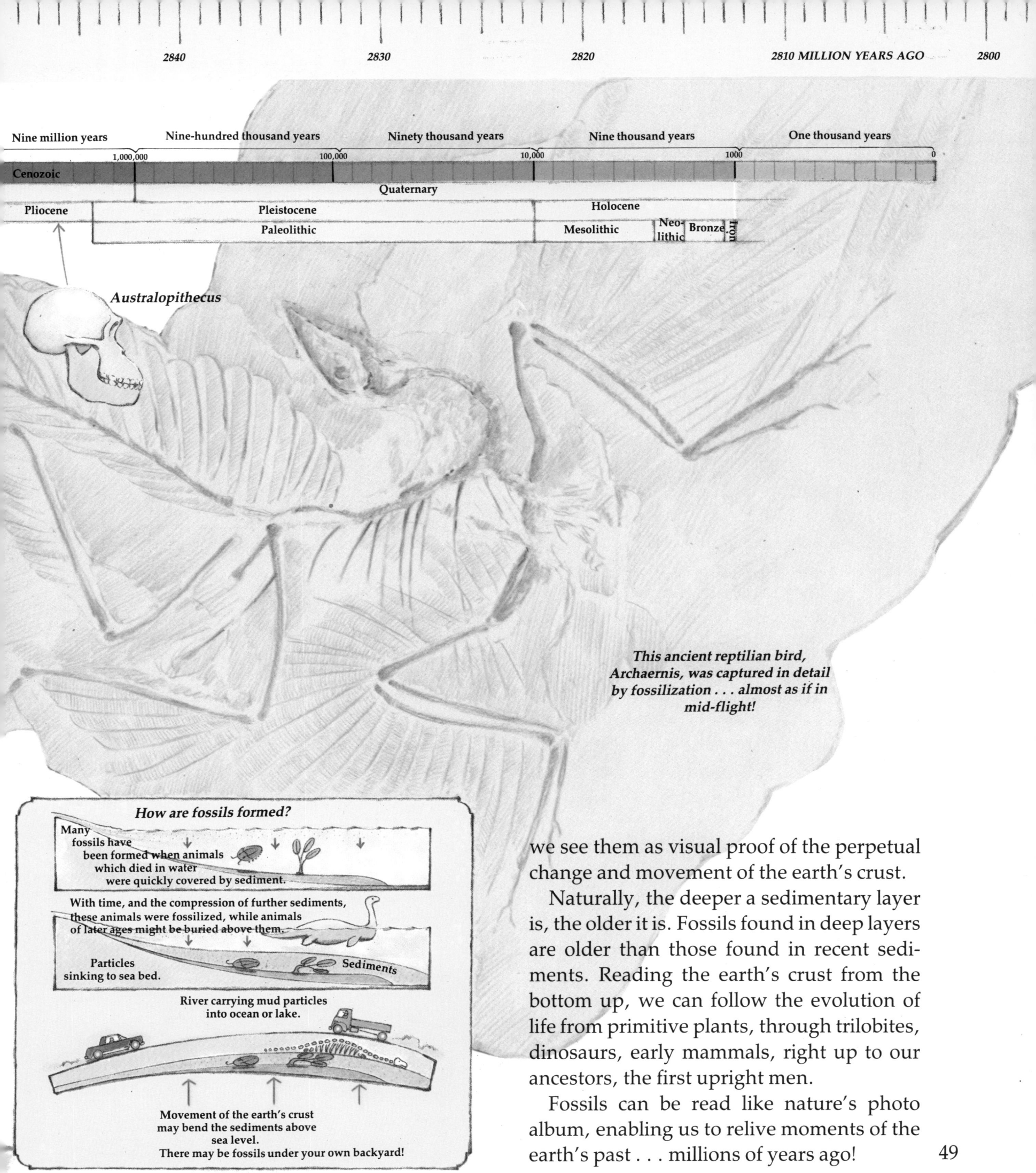

This ancient reptilian bird, Archaernis, was captured in detail by fossilization . . . almost as if in mid-flight!

we see them as visual proof of the perpetual change and movement of the earth's crust.

Naturally, the deeper a sedimentary layer is, the older it is. Fossils found in deep layers are older than those found in recent sediments. Reading the earth's crust from the bottom up, we can follow the evolution of life from primitive plants, through trilobites, dinosaurs, early mammals, right up to our ancestors, the first upright men.

Fossils can be read like nature's photo album, enabling us to relive moments of the earth's past . . . millions of years ago!

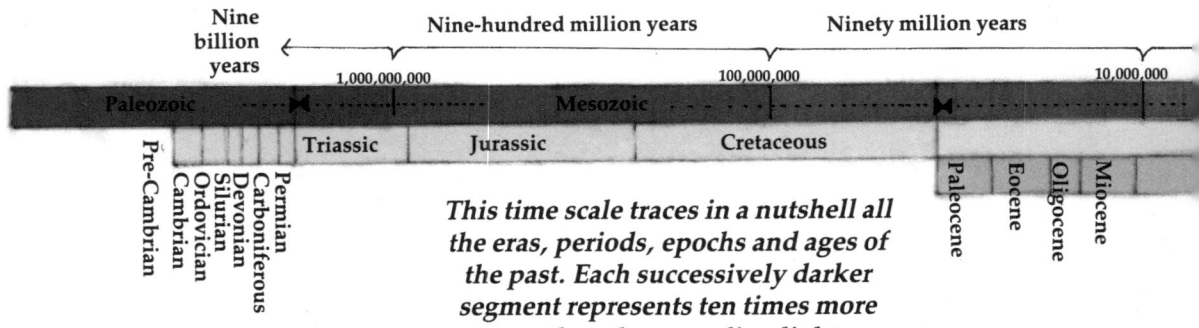

This time scale traces in a nutshell all the eras, periods, epochs and ages of the past. Each successively darker segment represents ten times more years than the preceding lighter segment.

. . . To the Uppermost Branches

There is magnificent diversity in the animal world. There are animals of every shape, color and size; flying, swimming or crawling on the earth. Even more fascinating is the order, or similarity, in animals.

All animals are made of cells. They all breathe. Many have similar bone structures. One group of animals within the mammal family has striking similarities with man himself. These animals have man's keen sense of vision, similar bone and skull structures, and fingers and toes capable of grasping and climbing, aided by thumbs. These animals are called primates and include tree-dwelling lemurs, tarsiers, monkeys and apes, as well as man himself.

Charles Darwin's theory of evolution has long been misunderstood by people, for they interpreted it to mean that man is descended from the apes we see in the zoo. This certainly isn't so. The evolution of apes is as long as the evolution of man. But somewhere, far, far back in time, the two species may have had a common ancestor.

Searching for man's ancestors and studying his evolution is called the science of anthropology. Anthropologists learn about ancient man the same way that paleontologists study ancient animals . . . through fossils.

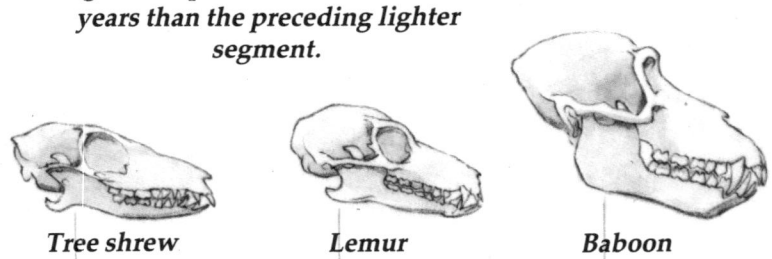

Although modern man is not a descendant of other present-day primates, these can give us an idea of how our distant ancestors may have evolved.

Here is a small dictionary to help you decipher the paleontologists' and anthropologists' difficult terminology. Names are generally derived either from Ancient Greek (Gr), or from Latin (Lat).

-cene, ceno (Gr): new, recent	Pleisto *(Gr): most*
Eo *(Gr): early*	Plio *(Gr): more*
Holo *(Gr): wholly*	-zoic *(Gr): life*
-lithic *(Gr): stone*	Australo *(Lat): southern*
Meso *(Gr): middle*	Homo *(Lat): man*
Mio *(Gr): less*	Erectus *(Lat): Upright*
Neo *(Gr): new*	Pithecus *(Gr): ape*
Oligo *(Gr): little*	Sapiens *(Lat): wise*
Paleo *(Gr): old*	*Cro-Magnon:* Name of a cave in France where remains were found.
Neanderthal: A valley in Germany where remains were found.	

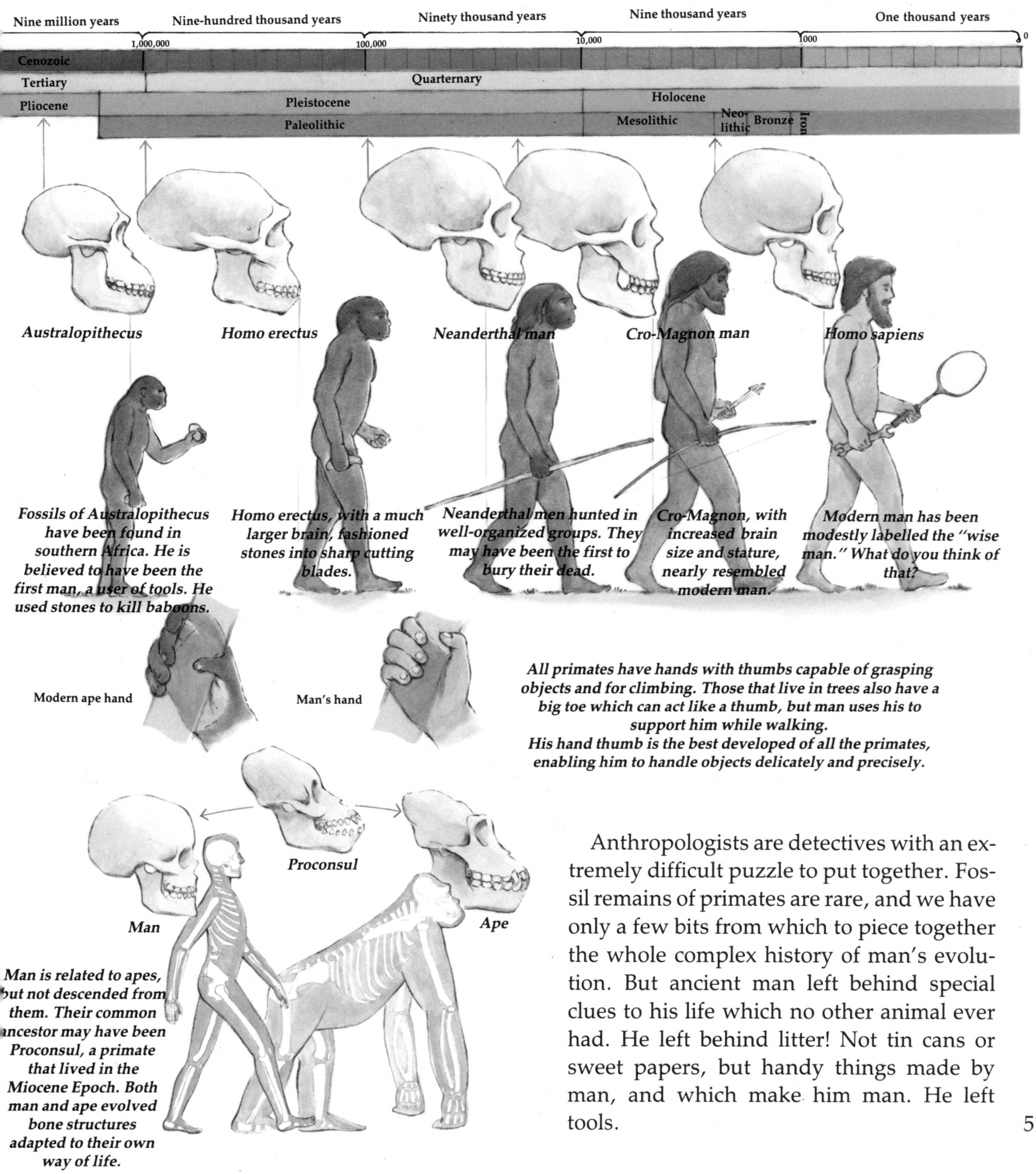

Anthropologists are detectives with an extremely difficult puzzle to put together. Fossil remains of primates are rare, and we have only a few bits from which to piece together the whole complex history of man's evolution. But ancient man left behind special clues to his life which no other animal ever had. He left behind litter! Not tin cans or sweet papers, but handy things made by man, and which make him man. He left tools.

Man the Maker

For millions of years life existed on earth and no animal made tools. Why did early man? He walked upright and could run, he had good eyesight. But he was nonetheless at a real disadvantage on earth.

First of all, man shared the planet with many other animals who were bigger, stronger and faster than he. Not only did he have to fight for food, he was in constant danger of becoming another animal's dinner!

Secondly, early man had to cope with severe changes in climate. During his evolution our planet several times became very cold. The seas retreated and turned into ice, covering most of the Northern Hemisphere during what we call the Ice Ages. Most plants and animals perished from the cold, but man coped and survived by using his head and his hands. He invented implements and tools which reached farther than his arm, gave strength to his hands, and which were sharper than teeth or claws. With these he fashioned shelter, clothing, and still better tools. We might say that man's inventiveness was triggered by his hungry stomach and his lack of a woolly or furry pelt!

What is remarkable about the first tools man made was that he had no examples to copy. By himself he "saw" in a branch or stick an extension to his arm. He "saw" in a stone a hammer, an axe or a knife. No one was there to show him how to tie a knot, or sew a hide. He found out everything by himself.

Other animals make things too. Beavers build dams, birds make nests, and bees build beehives. There is, however, a distinct difference between what other animals and man make. Other animals build from instinct. Their skills need not be learned. Also, they do not improve them.

Man, on the other hand, from birth must *learn* everything. From his parents, and others, he imitates and is instructed in all he

Early man shared his environment with other animals stronger and faster than himself. Man's tools, however, gave him an upper hand, and made him the dominant animal.

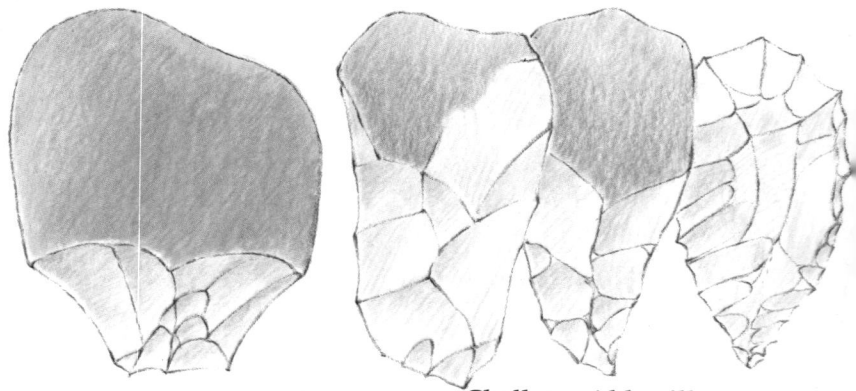

Oldowan Chopper
Two million years ago

Chellean, Abbevillean, Acheulean hand axes
600 thousand 400 thousand 200 thousand years ago

The first shovel was an animal's shoulder blade!

Tools started man on the road to master his environment. His first tools, no more than chipped stones, helped him to cut wood and animal hides.

Fire was one of early man's best friends. It kept him warm, protected him from other animals, made meat easier to cut, and made wooden spear tips harder.

Woolly mammoth Smilodon Woolly rhino

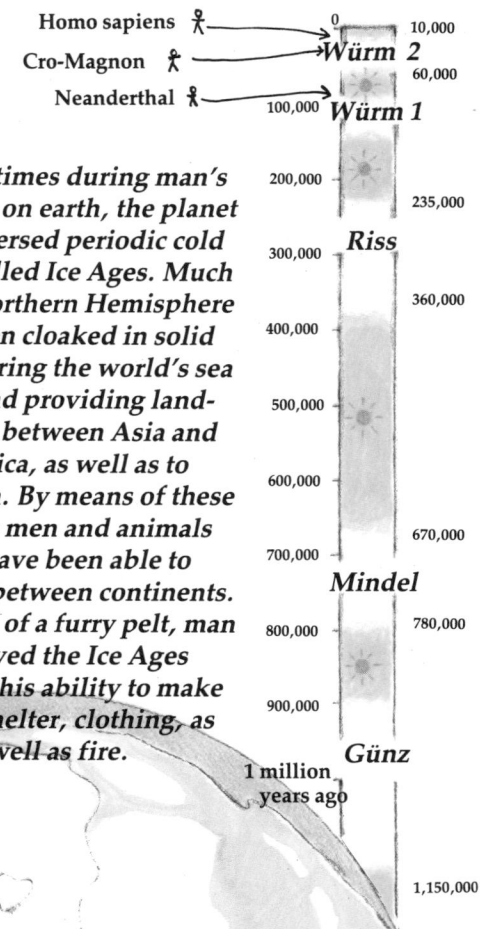

Several times during man's existence on earth, the planet has traversed periodic cold spells called Ice Ages. Much of the Northern Hemisphere was then cloaked in solid ice, lowering the world's sea level and providing land-bridges between Asia and America, as well as to Australia. By means of these bridges men and animals may have been able to migrate between continents. Deprived of a furry pelt, man survived the Ice Ages through his ability to make tools, shelter, clothing, as well as fire.

Although other animals can make things instinctively, man learns from experience and he can improve on his initial ideas: in this case, hand axe blades. Learning was at first extremely slow, for hundreds of thousands of years passed between the making of the chopper on the left and the knife blades to the right. But this was man's first step to putting himself on the moon!

Man found protection from the elements within the shelters and clothing, made by himself.

Knife blades
20-30 thousand years ago

Needles were made from bone.

Thongs were cut from hides.

Stone blades could be made by flaking.

Canoes were fashioned from tree trunks.

needs to go through life. He gains knowledge and experience which he can store in his memory. He can call on this memory to reconstruct what he's learned, or mix it to conceive new ideas. All this he does with his greatest gift, and most important "tool" . . . his incredible brain.

Man the Thinker

The brain is certainly one of nature's most incredible creations. Its capability seems to be as limitless as the universe.

The brain's function is to keep the organs of a body working properly and to keep that body alive. At the same time, for humans in particular, it is a "bank" for storing information as memory. Storing knowledge there enables us to learn and to put bits of information together to judge, decide, and get new ideas.

The brain is made up of several distinct parts, and each of these parts has evolved through millions of years to its present size according to its usefulness. Not all animals have brains, only the upper vertebrates, or animals with backbones. The brain of each type of animal has evolved to suit that animal's needs. A fish's brain, for instance, has an extra large portion reserved for eyesight, so the fish can see better underwater. Other animals have an extra-sensitive sense of smell or hearing. The human brain has developed a voluminous bank or warehouse to store all we need to know to go through life! This bank, known as the cerebrum, accounts for around 85 percent of our brain's weight.

What do we mean when we talk about the mind? The brain can be seen as all the different parts put together in our heads, but the mind is more difficult to describe. The mind is basically what the brain *does*. The mind is thought, memory, emotion, action, sensation, perception, and so on. Very little is really known about the mind, it is so complex. For instance, we don't know if the mind is physical matter, or if it is something immaterial and immortal – what is sometimes called the soul.

Knowledge is what the mind has stored as memory. You may think that knowing more makes you smarter, but this is not really true. Knowing more can give you more skills, as speaking many languages lets you talk to many more people. Knowledge is necessary to do a job well, and to make everyday decisions. But knowledge is not truth. Knowing that something is *so*, only means we *believe* it to be so. Saying "I know" means only "I think I know." What you know from the past may not be true in the present, or disproven in the future. Information you read or hear may not be correct in the first place. Understanding the limits of knowledge gives one an open mind.

And so what is intelligence? It used to be thought that the bigger one's brain, the more intelligent one was. This isn't so. Man's brain is big so it can store lots of knowledge. Encyclopedias and computers store lots of knowledge, but neither is intelligent. Intelligence, to put it simply, is "paying attention." An intelligent mind uses knowledge like a reference library, but it needs no books to "see" clearly.

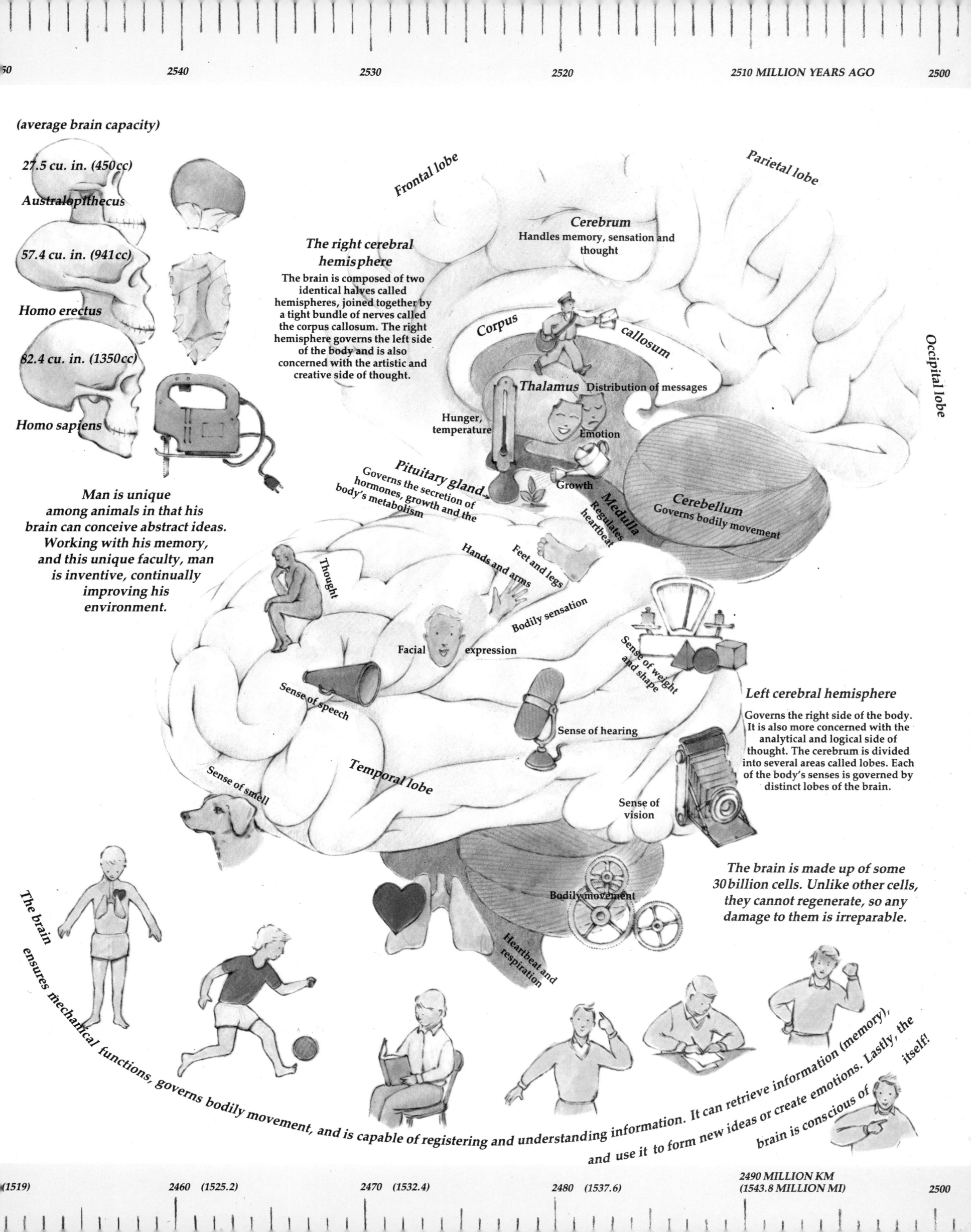
2540
2530
2520
2510 MILLION YEARS AGO
2500
(average brain capacity)
27.5 cu. in. (450cc)
Australopithecus
57.4 cu. in. (941cc)
Homo erectus
82.4 cu. in. (1350cc)
Homo sapiens
Man is unique among animals in that his brain can conceive abstract ideas. Working with his memory, and this unique faculty, man is inventive, continually improving his environment.
Frontal lobe
Parietal lobe
Occipital lobe
Cerebrum
Handles memory, sensation and thought
The right cerebral hemisphere
The brain is composed of two identical halves called hemispheres, joined together by a tight bundle of nerves called the corpus callosum. The right hemisphere governs the left side of the body and is also concerned with the artistic and creative side of thought.
Corpus
callosum
Thalamus
Distribution of messages
Hunger, temperature
Emotion
Pituitary gland
Governs the secretion of hormones, growth and the body's metabolism
Growth
Medulla
Regulates heartbeat
Cerebellum
Governs bodily movement
Thought
Hands and arms
Feet and legs
Bodily sensation
Facial expression
Sense of weight and shape
Sense of speech
Sense of hearing
Temporal lobe
Sense of smell
Sense of vision
Left cerebral hemisphere
Governs the right side of the body. It is also more concerned with the analytical and logical side of thought. The cerebrum is divided into several areas called lobes. Each of the body's senses is governed by distinct lobes of the brain.
Bodily movement
Heartbeat and respiration
The brain is made up of some 30 billion cells. Unlike other cells, they cannot regenerate, so any damage to them is irreparable.
The brain ensures mechanical functions, governs bodily movement, and is capable of registering and understanding information. It can retrieve information (memory), and use it to form new ideas or create emotions. Lastly, the brain is conscious of itself!
(1519)
2460 (1525.2)
2470 (1532.4)
2480 (1537.6)
2490 MILLION KM
(1543.8 MILLION MI)
2500

Man the Inquirer

Science has provided us with answers to many questions about our physical world, but numerous fields remain barely explored, or seem unattainable. The forces in the universe – those behind atoms, the actions of the mind, and the incredible order throughout all of nature – fill us with awe and wonder.

Prehistoric man had no science, and much less knowledge of the world than we have today. He must have been baffled and frightened by thunderstorms; amazed at the sight of fire, a rare occurrence. He watched the sun and moon travel across the sky, but had no idea why. The death of his parents and comrades would have left him confused.

It was evident to him that some other more powerful forces governed his environment. Was it not natural that man should wish to stay on good terms with these forces, that they might be favorable to him? Perhaps this is where man's spiritual beliefs began; but it is only a guess, for he left little evidence behind him.

Anthropologists have tried to piece together the meaning behind the few relics we have of man's early spiritual life. The most beautiful pieces of evidence are surely the paintings left deep inside caves. These magnificent, stylized pictures of animals were certainly not drawn just for fun, or even to be seen by others. They were painted in the most inaccessible part of a cave,

Early man had no scientific explanations to help him understand the world he lived in. In his wonderment and fear of nature's actions, he was certain of one thing: there was some greater power exerting its force over everything on earth.

An older member of a tribe, respected for his wisdom, may have been thought to have skills in communicating with superhuman powers. This wise man, or shaman, conducted rituals and was called on to take the members of the tribe through the rites of life – just as a priest today performs baptisms, weddings and funerals.

Bear skull burials may have been primitive sacrifices to ensure the continuity of game to hunt. The burial of deceased men, often with their belongings, testify to man's early belief in an afterlife.

Here is an orbiting electron of the atom whose

To ensure the continuity of the tribe, early sculptors may have made these Venuses to win the favors of a fertility god.

where not even light would penetrate. You have probably heard of voodoo dolls, into which medicine men stick pins to inflict a wound on whomever the doll represents. Prehistoric man probably believed that his painting had similar powers. By painting an animal, he "controlled" its spirit. He would sometimes draw arrows over the animal, probably to ensure its capture in the next hunt.

Early man also paid tribute to the powers who "made" the animals. He would offer the powers parts of the captured animal, usually the skull and some bones, by burying them carefully. This way he thought that the powers would continue to provide more animals to hunt.

There were no doctors to take care of people who were ill, and presumably many sicknesses were fatal. People didn't live long. To ensure that a tribe did not die out, it was important that mothers had as many children as possible. Early man may have carved the numerous little Venus statuettes which had been believed to ensure fertility and the continuance of his tribe.

The cave paintings and the statuettes are evidence of man's belief in magic. Special rituals were doubtless performed regularly, conducted by an older member of the tribe, called the shaman. The shaman may have communicated with the powers, and guided the tribe with his advice.

nucleus is on page 18, 33 ft (10 meters) away!

Man the Speaker

Most animals on earth communicate in one way or another. Blessed with senses to receive information, they have developed various ways of sending information as well.

Communications among animals are known as displays. Displays serve a variety of purposes. As a means of identification, a bird's call can attract a suitable mate. Its song can also warn others of impending danger. Other displays can indicate an animal's intentions.

Each animal has developed its own way of "speaking" to others, suited to its needs. An ant may show another ant where there is food by releasing scent on a trail. A bee, having found flowers with nectar, will do a dance back at the beehive, indicating the route to all the others. Deep at the bottom of the ocean there is no light at all, but some fish live there, equipped with their own lanterns. They are capable of making an electric current which lights them up like a bright neon sign!

"Badging" is communication, too. We can tell a robin by its bright red chest, and a zebra by its stripes. All these communications, however, are little more than signals. Animals cannot relate a story, or express an idea. They lack one thing: language. We humans take language for granted, but have you ever thought how you would live without it? How would you convey your wishes, or ask a question?

Without language, there would be no society, no culture, no arts, or ideas. Have you ever thought what language *is*? We can think in pictures, but mostly we think in language. Language is a way of thinking. It is also the expression of thought! Language and thought are woven like fabric. One weave supports the other. We do not know how language began. Man had certainly been speaking for hundreds of thousands of years before he began writing.

Languages are alive and change with time and where they are spoken. People of one language may borrow words from another, and drop old words which have become obsolete. Languages have been so mixed together that many languages share common, basic vocabularies: words which stand for the same thing, and which sound alike. Just as brothers and sisters share traits of the same parents, some words share traits of a parent language. Languages with a related basic vocabulary make up a family of languages, probably descended from a parent language.

There are several families of language on earth. One of the biggest is the Indo-European family, whose members include languages from Europe to India. Other families include the Sino-Tibetan, the Altaic, and the African Negro family, to name but a few. There is probably no original language, any more than there was an original man. Nor is any language better than another. Some languages sound musical, others a bit dry, but all languages are above all a means of cooperation between men.

Cooperation means understanding, working together, building together. Thanks to language, that is just what early man began to do.

Icelandic
Norwegian
Swedish
Danish
Gaelic
Gallic
English
Frisian
Dutch
Flemish
German
Breton
Gothic
Old Prussian
Lithuanian
Latvian
Polish
Czech
Ukranian
Germanic
Celtic
Slavonic
Indo-European
Indo-Iranian
Portuguese
French
Spanish
Latin
Italian
Romanian
Serbo-Croatian
Albanian
Bulgarian
Greek
Old Iranian
Sanskrit
Armenian
Pushtu
Persian
Baluchi
Punjabi
Bengali
Marathi
Hindustani
Gujarati

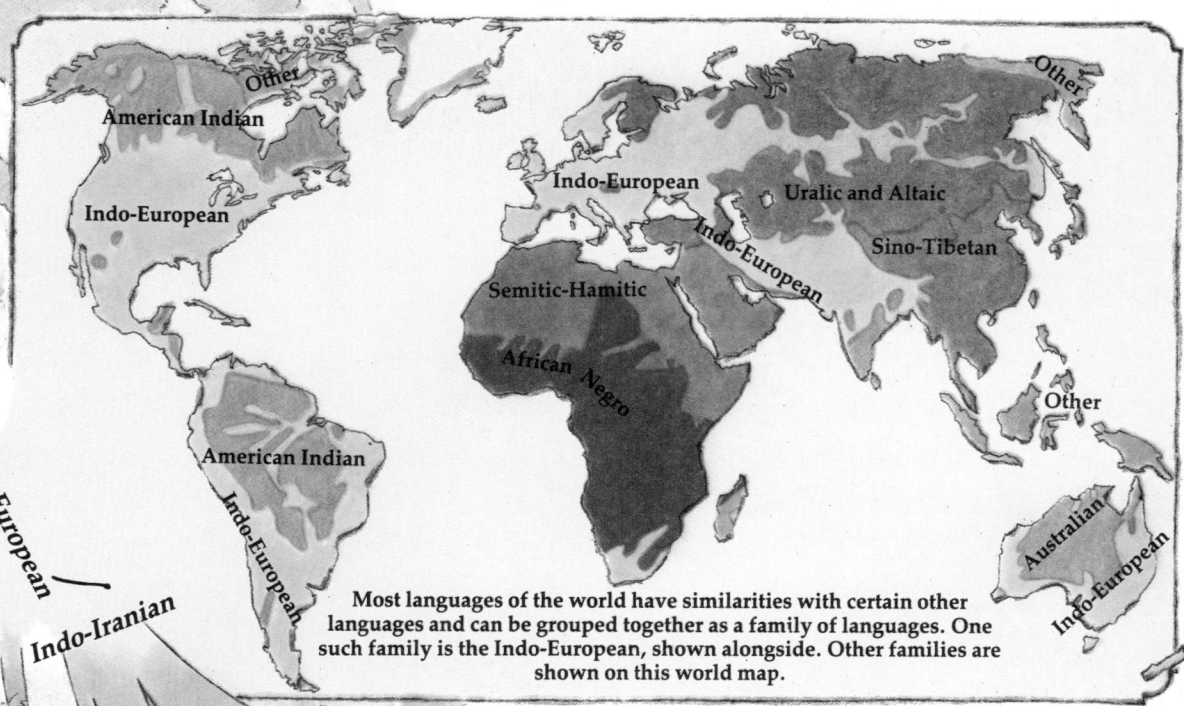

Most languages of the world have similarities with certain other languages and can be grouped together as a family of languages. One such family is the Indo-European, shown alongside. Other families are shown on this world map.

The United Nations comprises most of the nations on earth, as a forum for resolving problems between them. Of course, most of the world's languages are spoken here, but as long as there is a willingness to listen to others, nations have a chance to cooperate peacefully with one another.

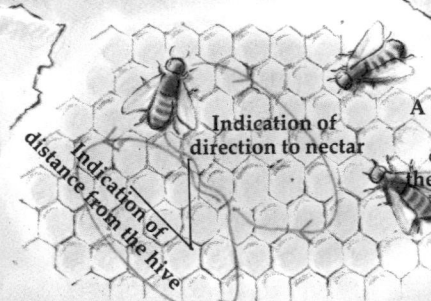

A bee returning to the hive tells its co-workers where there is more nectar by doing a dance.

The relation of several Indo-European languages can be seen clearly from the selection of words below:

German	English	Italian	Latin	Greek	Armenian	Sanskrit
Mutter	Mother	Madre	Mater	Mater	Mayr	Mátàr
Vater	Father	Padre	Pater	Pater	Hyar	Pitàr
ist	is	è	est	esti	e	asti
neu	new	nuovo	novus	ne(w)as	nar	návas
Knie	knee	ginocchio	genu	gonu	cune	jānu
drei	three	tre	tres	treis	erek´	tráyas
sechs	six	sei	sex	hex	vec´	sát

Animal communication spans from simple identification markings, as on the zebra, to instinctive transmission of information, as in the honeybee dance. Toothed whales and dolphins make groans and cries and receive echoes from reflecting objects. It is possible that they also have a language of their own with which they communicate with one another.

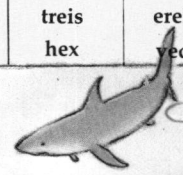

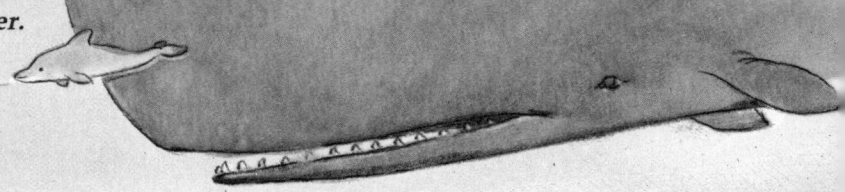

From Hunter to Herder

Early man lived as a hunter. He survived the Ice Age thanks to the skill of his hands, the cunning of his brain, and his gift for learning, aided by speech.

Generation after generation, he was always on the move, in the wake of the roaming herds he relied on for food. When the ice which covered much of the Northern Hemisphere retreated, as the earth warmed up, the face of the planet took on a new appearance. The melted ice filled the oceans and made them rise, covering numerous land-bridges which formerly joined the continents. Life on the planet changed too, as animals like the woolly mammoth and reindeer moved north and different, smaller animals came to live in the great forests which grew up from wasteland. Along wide rivers and lakes man not only hunted animals but caught fish, too, with traps, hooks and harpoons.

One day, returning from a hunt, someone may have brought back to camp the babies of

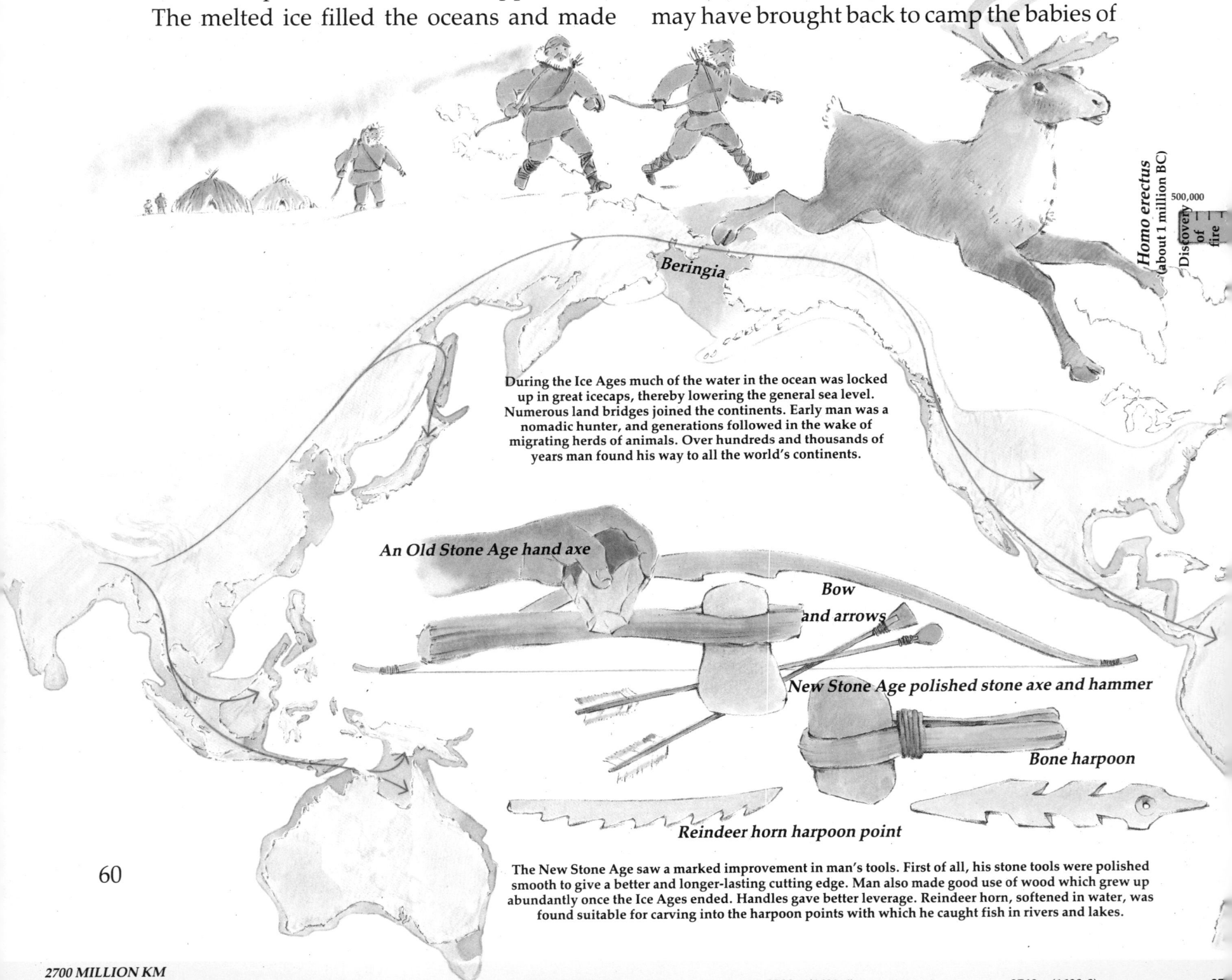

During the Ice Ages much of the water in the ocean was locked up in great icecaps, thereby lowering the general sea level. Numerous land bridges joined the continents. Early man was a nomadic hunter, and generations followed in the wake of migrating herds of animals. Over hundreds and thousands of years man found his way to all the world's continents.

The New Stone Age saw a marked improvement in man's tools. First of all, his stone tools were polished smooth to give a better and longer-lasting cutting edge. Man also made good use of wood which grew up abundantly once the Ice Ages ended. Handles gave better leverage. Reindeer horn, softened in water, was found suitable for carving into the harpoon points with which he caught fish in rivers and lakes.

the captured prey. These young animals may have been brought up by the tribe as pets, but it was evident, too, that once fully grown they would also make a good meal! Man had discovered that if he kept animals, he would no longer need to hunt them.

We have no idea when or how man first became domesticated, but it would bring a big change in the way he lived. First of all, he had more food. He tended goats which gave milk, pigs which gave meat, and sheep which also gave wool for clothing. Without the need to hunt, people could live longer in one place, and they built the first settlements, making huts from the materials at hand, be it mud, clay, grass or wood.

With better food and living conditions, people lived longer, and the population grew bigger. Children and old people alike found new tasks, such as tending the herd or gathering berries, fruit and wild grain – from which, it was discovered, bread could be made.

For the first time, man lived "at home." To distinguish this new sedentary life from the old nomadic one, historians have given this age the name Neolithic, or New Stone Age.

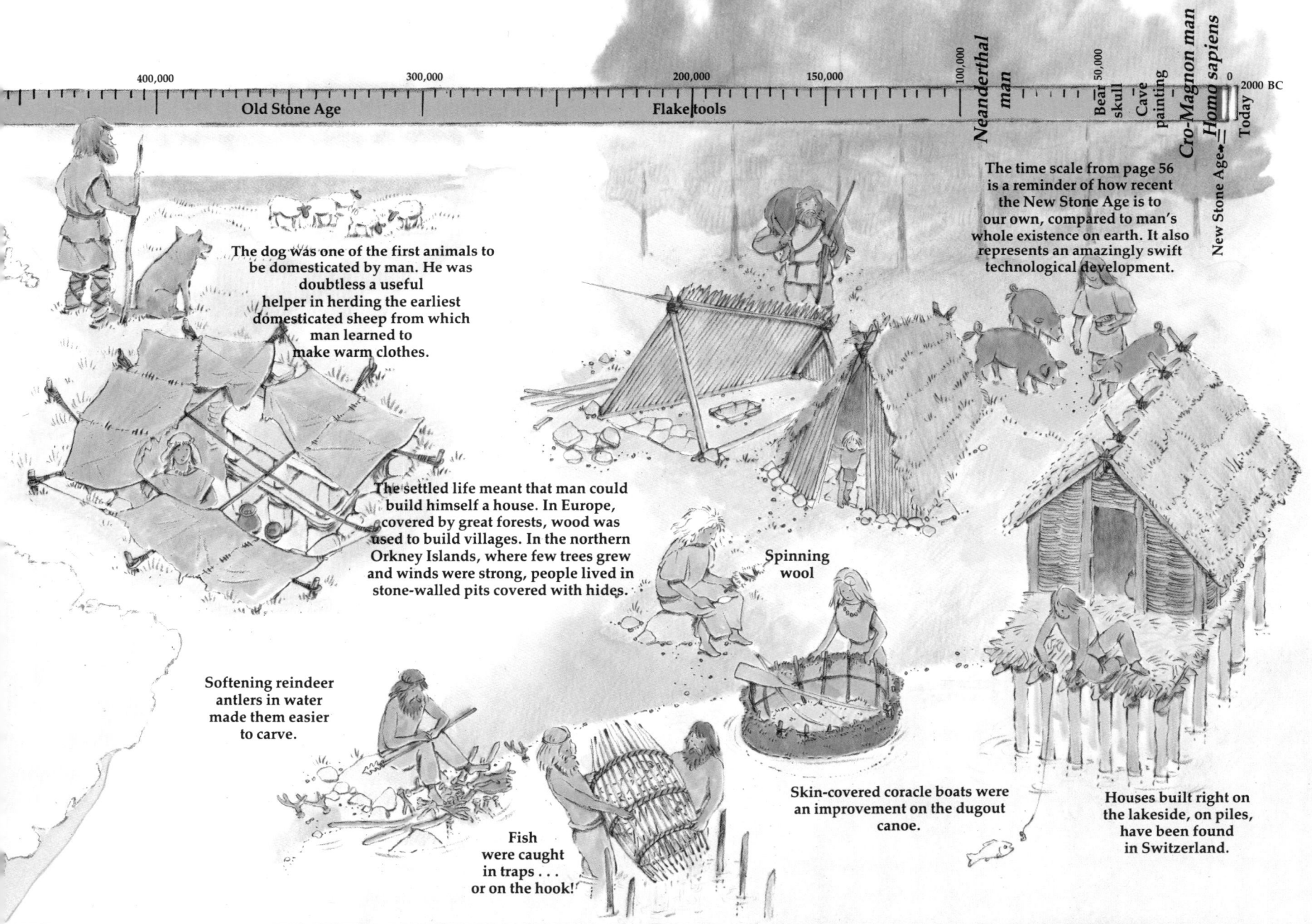

The time scale from page 56 is a reminder of how recent the New Stone Age is to our own, compared to man's whole existence on earth. It also represents an amazingly swift technological development.

The dog was one of the first animals to be domesticated by man. He was doubtless a useful helper in herding the earliest domesticated sheep from which man learned to make warm clothes.

The settled life meant that man could build himself a house. In Europe, covered by great forests, wood was used to build villages. In the northern Orkney Islands, where few trees grew and winds were strong, people lived in stone-walled pits covered with hides.

Spinning wool

Softening reindeer antlers in water made them easier to carve.

Fish were caught in traps . . . or on the hook!

Skin-covered coracle boats were an improvement on the dugout canoe.

Houses built right on the lakeside, on piles, have been found in Switzerland.

Of Herders and Harvesters

On page 35, we saw that rivers carry back to the sea the water that once originated there and fell as precipitation. Through the forces of friction and gravity, the rivers also wear away at the earth, eroding it and transporting mud, silt and bits of rocks and minerals downstream. Much of this suspended earth is rich in chemicals that plants need to grow. When this earth piles up on an alluvial plain, where the river meets the sea, it makes a good rich soil for plants to grow in. Similarly, should the river brim over after a season of rains, it will leave on the flooded lands this same enriching earth. It was on the banks of such flooding rivers that man learned the secret of making plants grow.

No one knows just how, when or where farming was started, but the earliest traces of it have been found around five rivers in the Near East and Asia: the Nile, the Tigris, the Euphrates, the Indus, and the Yellow River in China. All these rivers rejuvenated the soil on their river banks with their annual flooding and deposits of silt. There was probably no one place where farming first started. Doubtless, sedentary peoples who had mastered animal domestication had more time to observe their environment and take note of nature's cycles, and perhaps took time to experiment.

People gathered their first harvests where wild grains grew naturally, in the Near East, as early as 7000-8000 years ago. Grain stalks were cut with simple sickles, and the seeds were separated from the shell under a stone-studded sled dragged over the stalks. The nourishing seeds were chewed alone, or mixed with water as porridge, and eventually baked on hot stones as bread.

Man began to farm where he had a good chance of sucess: on the fertile river banks left by the rejuvenating floodwaters of certain rivers. Once planted in this fertile ground, seeds had no trouble in growing quickly into tall stalks.

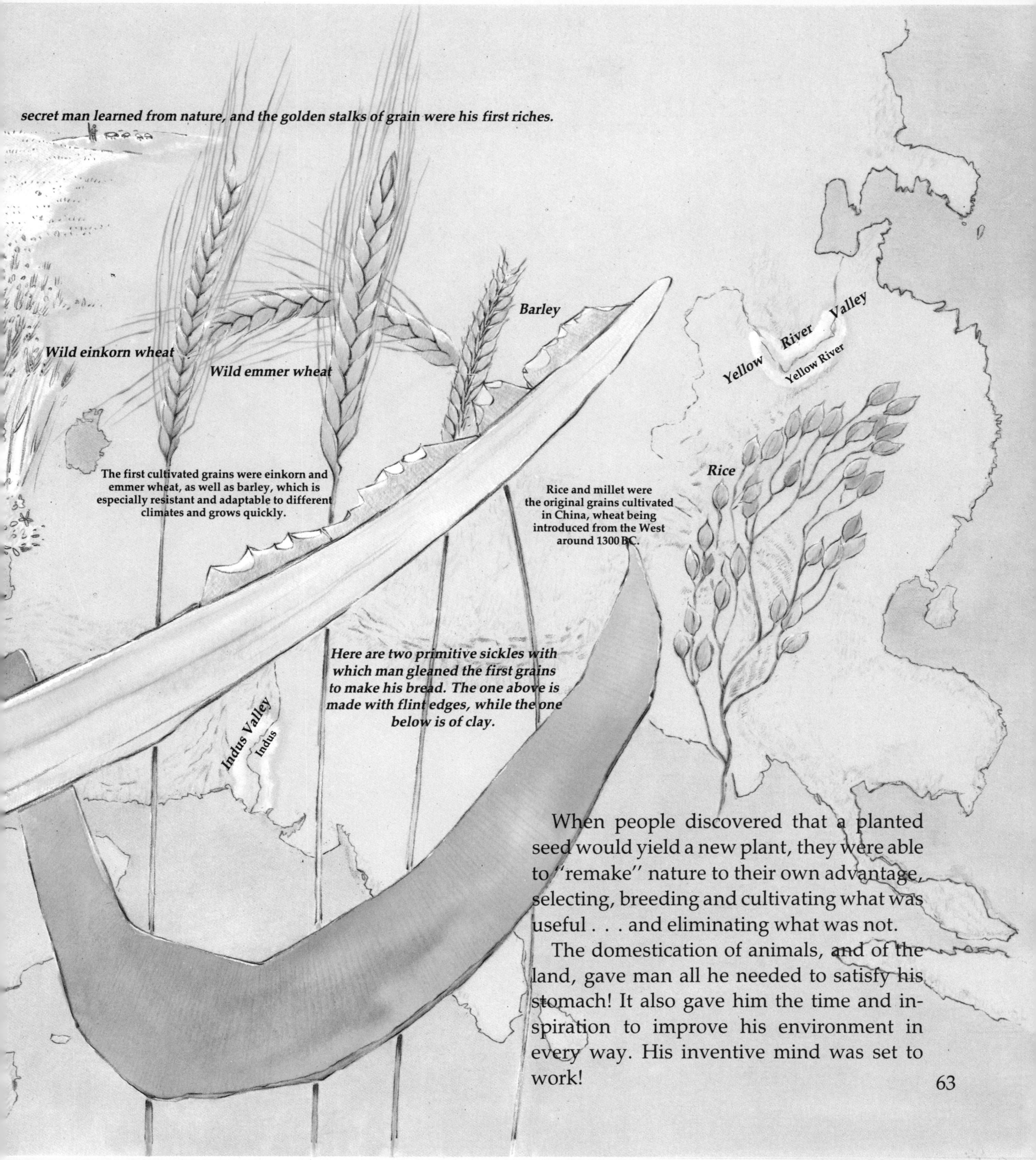

secret man learned from nature, and the golden stalks of grain were his first riches.

The first cultivated grains were einkorn and emmer wheat, as well as barley, which is especially resistant and adaptable to different climates and grows quickly.

Rice and millet were the original grains cultivated in China, wheat being introduced from the West around 1300 BC.

Here are two primitive sickles with which man gleaned the first grains to make his bread. The one above is made with flint edges, while the one below is of clay.

When people discovered that a planted seed would yield a new plant, they were able to "remake" nature to their own advantage, selecting, breeding and cultivating what was useful . . . and eliminating what was not.

The domestication of animals, and of the land, gave man all he needed to satisfy his stomach! It also gave him the time and inspiration to improve his environment in every way. His inventive mind was set to work!

Something Borrowed, Something New

Ever since Old Stone Age man made his first simple tools he has been constantly improving them. The inventions made today may be more complex, but the incentive and mental action behind them have been the same for thousands of years: the need to make things better, to do jobs more easily.

Most inventions have been made by borrowing from other things which already exist. Early man's flint-cutting blade was made easier to use by adding a handle. By varying the shape of both blade and handle, man made a variety of specialized and properly adapted tools. Other inventions, however, may be entirely new.

Each new invention eased the job to be done, and each gave man a little more mastery over his environment. On the other

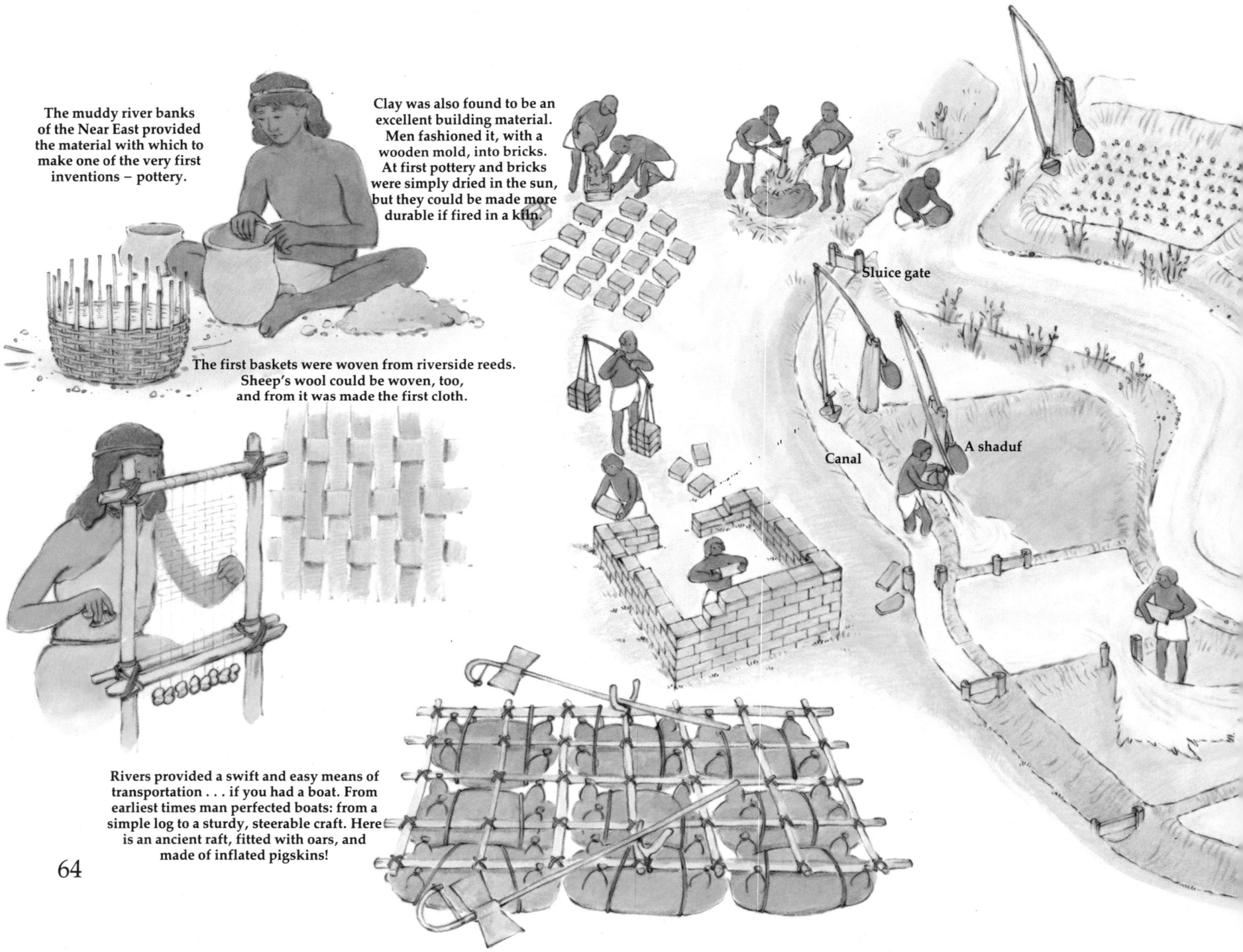

The muddy river banks of the Near East provided the material with which to make one of the very first inventions – pottery.

Clay was also found to be an excellent building material. Men fashioned it, with a wooden mold, into bricks. At first pottery and bricks were simply dried in the sun, but they could be made more durable if fired in a kiln.

The first baskets were woven from riverside reeds. Sheep's wool could be woven, too, and from it was made the first cloth.

Rivers provided a swift and easy means of transportation . . . if you had a boat. From earliest times man perfected boats: from a simple log to a sturdy, steerable craft. Here is an ancient raft, fitted with oars, and made of inflated pigskins!

hand most inventions, while solving one problem, created another! This is why invention has never ceased. Invention creates the need to invent!

When man travelled on his first boat, a drifting log, he needed to invent an oar to propel and steer it. This worked fine on a pond or river, but at sea he needed a sail.

A good house could be built from mud bricks, but many houses built together required notions of engineering, measuring and drainage.

Man enlarged his farmland with irrigation systems, but this required expert organization and measurement of time. He would have needed numbers and a means of recording them: the invention was called writing!

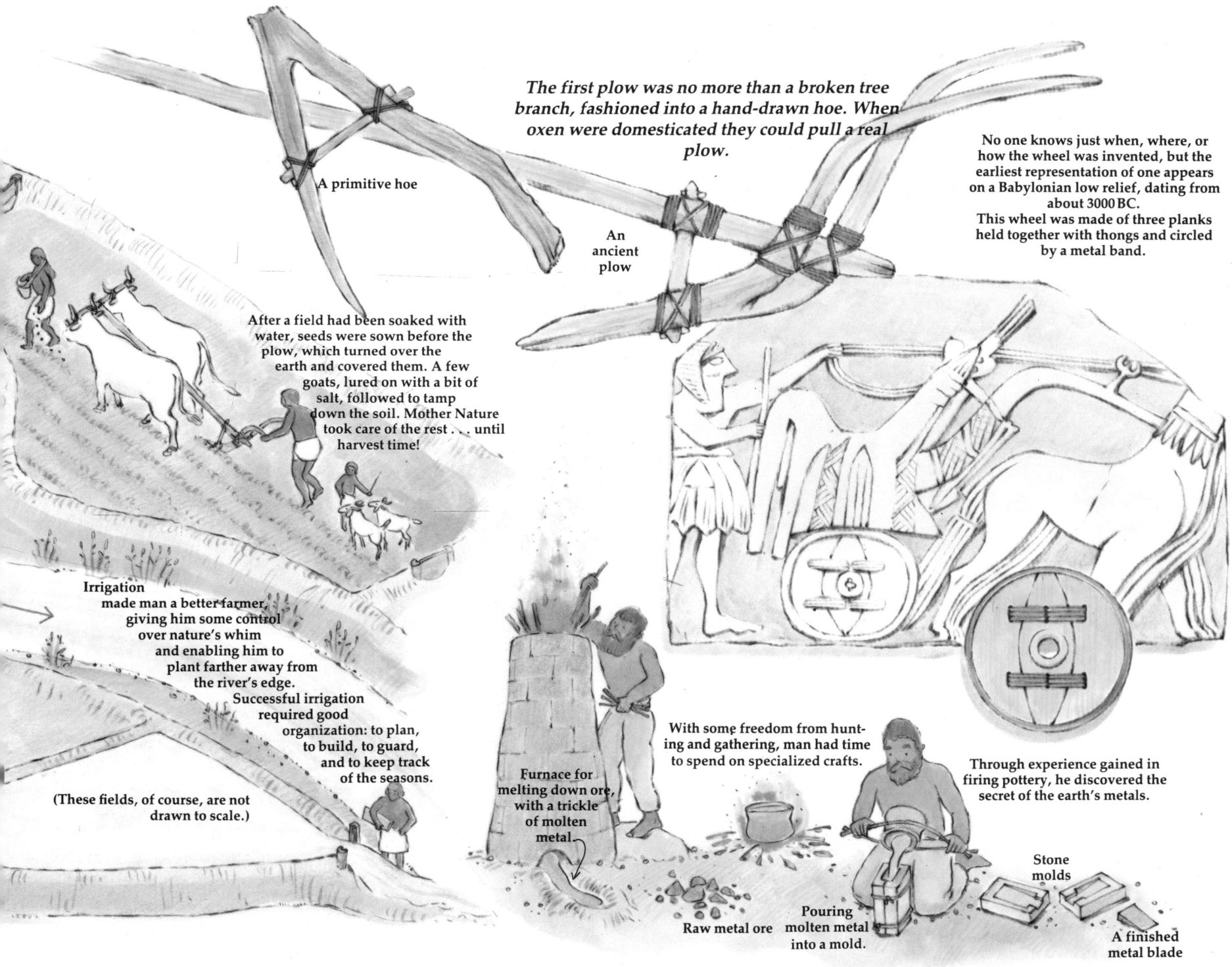

Reading, Writing and 'Rithmetic

Before he could write, man told stories with pictures.

This New Stone Age picture tells us vividly of a hunter's adventure, chased by his prey!

The Chinese written language uses a great number of separate symbols, each of which represent whole words or ideas. This one, which stands for eternity, is but one of some 40,000!

This Babylonian clay tablet is one of the oldest records of writing, dating from about 4000 BC. It was probably a record of accounts.

Our modern alphabet is the result of a continual development of symbols standing for single, separate sounds. Our word alphabet comes from the names of the first two Greek letters: alpha *and* beta.

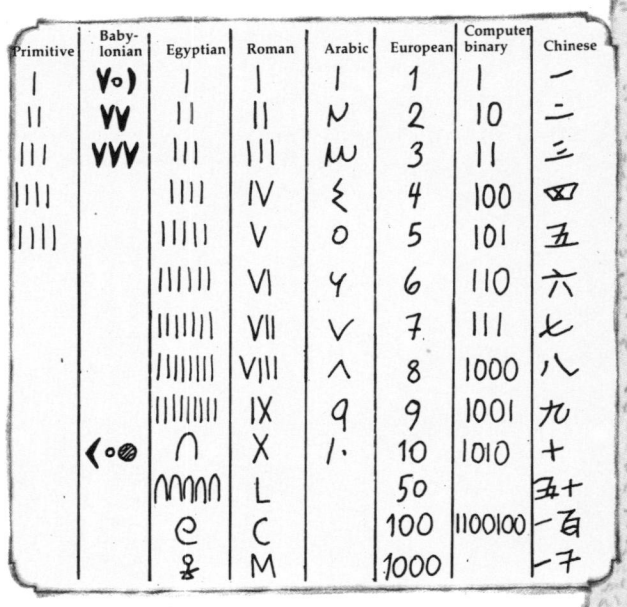

Primitive	Babylonian	Egyptian	Roman	Arabic	European	Computer binary	Chinese
I		I	I	1	1	1	一
II		II	II	٢	2	10	二
III		III	III	٣	3	11	三
IIII		IIII	IV	٤	4	100	四
IIIII		IIIII	V	٥	5	101	五
		IIIIII	VI	٦	6	110	六
		IIIIIII	VII	٧	7	111	七
		IIIIIIII	VIII	٨	8	1000	八
		IIIIIIIII	IX	٩	9	1001	九
		∩	X	١٠	10	1010	十
		∩∩∩∩∩	L		50		五十
		ᘓ	C		100	1100100	一百
		ⲝ	M		1000		一千

Counting is doubtless as old as writing. It developed just like writing, finding separate symbols for different quantities, along with the ingenious "place-value" system.

Writing is the one invention which made history . . .

Have you ever imagined how it would be not knowing how to read or write? If you have ever travelled to Greece, Russia, or the Near or Far East, and tried to read the road signs, you'll know just how important written language is. If you can't decipher it, you're lost! We learn how to read and write so soon in life that it seems as natural as speech, but for thousands of years people lived without reading or writing a word. How did they manage?

In prehistoric times people lived without writing because they didn't need it. However, when they learned to tend animals and began to farm, to build their first communities and cooperate with one another, something more than speech was needed. What people heard, they might forget; plans might be misunderstood; dates for planting and reaping might not be remembered. It be-

The written symbols on these clay tablets from the ancient Indus Valley civilization have not yet been deciphered.

Today, as many people with different languages to understand notice quickly, there has been a return to the use of simple pictograms.

(Hieroglyphs are read from right to left.)

PTOL M E S
PTOLEMAIOS
ΠΤΟΛΕΜΑΙΟΣ

For centuries the hieroglyphs of the Ancient Egyptians were a complete mystery. In 1801 a Napoleonic expedition unearthed a dark, basalt stone engraved in three languages: hieroglyphs, demotic (Ancient Egyptian script), and Ancient Greek. Called the Rosetta Stone, it was a trilingual dictionary which enabled the Frenchman Jean-François Champollion (1790–1832) to decode the Egyptian text. He discovered that the circled cartouches stood for the name of the then Pharaoh Ptolemy, and went on from there. Ancient Egypt, until Champollion's discovery, was literally a prehistoric age. It suddenly became one of the best-recorded periods of ancient history!

. . . for there is no history without writing!

In 1972 the United States sent a space probe, Pioneer 10, into the universe. Upon it is the plaque below, destined to tell any extraterrestrial people who might come upon it from where it has come.

came vital to write things down, so that everybody understood.

Writing did not come about in just one place only, but in different places at different times, as people began to need it. Nor was writing really invented. It evolved over thousands of years. Even the Ancient Egyptians lived with just the rudiments of writing – they didn't even have a real alphabet!

The simple scratches in clay and stone, and scribblings with a pen, offered possibilities no other tool possessed. They carried a person's words farther than the loudest cannon, and stayed alive long after his own death. Written accounts made trading much easier, and a ruler's voice could be heard over all his land. Indeed, writing was present in everything that man built, believed, created and planned. It was the cornerstone, the key, to civilization.

Enter Civilization!

Civilization is the largest stage in man's development. It appeared about five to six thousand years ago, and we live in it today. Our present civilization travels faster, communicates better and knows more than any civilization of the past, yet it is basically not very different from those that grew up around the original "cradlelands."

In spite of all the technology man has created, and all the science and history he has learned since the dawn of civilization, man has not changed. Knowledge may have changed our *way of life*, but it has not advanced *life* at all.

It is quite possible, of course, that man has not yet reached a final development, and our descendants of the year 4000 may write of our present age as "the last years of the New Stone Age"!

What does civilization mean? The word comes from the Latin word *civis*, meaning "citizen," the inhabitant of a city. Civilization, it would seem, is culture based around cities. But for the key to understanding what civilization *is*, and how it may have come about, we need to ask further: "What is a city?"

Probably you picture a place with big buildings and noisy traffic. But before that, what is it that all cities, towns, and villages have in common? They are places where people live together and work together, at a *variety of jobs*. Each citizen is a specialist in some kind of work.

Let us look back at New Stone Age man. What happened when he began to farm? First, man changed from a hunter and gatherer of food to a producer of food. As the population began to grow, being better fed, better sheltered, and better clothed, there were more mouths to feed, and man enlarged his arable land by means of irrigation. This early invention challenged him to plan and organize for the first time. Land had to be measured, workers delegated to dig

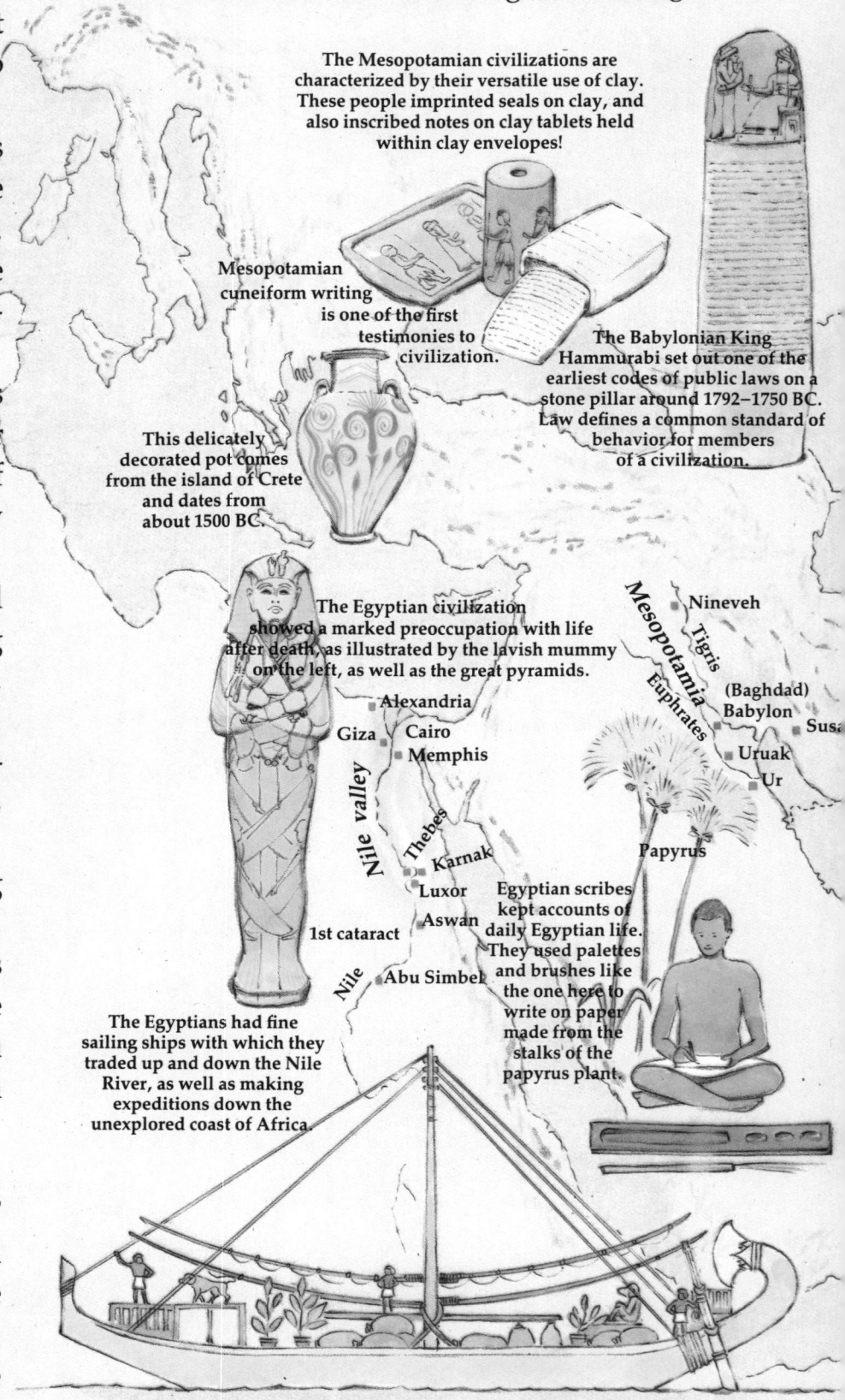

The river valleys where the first towns grew up are known as

learn

ditches and food to be distributed to them. Seasons had to be carefully watched to know just when to plant and harvest.

So it happened that not everyone was a farmer. There were engineers, laborers, administrators, scribes and sky-watchers. The community's work was divided into a variety of jobs. Each person became a specialist in his field . . . and so man had civilization!

The wheel made travel and transport easier and promoted trade between distant towns. This representation, dating from about 2600 BC, is from the Sumerian city of Ur.

Here is an example of Chinese pottery from the New Stone Age , made about 5000-3000BC in Yang Shao.

Pottery was one of the first techniques to be mastered by early civilizations. This pot is from Baluchistan, near the Indus Valley.

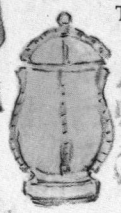

The Ancient Chinese were master metallurgists, using bronze. These vessels were for serving wine.

Mesopotamian civilizations built their great monuments largely with clay bricks, like this decorative low relief of a bull at Babylon. The Ancient Egyptians, on the other hand, built their monuments from great blocks of quarried stone, reserving clay bricks for simpler, domestic structures.

A self-sufficient tribe . . . and a civilized society.

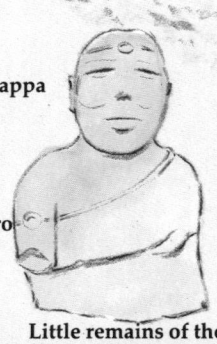

Little remains of the ancient civilization of the Indus Valley. This stone sculpture from Mohenjo Daro is one of the rare remnants of these people.

Soldiers Architects Governor and pan bearer Queen and bearers

Carpenter, sculptor, painter Scribe Brickmaker Fisherman Musician

Civilization is a society of specialists, each dependent on one another to go through life!

Farmers

Slaves

the cradlelands of civilization.

Of Business and Bondage

learn

People living in civilization are dependent on one another. Each person provides a particular product or service for the others, and receives other products and services in return. Farming provided the first surpluses of food that gave man the time to work at other tasks. One of the earliest industries, metalworking, a difficult and time-consuming activity, became possible only when farmers could produce enough to support people to work metal.

Metalworkers and farmers might barter their products . . . so many tools for so much grain, for instance. However, civilization became more complex and trades more specialized. It was necessary to find some common means of exchange. So money was invented.

What is money? Above all, money is a convenience. Have you ever tried to buy something without it? Imagine you need some new buttons, but only have apples to buy them with. You would have to find someone with extra buttons, who would like to have some apples! Of course, trade like this is impossible, and money solves the problem. Money separates the act of buying from that of selling. You can buy buttons, and the button-man can buy what he wants, when he wants. He accepts your money because he knows other people will easily accept it, too. Thus, money has value because everyone agrees that it does.

Anything rare enough and acceptable to all can be used as money. Indians traded with beads; schoolchildren with marbles; and even cigarettes could buy you what you wanted during the last world war when they were rare and desirable. But from earliest times metal was found to be the most practical money. It could be divided into small bits, was easily carried, and could be put to a variety of uses as well: to make tools, weapons, containers or jewelry.

When jobs became specialized, with each person skilled at one task, a community's productivity could increase. It could sell what it made in excess to other communities and become wealthier. The more hands that were put to work, the faster and better production became. Labor had to be as cheap as possible, and free at best. Man had learned to harness beasts of burden; surely he could harness his own kind, as slaves?

Societies condoned slavery when they could produce enough food to feed the extra mouths, and needed extra manpower to build up their civilization. A slave was someone owned as the personal property of another, deprived of any rights and obliged to work involuntarily, for free. The earliest slaves were probably the conquered subjects of a rival community; but convicted criminals, and people who had run up unpayable debts could also be made slaves. A debtor might even sell his wife and children as slaves!

Slavery provided much of the manpower that built the cities of Mesopotamia and the temples and pyramids of Egypt. Slaves worked the galleys of the Greek and Roman navies. Reaching a peak in Roman times, slavery persisted for centuries afterwards. The medieval peasant, or serf, had little more rights than an ancient slave.

Only in the last centuries have efforts been made to abolish slavery. But it still persists today in forced labor camps in many countries of the world.

Barter Exchange
An apple
for a button.
Monetary Exchange
Money
for a pen . . .
for a
button . . .
for an apple.
Money separates the acts of buying and selling. As such, it is a promise of payment. The man who buys a pen with money promises the pen vendor that he will be able to use the same money to buy buttons, apples or anything else! Money is a convenient means of exchange.
Coin representing Alexander the Great
Ancient Athenian coin
Ancient Roman coin depicting Caesar
Money does not make the world go round, but it almost does! Money provides the opportunity for each person to do a different job. It allows the division of labor which is the backbone of civilization.
Roof tiles made by potters
Seafaring merchant
House made by carpenters and masons
Delivery men
Shopkeeper
Soldiers
Market traders
Baker
Entertainer
Road made by engineers
Slave dealer
Fishermen
Water bearer
Peddler
Hunter
Litter bearers
Overseer

Keeping Time with the Sky

On page 28, we saw how the earth's tilt, its rotation, its orbit around the sun and the orbit of its moon make a giant celestial clock which tells us night from day, and the season of the year. Long before mechanical clocks man "told time" by the sky.

Time is told by recurring cycles. A simple cycle to follow is that of day and night, and day again. We can keep track of groups of days by means of a calendar, but before the use of writing people counted groups of days by following the cycle of the moon.

When man became civilized and began to farm by the banks of rivers it was necessary to keep track of a longer cycle which told him the seasons to sow and to reap, and warned

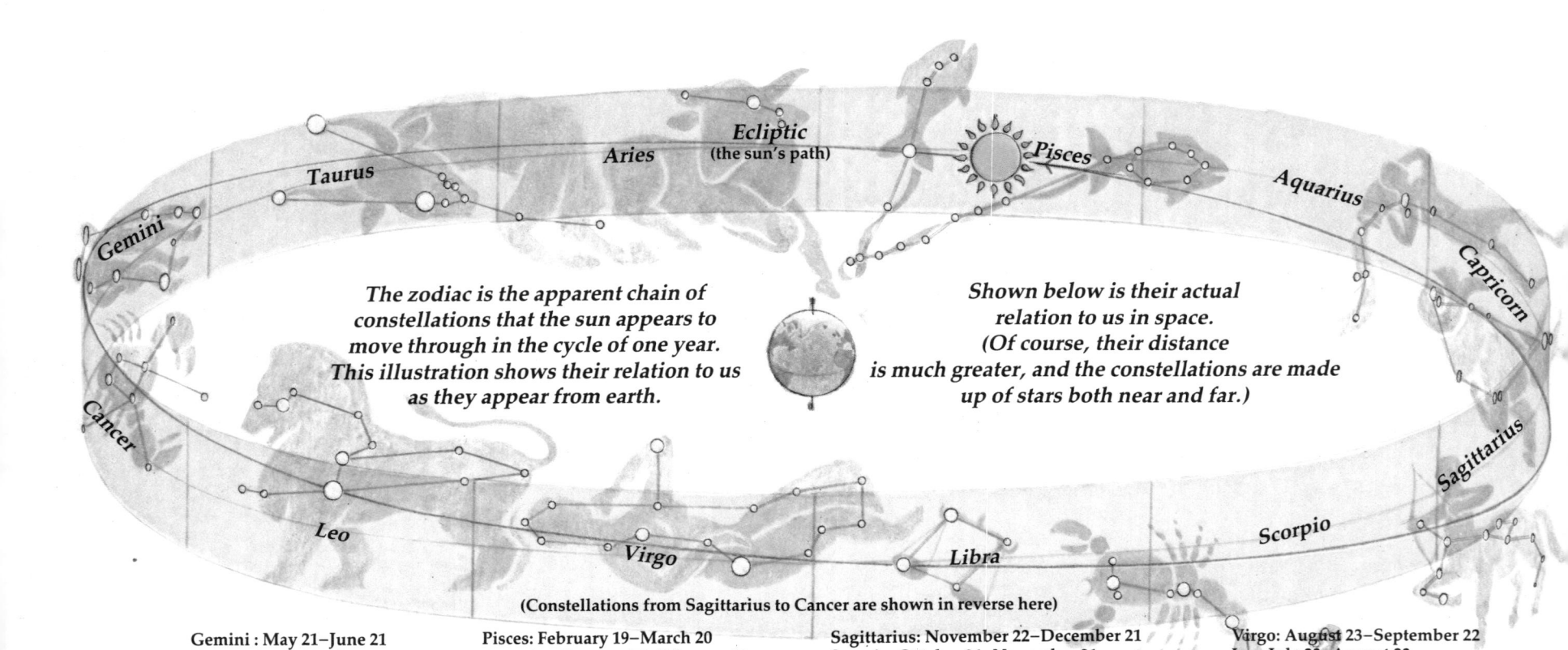

Gemini : May 21–June 21
Taurus: April 20–May 20
Aries: March 21–April 19

Pisces: February 19–March 20
Aquarius: January 20–February 18
Capricorn: December 22–January 19

Sagittarius: November 22–December 21
Scorpio: October 24–November 21
Libra: September 23–October 23

Virgo: August 23–September 22
Leo: July 23–August 22
Cancer: June 22–July 22

To read the time of year, man chose the night sky as a clockface. Groups of stars, constellations, served as numerals. Man noticed that at different times of the year the sun, rising and setting at different points on the horizon, could be found at different points on the clockface of constellations. Man thought the sun moved across a cycle of twelve

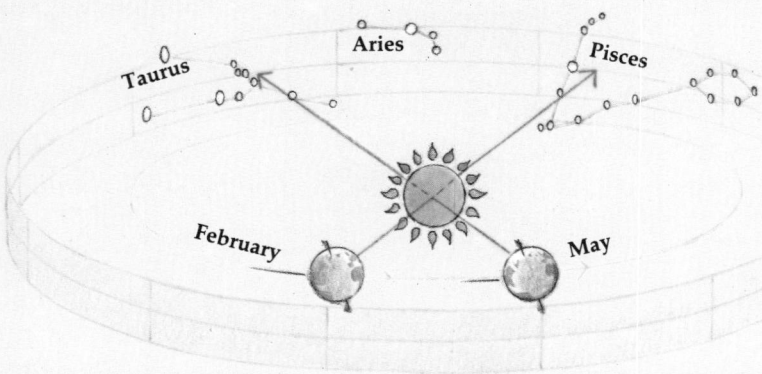

constellations, which were called the zodiac, in the space of one year. We know today that it is not the sun which moves through the zodiac. Our point of view from earth makes it appear to move as we orbit the sun. The sun blocks our view of the constellations behind it . . . a different constellation for a different time of year.

It is not possible to see directly on which constellation the sun is resting. To find out, the ancients watched the first constellation to rise up at sunset, directly opposite the setting sun. If the constellation was Taurus, then the sun was in the constellation directly opposite; in Scorpio.

It must be early November.

when the river would flood: a cycle called the year.

The cycle of the year (365¼ days) does not divide into a full number of lunar cycles (29½ days). To make a proper calendar, you have to make some months longer than the moon cycle. Julius Caesar is credited with having established the first practical calendar, and we still use it today (modified by Pope Gregory in 1582), it works so well.

A modern attempt at a world calendar with more regular months has been proposed. This calendar has the advantage that each day of the year, and hence all holidays, fall at the same place every year. That, it seems, is what people want to know today!

Planets	Latin	Italian	French	English
Sun	DIES SOLIS	DOMENICA	DIMANCHE	SUNDAY
Moon	DIES LUNAE	LUNEDÍ	LUNDI	MONDAY
Mars	DIES MARTIS	MARTEDÍ	MARDI	TUESDAY From old English *Tiw*, the god of war
Mercury	DIES MERCURII	MERCOLEDÍ	MERCREDI	WEDNESDAY From Old German *Woden*, the messenger god
Jupiter	DIES JOVIS	GIOVEDÍ	JEUDI	THURSDAY *Thor*, the god of thunder
Venus	DIES VENERIS	VENERDÍ	VENDREDI	FRIDAY From Old German *Fria*, the goddess of love.
Saturn	DIES SATURNI	SABATO	SAMEDI	SATURDAY

The days of the week get their names from the seven planets known in Roman times and called after gods.

After the French Revolution in 1789, the revolutionaries felt the calendar could use a change, too! A new Republican Calendar was devised of twelve months and thirty days, with five dateless carnival days at the end. It was too difficult to translate dates when dealing with neighboring nations, so this original calendar fell quickly into disuse.

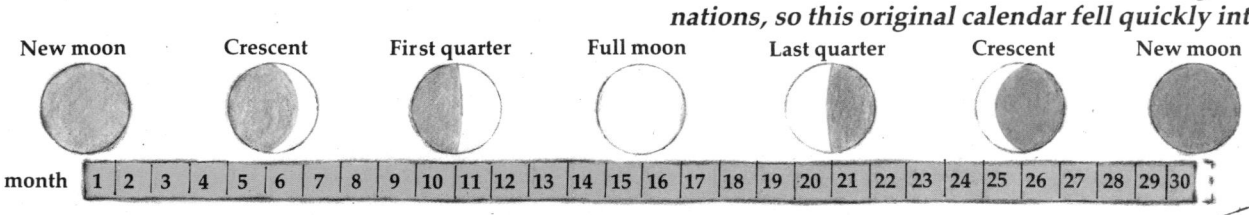

The moon has a cycle short enough to count groups of days. The cycle from new moon to full moon and back again takes 29½ days; a cycle called a month. Half a month, or 14 nights, is called a fortnight.

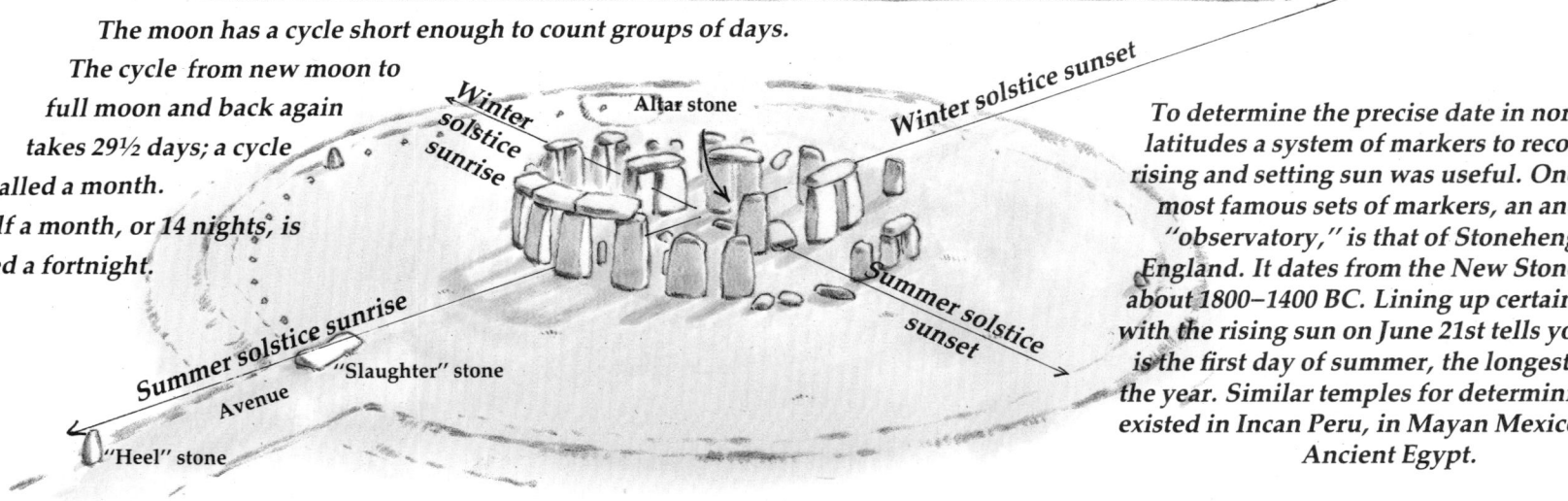

To determine the precise date in northern latitudes a system of markers to record the rising and setting sun was useful. One of the most famous sets of markers, an ancient "observatory," is that of Stonehenge in England. It dates from the New Stone Age, about 1800–1400 BC. Lining up certain stones with the rising sun on June 21st tells you that it is the first day of summer, the longest day of the year. Similar temples for determining time existed in Incan Peru, in Mayan Mexico and in Ancient Egypt.

Brilliance from Dark Ages

Here are some waterwheel types

Overshot

Breastshot

Undershot, or stream

The first windmills appeared in Europe in the 1100s, probably adapted from windmills in central Asia. Vertical watermills were first built on the Tiber, in Rome, in AD 536. The elaborate gearing used gave men the idea for making the first clocks.

The Roman chariot horses above strangle themselves the harder they pull. The shoulder harness, below, puts the pressure in the proper place.

Moldboard

Shoulder harness

With sturdier plows and more powerful horses, and thanks to proper harnessing, farming tasks were speeded up.

Fallow (or unsown field)

Wheat or rye

Barley or beans

Medieval farmers practiced crop rotation, which allowed the soil to rest and rejuvenate after providing a year's harvest.

Horseshoes gave hooves a better hold on the ground.

The energy needed to build the great, ancient civilizations of the Mediterranean came from manpower: the muscles of the abundant slaves who carried out every varied task necessary to till the land, man the ships and build the cities. Although they were skilled engineers, superb artists and able administrators, the ancient civilizations of Egypt, Greece, and Rome added few technological innovations.

The period following the fall of the Roman Empire, the last of the great, ancient civilizations, is sometimes called the Dark Ages. Often thought of as a sombre age of stagnant minds, barbaric invasions and poverty, these times nonetheless witnessed the birth of a whole host of inventions to ease work and quicken travel.

New plows with iron blades and moldboards were made, strong enough to turn the wet and heavy soil of northern Europe. Horses were stronger and worked faster than the slow Mediterranean oxen, thanks to proper harnesses and sturdy iron

horseshoes. Stirrups made riding easier, and the mounted soldier now had the leverage to strike a forceful blow with his lance.

Mills powered by water or wind, and using ingenious gearing, sprang up all over the place to grind grain, pump water and saw wood.

Ships were built stronger, and were equipped with true rudders and lateen sails, which gave them the strength and maneuverability to sail the high seas. The novel compass guided the mariner on his way.

In spite of their widespread use, the origins of these inventions went undocumented. It would seem, though, that many came from the East: Asia, China and the Arab world. These lands also brought to Europe, via adventurous overland traders, silks and spices, and legends of splendid, golden cities. The prospect of wealth, free for the taking, prompted the royal houses of Europe to seek sea routes to the "treasure chests" of the East. While searching for gold, they discovered the world!

Conquest and Exploration

Judging from maps of the period, such as the Ptolemaic map on page 12, the world known to medieval Europeans was a small and cozy place. Yet although on paper the "world's edge" appeared to lie just beyond the horizon, Europeans were in contact with goods brought from well off the map . . . from the Indies, and the Orient.

Although no one from Europe had really been there, people knew of it from Arab traders who plied the coastal waters of the

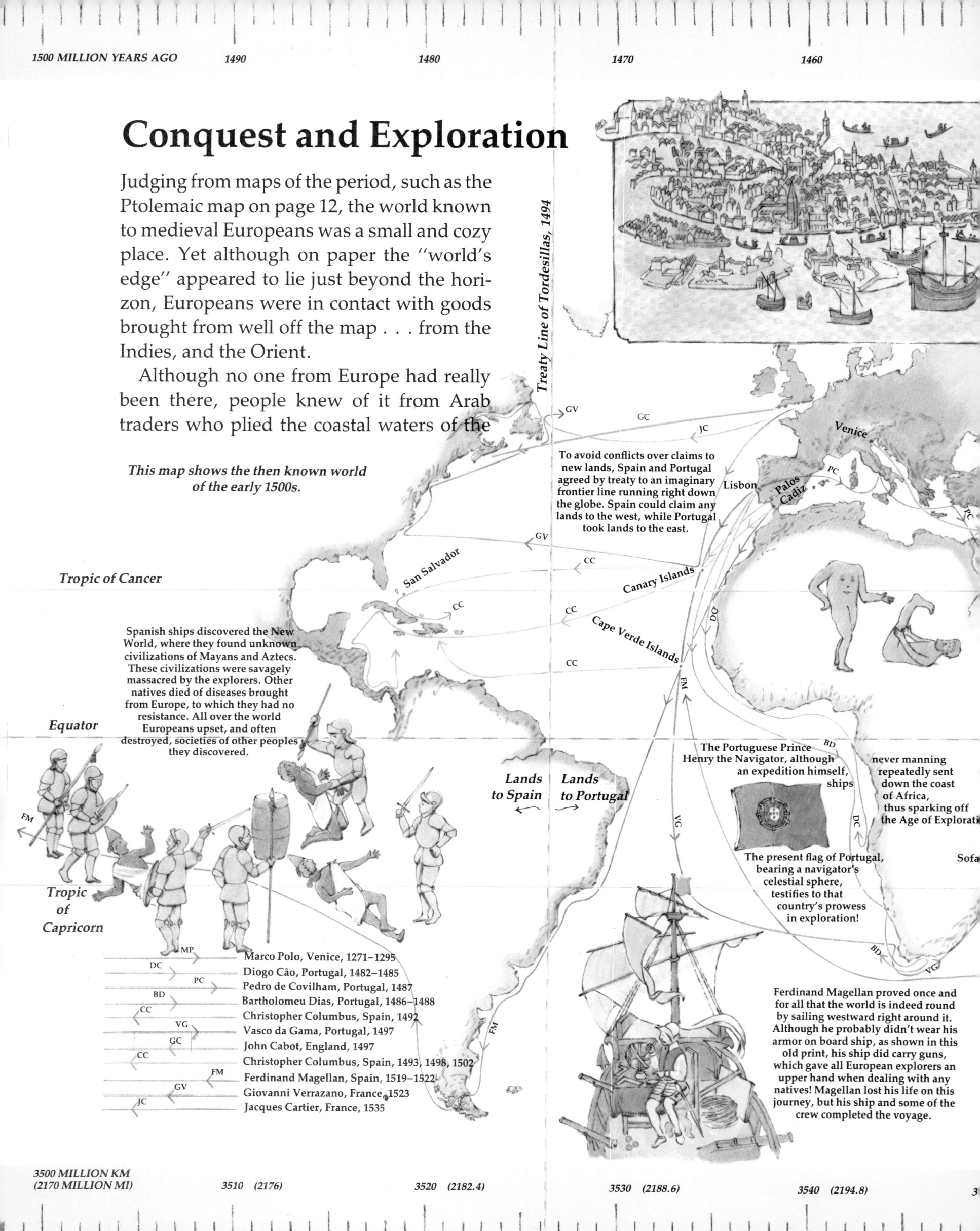

This map shows the then known world of the early 1500s.

Spanish ships discovered the New World, where they found unknown civilizations of Mayans and Aztecs. These civilizations were savagely massacred by the explorers. Other natives died of diseases brought from Europe, to which they had no resistance. All over the world Europeans upset, and often destroyed, societies of other peoples they discovered.

The Portuguese Prince Henry the Navigator, although never manning an expedition himself, repeatedly sent ships down the coast of Africa, thus sparking off the Age of Explorati

The present flag of Portugal, bearing a navigator's celestial sphere, testifies to that country's prowess in exploration!

Ferdinand Magellan proved once and for all that the world is indeed round by sailing westward right around it. Although he probably didn't wear his armor on board ship, as shown in this old print, his ship did carry guns, which gave all European explorers an upper hand when dealing with any natives! Magellan lost his life on this journey, but his ship and some of the crew completed the voyage.

Indian Ocean and brought to the Eastern Mediterranean ports exotic and rare goods from the East, and doubtless no less fabulous tales.

The powerful cities of Genoa and Venice held a monopoly on trade in the Eastern Mediterranean, and it was through these cities that silks, spices, pepper, tea, gold and ivory found their way into Europe. It was from Venice that the young Marco joined his father, a trader named Nicolo Polo, on a journey by land into Asia. Their trip took them all the way to China, and Marco returned home aged only twenty-four years. He wrote of his amazing adventures in strange lands in a book called *Il Milione*, and his experiences became known all over Europe.

A copy of Marco Polo's book fell into the hands of a Portuguese prince in 1428. Already imbued with a spirit for discovery, and sending sailing expeditions southward along the coast of Africa, it occurred to him that if one sailed far enough, one might actually round the African continent and sail eastward to the riches of the Orient, breaking the Venetian monopoly on trade with the East. Later known as Henry the Navigator, the prince sent ships farther and farther away, and after his death a Portuguese ship, sailed by Vasco da Gama, finally reached the Indian shore.

The Spanish royal house, also tempted by the possibility of enrichment through eastern trade, consented to equip a Genovese navigator who claimed India could be reached by sailing west. Indeed, the sailor Columbus did touch land, but instead of finding India, he found a New World. Spain found that this new territory held riches of its own, and began setting up colonies all around it.

The oceans soon teemed with ships under many flags: Dutch, English, French, all seeking ports with which to trade, and lands to claim as colonies. There were lands of every description: in size, shape and color . . . and as many different types of people, too!

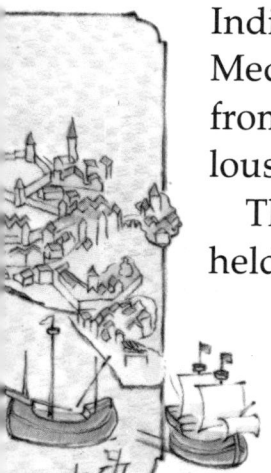

At the time of Marco Polo, Venice was the link between the world of the East and the West and became wealthy through this monopoly of trade.

Marco Polo accompanied his father on a trip through Asia, which he recounted in his book, *Il Milione*. It inspired interest throughout Europe in the lands of the Orient.

Kashgar
Shangtu
Peking
Tabriz
MP
Yunnan
Chuanchow
Pagan
PC
Calicut
VG
Malindi
North star
FM
Sun
Horizon

Two new instruments helped navigators to find their position at sea. The cross-staff was used to sight the sun by day, while the circular astrolabe sighted the north star by night. By moving the sighting stick to line up either reference, the navigator could read off on his instrument's scale his exact latitude on the globe.

Variety and Acceptance

The explorers who pushed back the horizons of the globe and discovered new lands also found different types of people wherever they went. In some places the native inhabitants were generally tall; in others, they were short. The shape of their eyes, the color of their skin and of their hair was different.

What makes people around the world different? Anthropologists today believe that there was no original human type, but that people developed biological characteristics best suited to their environment, depending on where they lived. Very ancient human fossils found around the world, showing different bone structures, support this theory. People with biological differences are known as different races, although all the different races belong to the one species, Homo sapiens.

When Europeans colonized the world in the sixteenth and seventeenth centuries, the original local races became mixed with the European one, giving us the endless variety of types of people we can see around the world today.

The color of people's skin or their physical characteristics are not the only ways in which they might be different from others. There is another, invisible, distinguishing feature. In 1900 it was discovered that there are four different types or groups of blood. Each of us inherits his blood group from one of his parents. It was found that some blood types were more predominant in some places of the world than others, just as skin types are.

People of different races have tended to nurture a mutual dislike for one another. People often dislike, or fear, what they don't know, or what is unusual to them. People who are hostile to another race are called racist. They are always finding fault in other races, perhaps to cover up their own doubts about themselves!

Acceptance (and not just tolerance) of all the different peoples of the earth, and respect for their ways and customs, shows you have real understanding for the whole world . . . not just a personal view.

No one of us is superior or inferior, and if we are all a bit different, so much the better! It would be boring if everyone were the same.

Do you like ice cream? If so, you are probably delighted that there are more flavors than just vanilla!

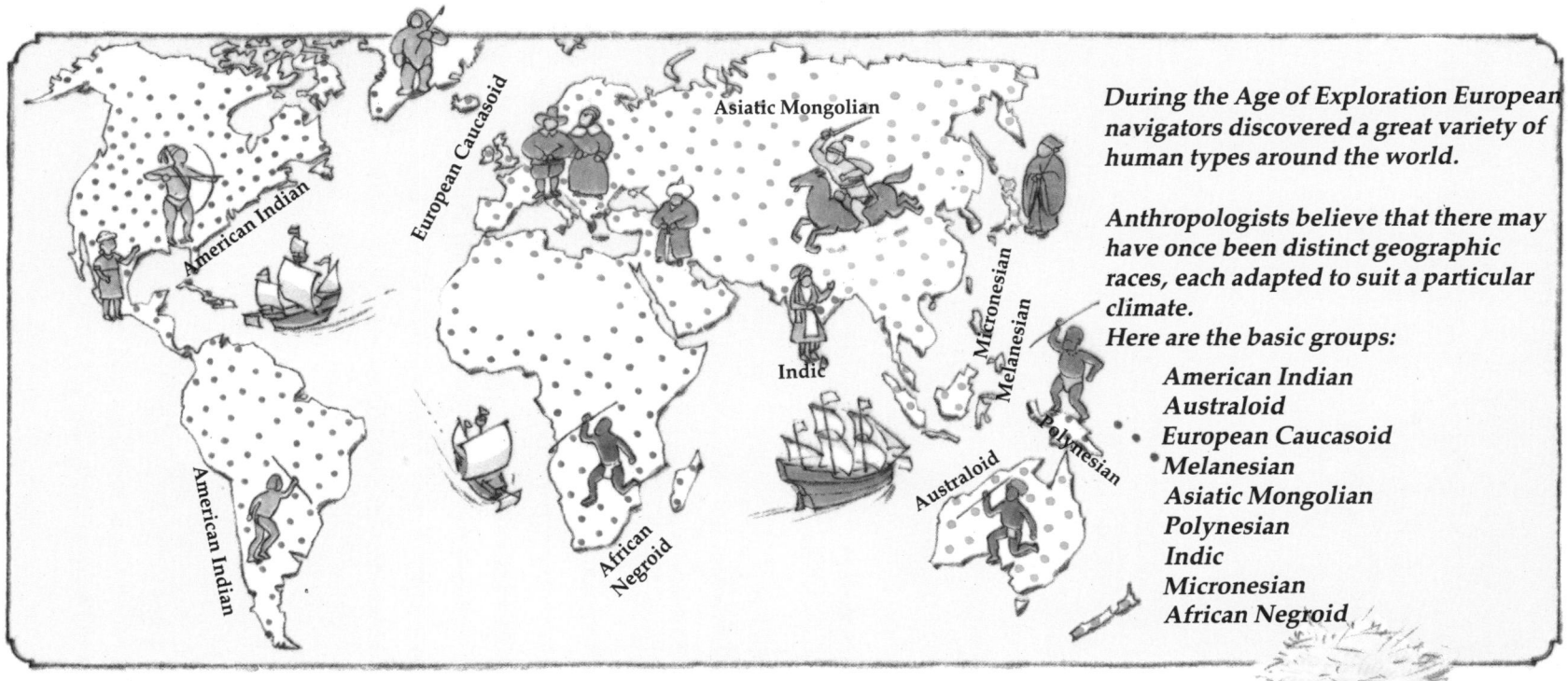

During the Age of Exploration European navigators discovered a great variety of human types around the world.

Anthropologists believe that there may have once been distinct geographic races, each adapted to suit a particular climate.
Here are the basic groups:

- *American Indian*
- *Australoid*
- *European Caucasoid*
- *Melanesian*
- *Asiatic Mongolian*
- *Polynesian*
- *Indic*
- *Micronesian*
- *African Negroid*

People may be distinguished by their skin color, hair, eyes and nose types; but be we black, yellow, red or white, we are all members of the family of people on earth!

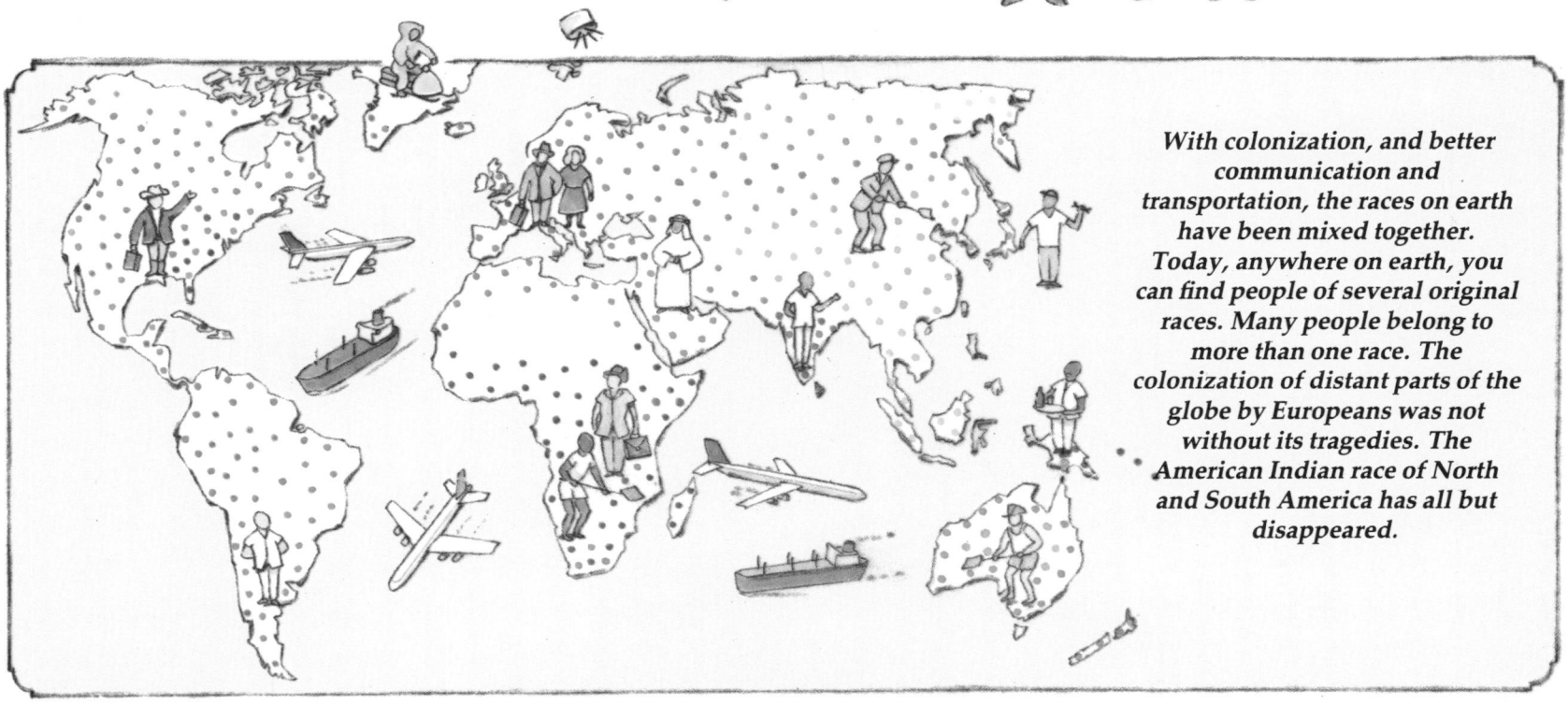

With colonization, and better communication and transportation, the races on earth have been mixed together. Today, anywhere on earth, you can find people of several original races. Many people belong to more than one race. The colonization of distant parts of the globe by Europeans was not without its tragedies. The American Indian race of North and South America has all but disappeared.

Function and Expression

From the moment that man made his very first tool, he has been an artist. In remaking his environment to suit his needs, he took natural objects out of their context, and reorganized them, or transformed them to his imaginative wishes. Nature, however beautiful it is, is never art. Only man makes art, and he does it by transforming nature. Of course, not everything man makes can be called art . . . far from it! So what does art mean?

Defining art is much less easy than recognizing it. Each one of us, with his individual background and sensitivity, could give a quite different definition. Even just recognizing art is largely a matter of personal taste!

Some things, like painting and sculpture, are done deliberately as works of art, to be admired for their beauty or for what they express. Other things are made with a practical function, but we can still admire the artistry of fine craftsmanship and sensitive proportions. Early man, for instance, made his arrowheads with such skill that we can find artistry in their design. The man who made them, however, may not have given art a moment's thought!

Although this is over-simplifying things, something done artistically is something done well. Artistry might be defined as something done in an outstanding way!

Of all the different arts, architecture best combines the dual beauty of function and expression. The first purpose of a building is to serve a function: to house some sort of activity within it. Churches, or houses, or factories look alike because they all do the same job. If a building is well suited to its purpose, it has lived up to the first beauty, that of function. If, at the same time, it has been built with care and thought, with pleasing proportions and appropriate materials, the building has become expressive.

Society prescribes the role architecture takes. Buildings can tell us much about the people who used them. The great pyramids of Ancient Egypt, the cathedrals of the

Birth of Venus, by Sandro Botticelli, about 1485

The human figure, and the nude in particular, is important subject matter in Western art. Oil painting gives a realistic rendering of space, volume and surface: a goal which Western painters sought in a scientific manner. However, artists do not always seek realistic representation, but often synthesize what they have seen into abstract forms which become purely expressive.

Reclining figure, by Henry Moore, 1945–6

Islamic bowl, 10th century

Anatolian carpet, circa 1600

The Islamic religion shuns the pictorial representation of humans, so much Islamic art is non-figurative. Highly decorative tapestry is a hallmark of Islamic art, and calligraphy, the art of fine writing, such as on this bowl, is considered an important art.

Middle Ages, the towering skyscrapers of our own age, were all built with different intentions; but the grandeur of all three examples tells us that each one represented an important aspect in the life of a society. Pyramids were monuments to posterity. Cathedrals testify to man's faith. Skyscrapers are built for business. Their function *is* their expression.

Rhythm and Punctuation

Painting, sculpture and architecture are known as spatial arts, for they owe their existence to a play of surfaces and volumes, light and shadow, which occupy space. Art, however, is not confined to spatial dimension alone. It is also concerned with the dimension of time.

The arts of literature, poetry, music, dance and theater might all be called temporal arts, for they all make use of the passage of time to tell us a story, or arouse our emotions.

A good storyteller will manipulate time, punctuating some passages with details or wit, to build up our interest in his tale before unveiling its outcome. A writer does just the same, but through the medium of the printed word. A poet uses time rather like a musician or dancer, giving his words a rhythm and rhyme, tickling our mind through a careful selection of words.

Music is unlike any other art, for in no way does it imitate, or refer to, any audible or visual thing in nature. Music speaks directly to our emotions. We feel some music as happy, other pieces as sad, or serious. Music sounds fast, slow, boisterous or gentle. Music is the art which is perhaps most strongly concerned with time, with its measured cadence and regularly repeated rhythm. It also serves as a support, or accompaniment, to other arts: song, dance and theater.

Dancing may well be the oldest of all the arts, originating in the natural urge to move and jump to the sound of clapping hands or drumbeats. Dances have also been used all over the world, and since ancient times, as rituals to ensure nature's assistance and goodness to man. It was probably as a derivation, or even parody, of such ritual spectacles that the theater itself was born.

Like so many beautiful things – a flower, a ripe fruit, a rainbow – the temporal arts last but an instant; and unless they can be somehow preserved, they are only as lasting as our memory. Today we take for granted our records, tapes, television, radio and movies,

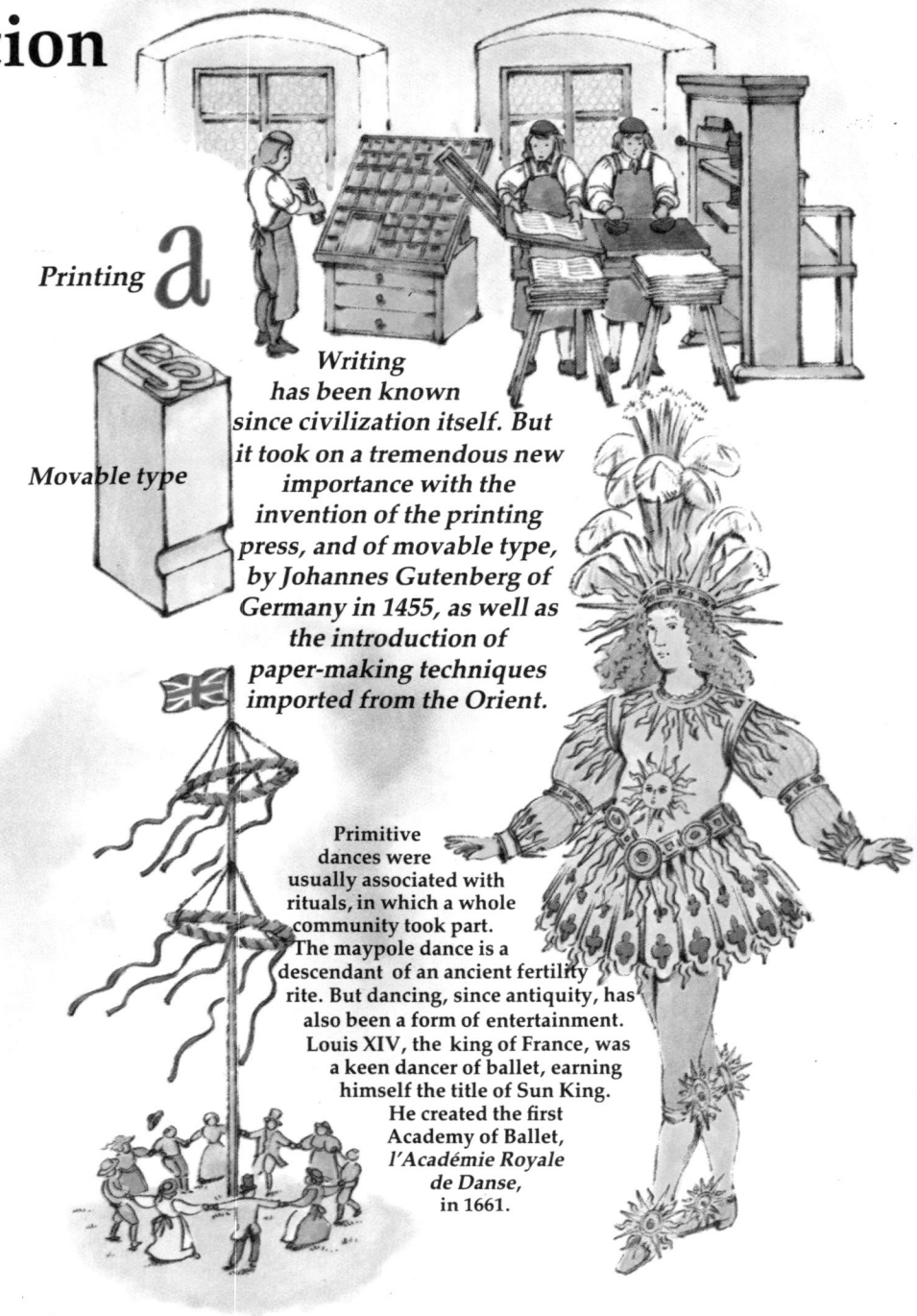

Writing has been known since civilization itself. But it took on a tremendous new importance with the invention of the printing press, and of movable type, by Johannes Gutenberg of Germany in 1455, as well as the introduction of paper-making techniques imported from the Orient.

Primitive dances were usually associated with rituals, in which a whole community took part. The maypole dance is a descendant of an ancient fertility rite. But dancing, since antiquity, has also been a form of entertainment. Louis XIV, the king of France, was a keen dancer of ballet, earning himself the title of Sun King. He created the first Academy of Ballet, *l'Académie Royale de Danse*, in 1661.

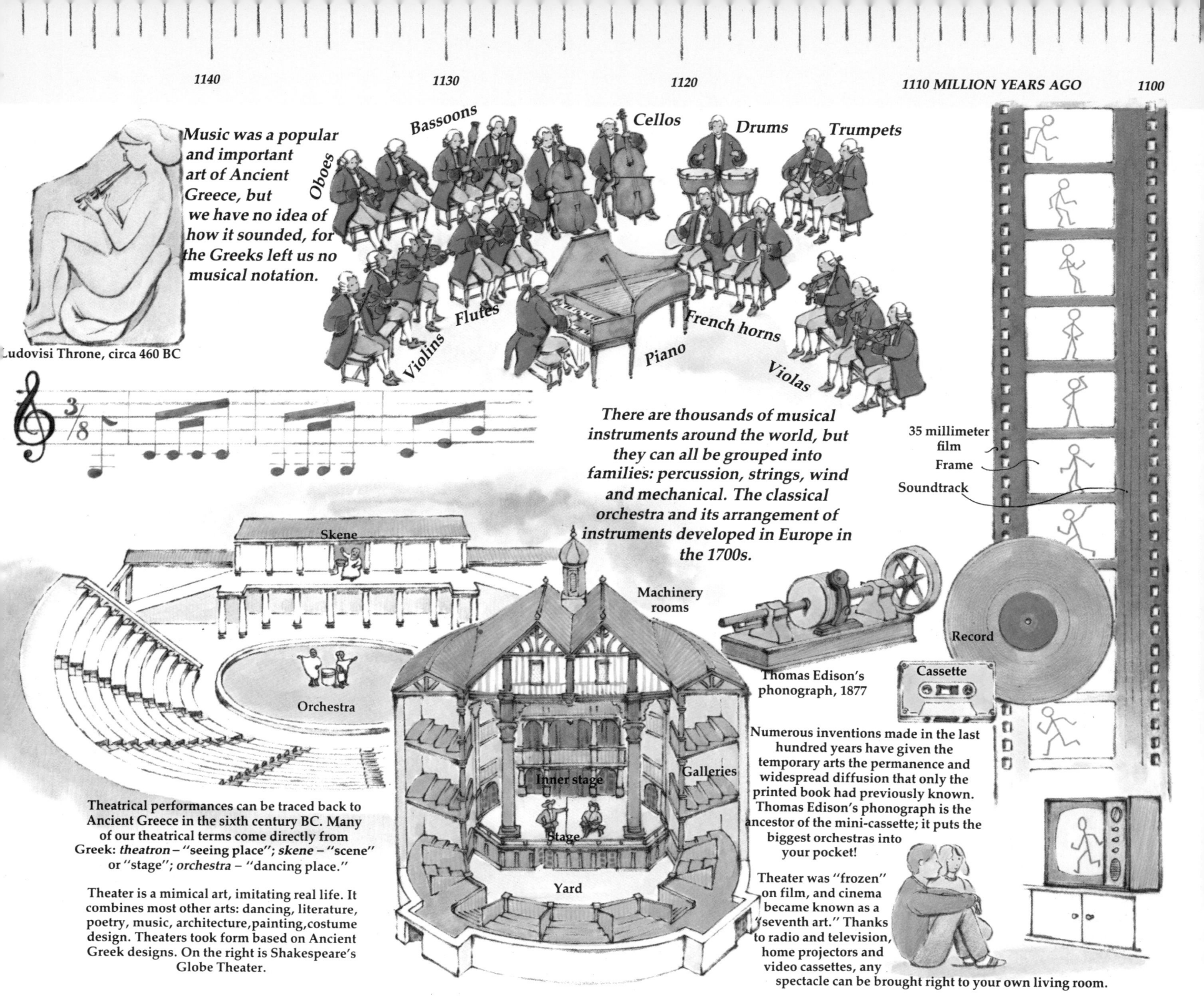

which keep us in constant touch with the temporal arts. It is hard to imagine what it would be like to live without these inventions . . . and yet they are all only one or two generations old.

Without records the only music we would know would be what we could hear played live. We would have to go to a theater whenever we wanted to see a play. And just imagine if there were no books! Why, the only stories we'd know would be those we were told!

Recording, through printed words, tapes and films, has given us an immeasurably larger library of artistic knowledge than any of our ancestors could possibly have hoped to grasp in a lifetime. Don't you think we're lucky?

God and Religion

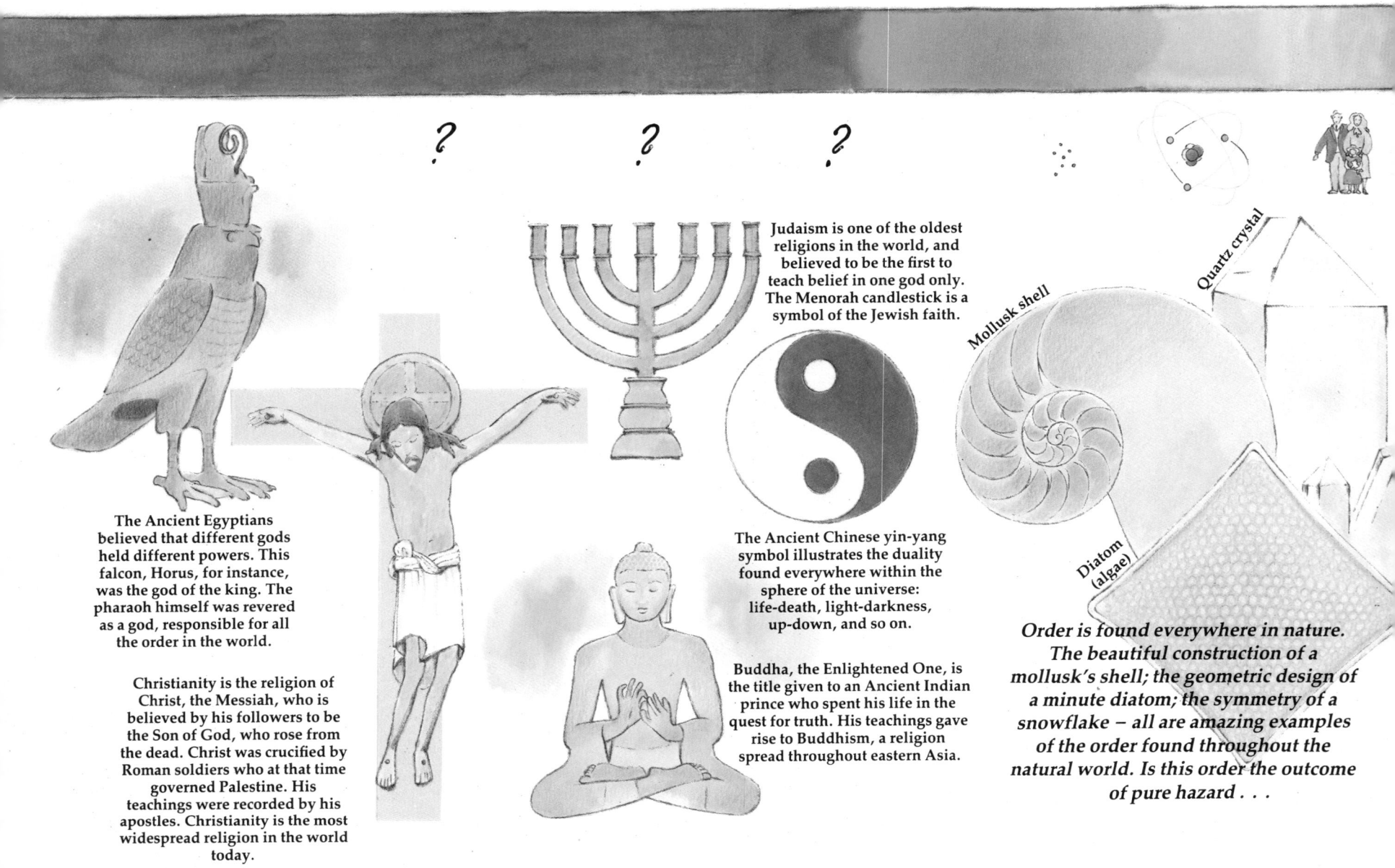

The Ancient Egyptians believed that different gods held different powers. This falcon, Horus, for instance, was the god of the king. The pharaoh himself was revered as a god, responsible for all the order in the world.

Christianity is the religion of Christ, the Messiah, who is believed by his followers to be the Son of God, who rose from the dead. Christ was crucified by Roman soldiers who at that time governed Palestine. His teachings were recorded by his apostles. Christianity is the most widespread religion in the world today.

Judaism is one of the oldest religions in the world, and believed to be the first to teach belief in one god only. The Menorah candlestick is a symbol of the Jewish faith.

The Ancient Chinese yin-yang symbol illustrates the duality found everywhere within the sphere of the universe: life-death, light-darkness, up-down, and so on.

Buddha, the Enlightened One, is the title given to an Ancient Indian prince who spent his life in the quest for truth. His teachings gave rise to Buddhism, a religion spread throughout eastern Asia.

Order is found everywhere in nature. The beautiful construction of a mollusk's shell; the geometric design of a minute diatom; the symmetry of a snowflake – all are amazing examples of the order found throughout the natural world. Is this order the outcome of pure hazard . . .

Today we have more knowledge about the earth and the universe than any previous generation. What has knowledge taught us? You might think that it makes us feel smart, but in fact knowledge makes us very humble.

Physicists have broken down atoms into even smaller particles, and they still haven't met the ultimate "brick" of all matter. Astronomers are pushing back the horizon of the universe in space and time but have come nowhere nearer its "edge." When men knew very little of the physical world, they explained things through theories. But now, with so much more knowledge, we can only account for how little we really know!

Throughout history, and around the world, people have always accounted for what they couldn't understand as the work or will of God. God has been given many shapes and many different names but he is generally believed to be a supreme being

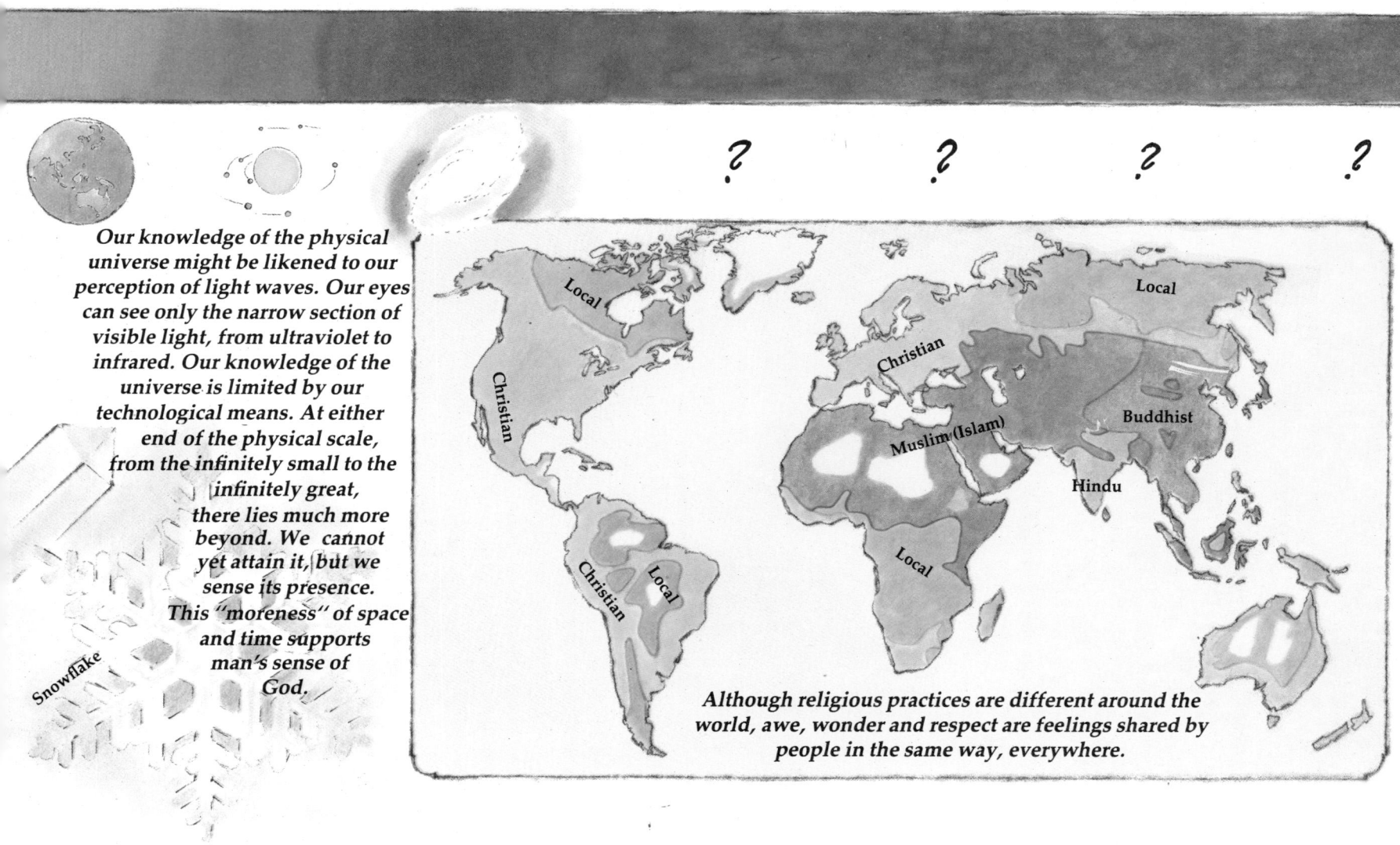

. . . or is there more to nature than that?

who has created all the order in the universe.

Men use language to communicate with one another. Religion is a communication between man and God. Languages are based on many different symbols which make up an alphabet, all arranged according to rules to make a common grammar. Religions make use of all sorts of symbols through which man seeks communication with God. Religious symbols are also arranged and used according to rules. These make up a common grammar for all users of a religion to follow.

Like languages, all religions are made by man. Although they are different the world over, no one religion is better than another: each speaks in its own way to God.

You have probably heard people discussing whether God exists or not. Everyone seems to have an argument defending his own point of view. The truth is, however, that no one really knows.

Mores and Culture

As well as being a vehicle of communication, most religions also serve as a basis of conduct in our daily lives. Religions lay down guidelines which advise us how we should live. Such guidelines, defended by society, are called mores, from the Latin word for custom.

Mores are customs which have been handed down over many generations, and to which society has attached an almost sacred importance. In the Christian world, mores permit a man to have one wife only; whereas in the Islamic world, he may have several. The Islamic man, however, is allowed no alcohol – his mores forbid it.

Lesser customs, such as tipping one's hat or shaking a hand, are known as folkways.

We have looked at the fruit of human thought: language, art, architecture, music, technology, religion. All these things, and many more, make up what is called culture. Culture is the sum of elements that make up a particular way of life for a whole society. Culture is inherited. Each one of us has to

When we play a game we abide by a mutual set of rules which make the game possible. Without rules the game cannot be played. In life each person abides by common rules, moral or legal, which allow the community to live peacefully and harmoniously.

Codes of behavior are closely tied to religion. Moses is believed to have received the Ten Commandments directly from God while on Mount Sinai in Palestine. The Babylonian ruler Hammurabi similarly received a code of laws from the sun god Shamash. He had them written down on a stone pillar decorated with a bas-relief.

"In everything, do unto others what you would have them do unto you."

This Golden Rule, found in the Bible, is found in most other religions, too. It is called the Golden Rule because it seems to excel all other rules of conduct in its simple recognition of equal respect for all men, by all men.

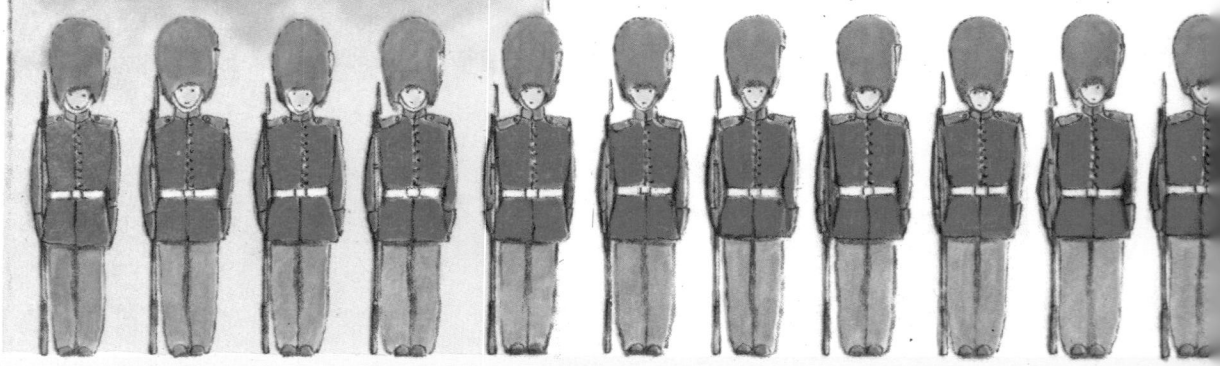

learn everything from childhood: first we imitate the ways of our parents, and later we pick up the customs of all the other people around us.

There are thousands of cultures all around the earth. Each is a mixture of innovative ideas, or acceptance of change, as well as inherited traditions, or unwillingness to change.

The network and rapidity of communications today has brought each one of us into contact with cultures from all over the world. While the customs of other people may look strange to us, many of ours must seem funny to others!

Communication has influenced every culture. A custom may be dropped by society and replaced by one from abroad. Although the mixing of cultures has "killed" some traditions, their loss has given us a renewed sensitivity towards them for their historical value.

The diversity of cultures is full of interest and beauty.

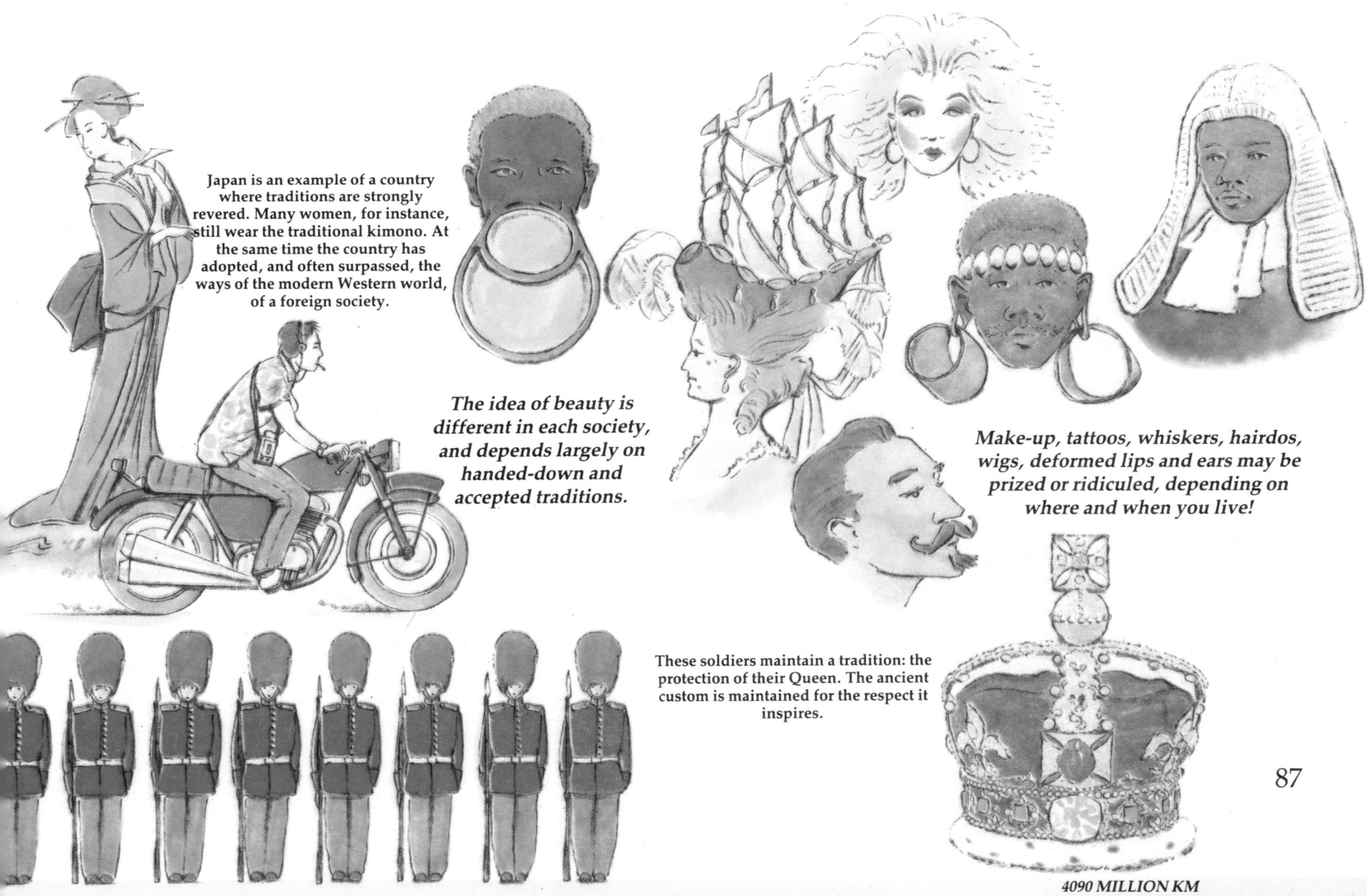

Japan is an example of a country where traditions are strongly revered. Many women, for instance, still wear the traditional kimono. At the same time the country has adopted, and often surpassed, the ways of the modern Western world, of a foreign society.

The idea of beauty is different in each society, and depends largely on handed-down and accepted traditions.

Make-up, tattoos, whiskers, hairdos, wigs, deformed lips and ears may be prized or ridiculed, depending on where and when you live!

These soldiers maintain a tradition: the protection of their Queen. The ancient custom is maintained for the respect it inspires.

Power and Administration

What do you do for your family? Perhaps you have certain chores which you do regularly, like cleaning the car, mowing the lawn, or doing the dishes. Maybe you even babysit for your little brother or sister. You have responsibilities, and by carrying them out you cooperate with your parents to help make a harmonious family.

The family is society's oldest institution and its basic unit. In a way, it is a miniature government. It is an exercise of cooperation among separate members towards a common goal.

There are several ways of running a family. Sometimes the father is the dominant figure, holding all the power and making all the decisions. This type of family is called patriarchal. In other cases both mother and father make decisions together, and might take notice of their children's ideas, too. Such a family is egalitarian.

The family probably served as a model for the earliest governments. At the simplest level, government is a means of cooperation among a number of families. The ways of administering a government are as different as the ways of running a family.

Throughout history, and in many places today, most governments have tended to be modelled on the patriarchal family. One person or a small group of people holds all the power and makes all decisions by themselves. Monarchies, dictatorships and

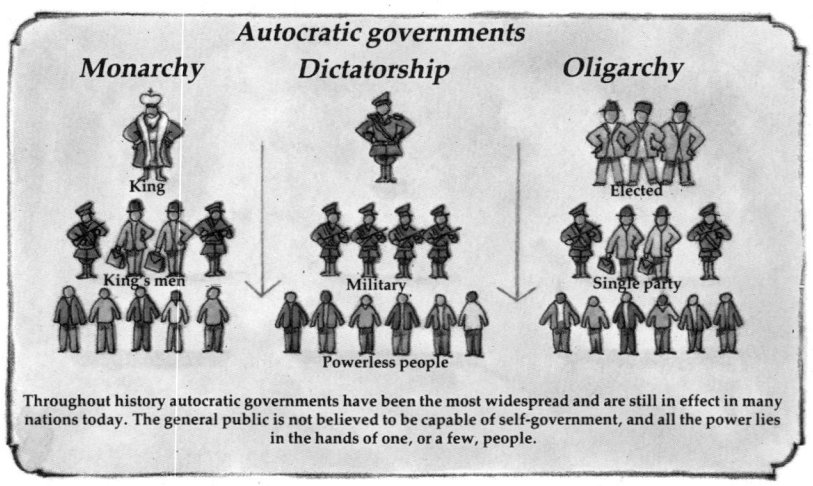

Throughout history autocratic governments have been the most widespread and are still in effect in many nations today. The general public is not believed to be capable of self-government, and all the power lies in the hands of one, or a few, people.

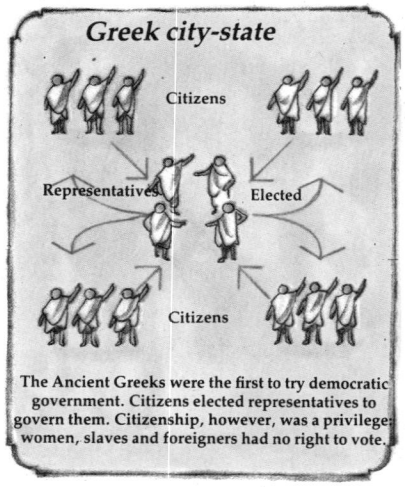

The Ancient Greeks were the first to try democratic government. Citizens elected representatives to govern them. Citizenship, however, was a privilege: women, slaves and foreigners had no right to vote.

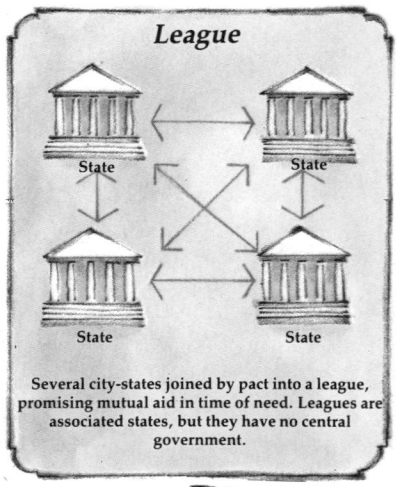

Several city-states joined by pact into a league, promising mutual aid in time of need. Leagues are associated states, but they have no central government.

Many nations today are made up of separate states that have united together as one nation. Switzerland is an example.

What governments do

The tasks a particular government has to do depend on what that government represents. Taking Italy as an example, municipal government is concerned with looking after the well-being of a community. It is responsible for the provision of water, for sanitation, and for local transportation and schools. Roads, which serve a number of communities, fall under the administration of a provincial or regional government. Central or state government deals with matters on a national level; defense, foreign affairs, and the printing of money, for example.

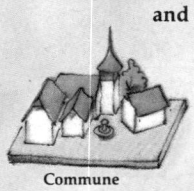

empires fall into this category.

The other type of government, more egalitarian, spreads the power by giving a share of it directly to the people governed. In history the first such governments were the Greek city-states. We call such governments democracies, from the Greek words *demos*, "people" and *kratos*, "power." A republic means the same thing, but comes from the Latin words *res publica*, or "public thing."

Most democracies were created in this century. However, in many places only the name is adopted, mock elections and single-party representation belying a government where only a few men really hold the reins.

Governments exist on every level: tribe or clan; municipal governments; cantonal or regional governments; and nations.

Nations are large groups of people who have a common bond: through geography, language, religion, an idea or common interest. Sometimes nations bond together in federations to cooperate within particular fields, such as trade or defense.

Government is not an end in itself. It acts as a service to its citizens. It provides protection, agrees to a common law and administers justice. It also carries out projects for the public good, such as building roads, schools, and hospitals. Government is a tremendous convenience to civilization . . . but it can also be a curse.

Fear and Aggression

We all get angry. Nearly every day there is some little thing that annoys us. If pushed too far, we feel like hitting or breaking something, or letting off a lot of noise. Usually, when our fury has calmed, we can't understand what we got all worked up about – our anger seems so silly! Have you ever wondered why we get angry at all, and why we get aggressive?

We usually get angry because something, or someone, gets in the way of our plans, or steps on our ideas. We make ourselves angry because we have our *own* idea of how things *should* be, which conflicts with the way things *are*. We are all self-centered. We all have an ego, a preconceived idea of ourselves; our ego gets stepped on, and we get angry. Anger is man-made.

People let off their anger with aggression. If you're insulted, you bark back; if you're hit, you strike back. You defend yourself. Some people are always aggressive. They bully, tease, steal or vandalize. Why? They have a hidden anger and let it out; or they have a hidden fear, some insecurity which aggressiveness covers up.

Many animals hunt for their food. They need space to hunt in. Such animals reserve territorial rights, a space to hunt that is off limits to others. If another animal infringes their right, then the defending animal will make an aggressive display to frighten off the intruder.

People, too, need food and space. We are no longer hunters, but throughout history nations have intruded on their neighbors in quest of more food, or wealth, or more land to extend their activity.

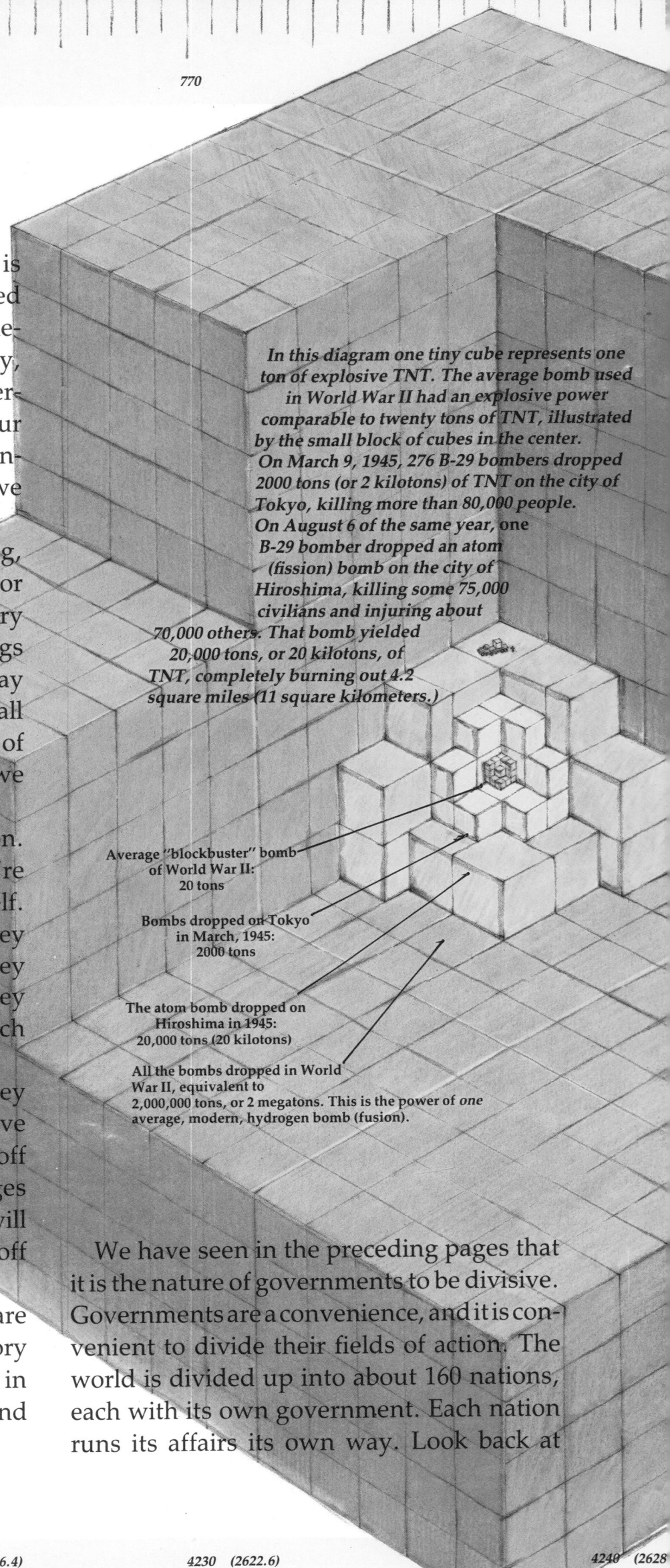

In this diagram one tiny cube represents one ton of explosive TNT. The average bomb used in World War II had an explosive power comparable to twenty tons of TNT, illustrated by the small block of cubes in the center. On March 9, 1945, 276 B-29 bombers dropped 2000 tons (or 2 kilotons) of TNT on the city of Tokyo, killing more than 80,000 people. On August 6 of the same year, one B-29 bomber dropped an atom (fission) bomb on the city of Hiroshima, killing some 75,000 civilians and injuring about 70,000 others. That bomb yielded 20,000 tons, or 20 kilotons, of TNT, completely burning out 4.2 square miles (11 square kilometers.)

We have seen in the preceding pages that it is the nature of governments to be divisive. Governments are a convenience, and it is convenient to divide their fields of action. The world is divided up into about 160 nations, each with its own government. Each nation runs its affairs its own way. Look back at

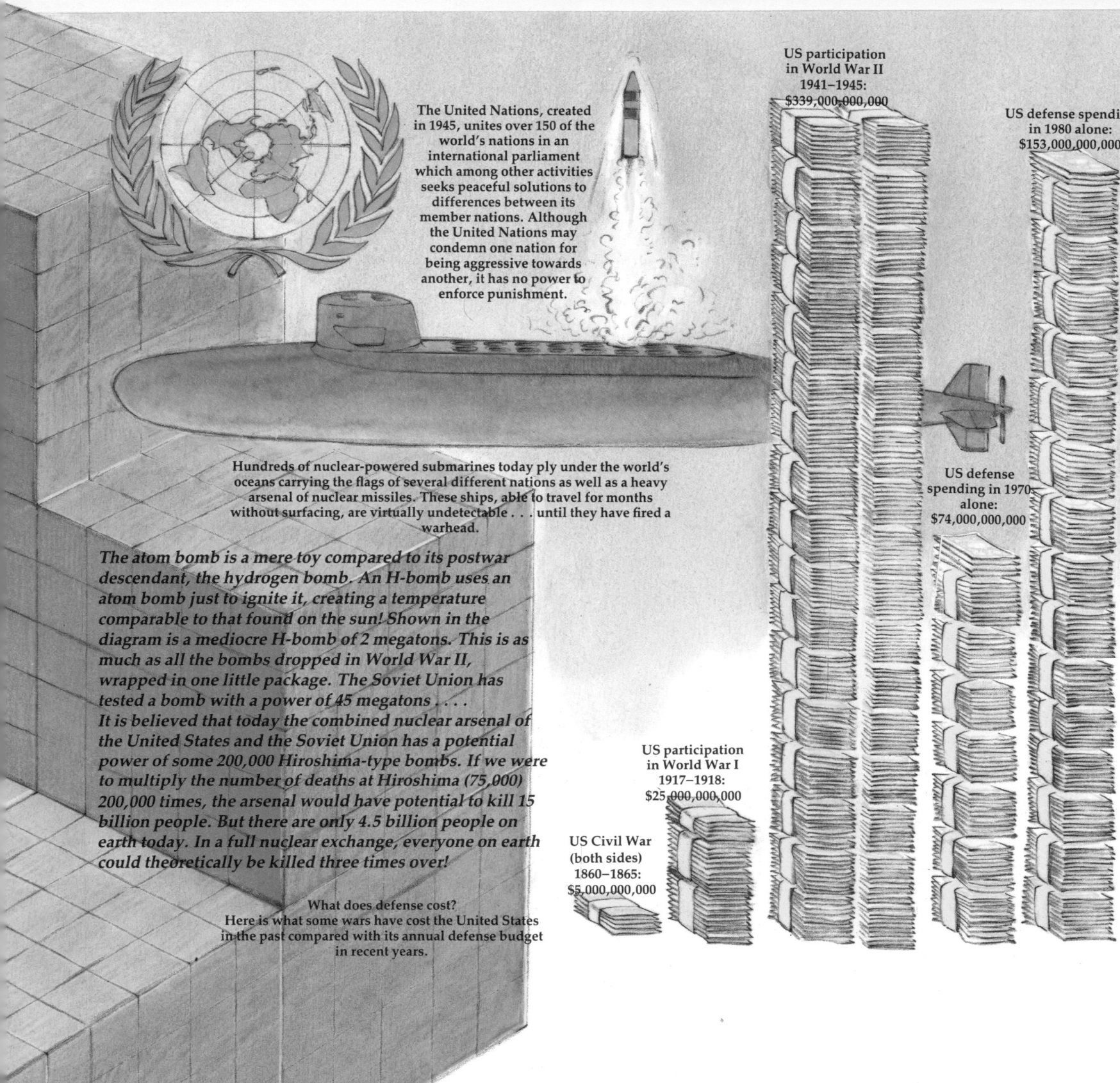

pages 38 and 39, the map of the earth. Can you find any nations? Can you see any political frontiers? Nature made none. Nations are man-made; they are ideas.

Nations are like individuals: after all, they are made up of people. The people of a nation share a common bond which makes up the self-centered ego of the nation itself, sometimes called the national interest. If that national ego gets upset by an insult, a provocation, or is aggressive due to internal problems, it can get angry just like a person. It strikes out and breaks things . . . it makes war.

Resources and Conservation

You have seen pictures of astronauts in space. The very first missions could be counted in hours, but now men can stay aloft for several weeks. There is no food, water or air in space, so, of course, astronauts have to carry with them everything needed to live. Room for all these supplies is necessarily limited, so when they run low the mission is over, and the astronauts head home to planet earth.

Seen from space, our earth looks like a spacecraft, too. It floats alone in the deep universe carrying all the necessities of life on its back. Room on it is limited, too. The biosphere, that thin skin on the earth's surface capable of supporting life, is a tiny, delicate place, with only so much food and space to go around. The biosphere is the earth's unique wealth. No other planet, as far as we know, has one. There is air to breathe, water to drink, plants and animals; mineral riches, metals and fuels are stored within its crust. These riches provided by nature – animal, vegetable and mineral – are called natural resources.

The resources on our "spacecraft" support a very demanding and voracious "astronaut" – man himself. Since he boarded the craft, man has been rearranging it to suit himself better, and he has crowded it with offspring at a frighteningly rapid rate. He's burning all his fuel and consuming his food, water and air as if at a gargantuan banquet! His mission in space won't last long . . . reserves aboard ship are limited!

Man is a burden on the earth because he is a waster. He takes from nature, but is often incapable of returning properly what he has

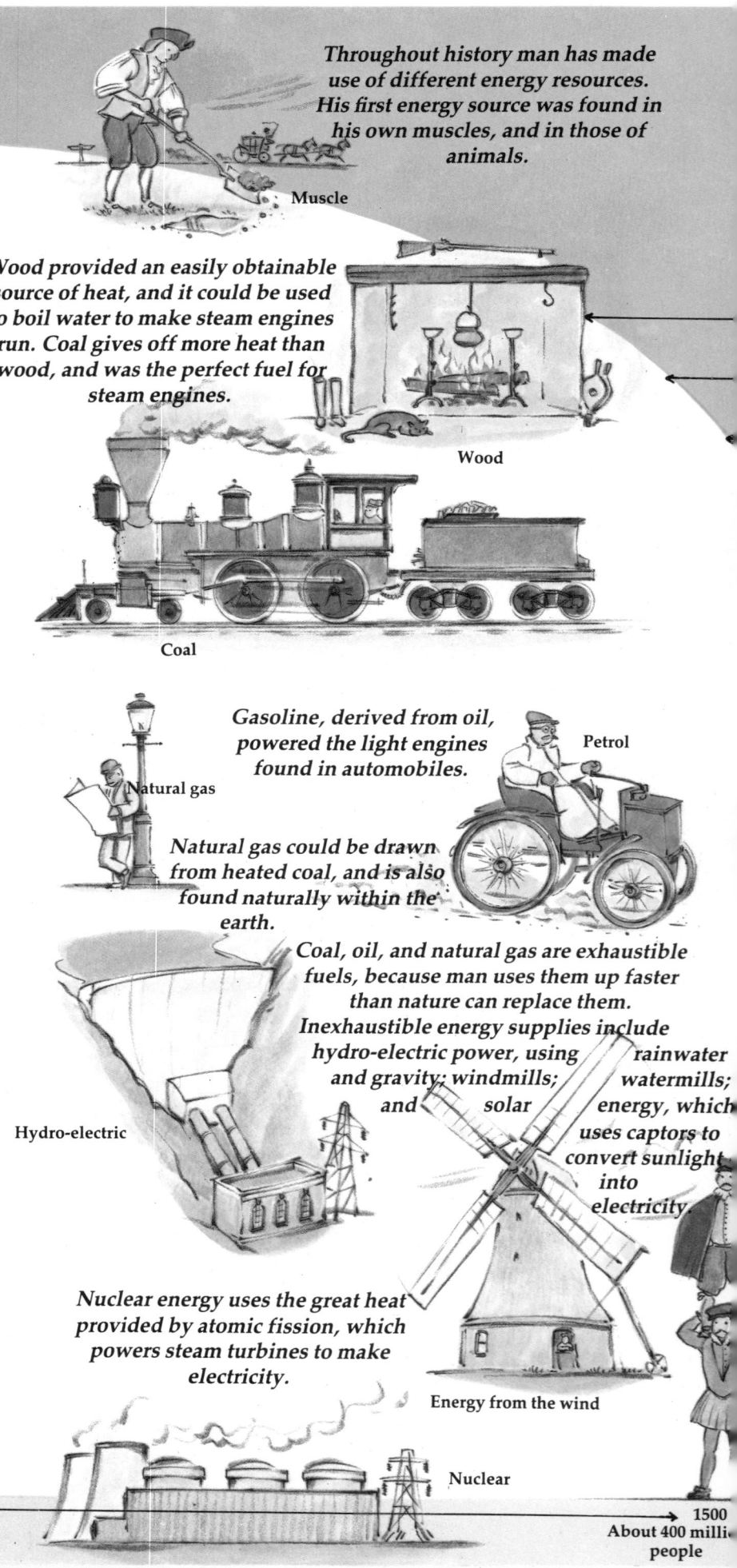

borrowed. Nature is a rejuvenating system, but it takes time. It takes thousands of years to make a seam of coal or oil; hundreds of years to make an inch of fertile soil; dozens of years to make a tall tree. But nature cannot rejuvenate if man takes away, or ruins, her building blocks.

Our spacecraft has been equipped for life, but *we* are the astronauts; each of us is responsible for our ship. If our supplies run out, there is no place to go to fetch more.

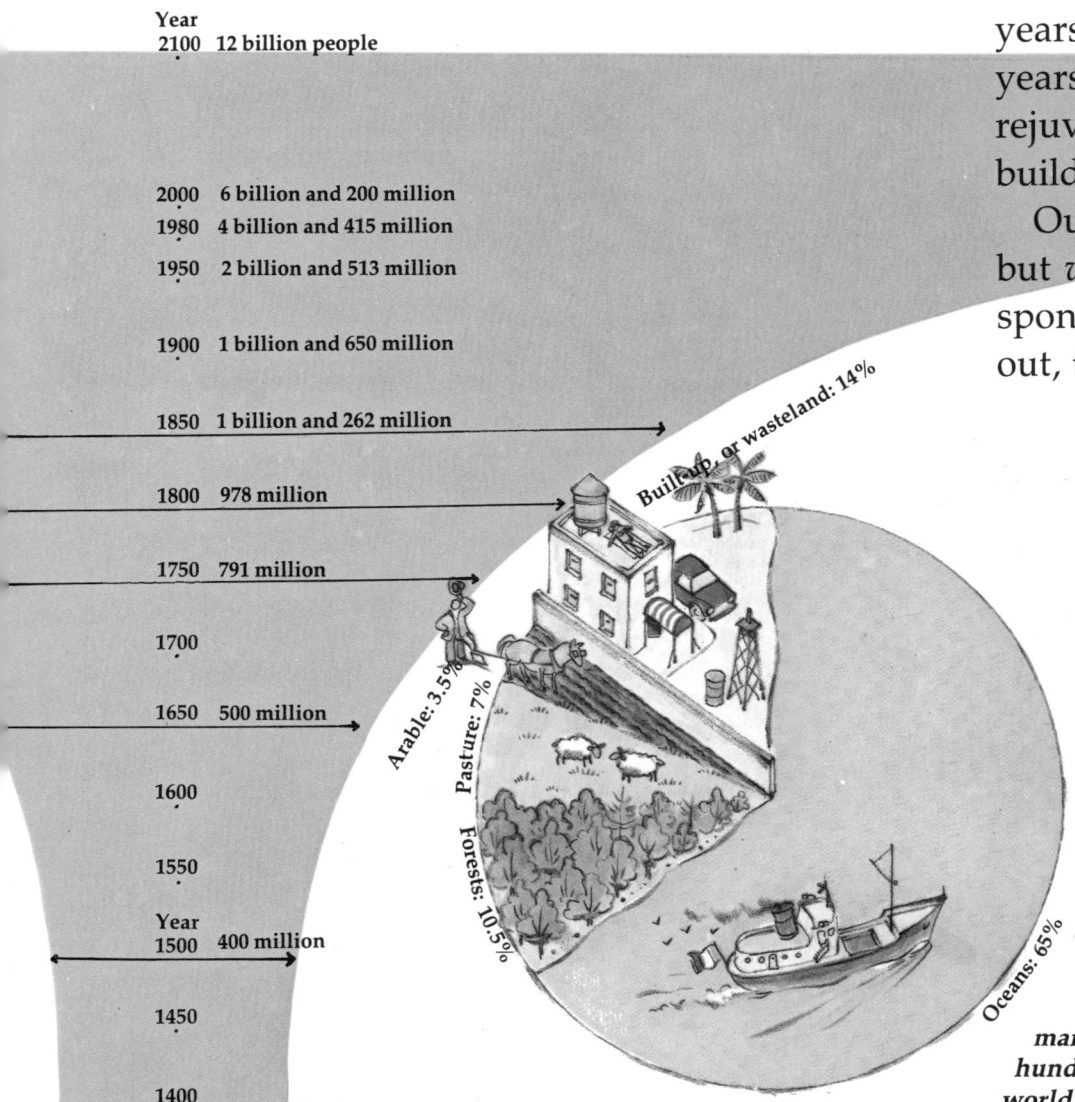

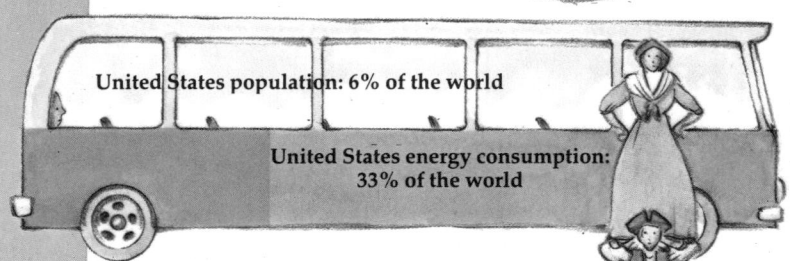

The industrialized nations of the world are the greatest users, per capita, of energy. Based on the statistics above, 6 Americans use up as much energy as 47 people elsewhere in the world.

The population explosion is illustrated by the graph above left. The great majority of births are in the developing countries of Asia.

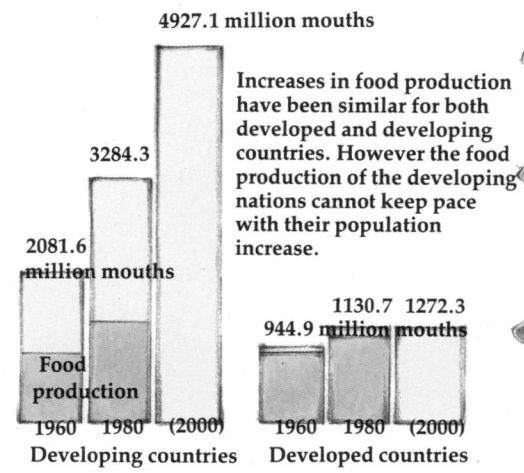

Increases in food production have been similar for both developed and developing countries. However the food production of the developing nations cannot keep pace with their population increase.

The earth is now supporting more than twice as many people than at the turn of the century. There may be twice as many more within the next one hundred years. 35% of the present world population is under the age of 15, while only 5.8% is over the age of 64. Millions more children will appear soon. Where will we house them; and will they find a job?

The earth's surface can be divided up roughly in the proportions shown above left. Compared with other land, very little is available for farming. Through irrigation and improved farming techniques food production can be increased, but there is nonetheless a limit to what the earth's surface can grow.

250 years to double — 1750 About 800 million people — 150 years to double — 1900 1 billion and 600 million people — 65 years to double — 1965 3 billion and 200 million people — ? 6 billion and 400 million

From Cotton to Computers

Where do you live, and what do you do? Chances are that if you don't live *in* a city, you probably live near one. Your parents may work in a factory or an office, but few of us work on a farm.

Eli Whitney's cotton gin of 1793 separated seeds from raw cotton much faster than by hand, thus accelerating cotton production.

The Industrial Revolution began in the textile industry in the late 1700s, when Great Britain was importing raw cotton from abroad, notably from India and the new American colonies. Cotton has to be cleaned, spun and woven to make cloth. The invention of machines which took over tasks formerly done by hand sped up the production of cotton and made it cheaper. Factories were built near fast rivers so that waterwheels could provide power for the new machines.

Industry was given a real boost with the invention of the steam engine, conceived by Thomas Newcomen and fully developed and marketed by James Watt. The steam engine provided power for almost any task. Steam locomotives and steamboats improved transportation and trade developed. Coal and iron ore were mined in greater quantities to supply fuel and metal to the new, industrialized society.

Most of us live in standardized houses, with prefabricated windows and doors. Much of our food is processed and packaged in factories, and so are our clothes. Most of our information about the world around us comes from the mass media: television, radio, newspapers and magazines. We can chat with friends over the phone, hundreds of miles away!

This is a very recent way of life. Until only 200 years ago the vast majority of people lived in the country and worked on a farm. Just about everything they might need would be made in their own village: from the timber posts to make a house to the wool from which the women made clothes. People would exchange news in the village square, or at the occasional country fair, and none of their friends were much farther away than shouting distance!

What happened in between? Back on page 62, we saw how man, given certain favorable conditions, discovered how to farm. Farming totally changed man's way of life, and with it he made an agricultural civilization: a diversity of jobs and trade, all thanks to the bounty of agriculture. It was an Agricultural Revolution!

Two centuries ago, starting in Britain, general conditions favored incredible new changes which revolutionized man's life just as agriculture had done centuries before. These changes are known as the Industrial Revolution: a way of life devoted to industry, and made possible by it. The great discovery of the Industrial Revolution was

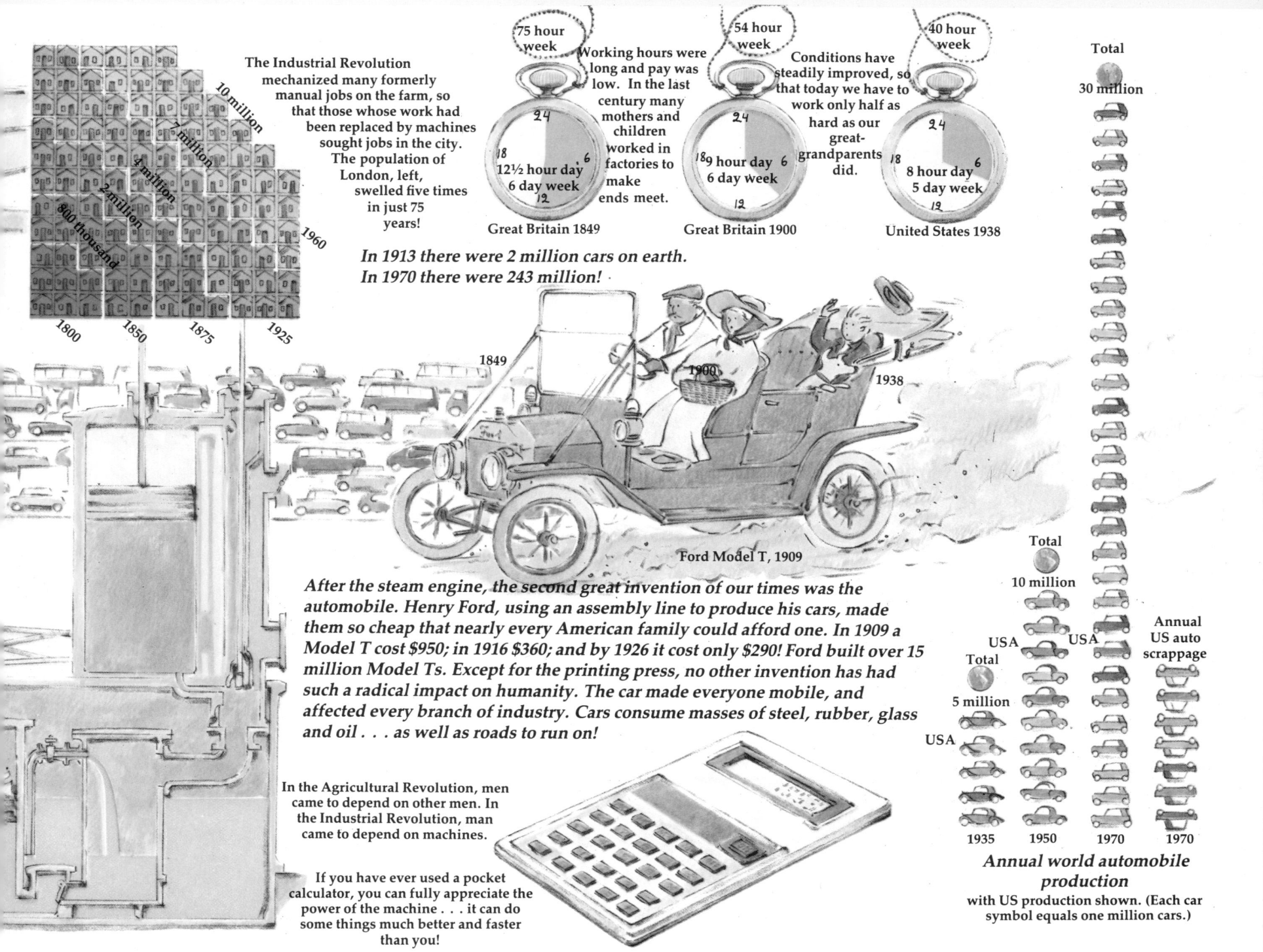

that machines could do work quicker, better and cheaper. Everything in people's lives, at some point, was handled by machines. Clothes were made by machines; wheat was harvested by machines; merchandise, and people themselves, were transported by mechanical machines. Man had made an industrial civilization.

We live in it still today. The superiority of a machine's work to a man's has meant that each time a new machine was invented, the man lost his job. This is still happening today.

Machines today not only do mechanical work faster, they can "think" faster too, retrieving information and performing complicated calculations in the blink of an eye. In the past, because machines increased production, lowered prices, and thus increased demand, people put out of work were eventually reintegrated into another job. Will this be the case in the future?

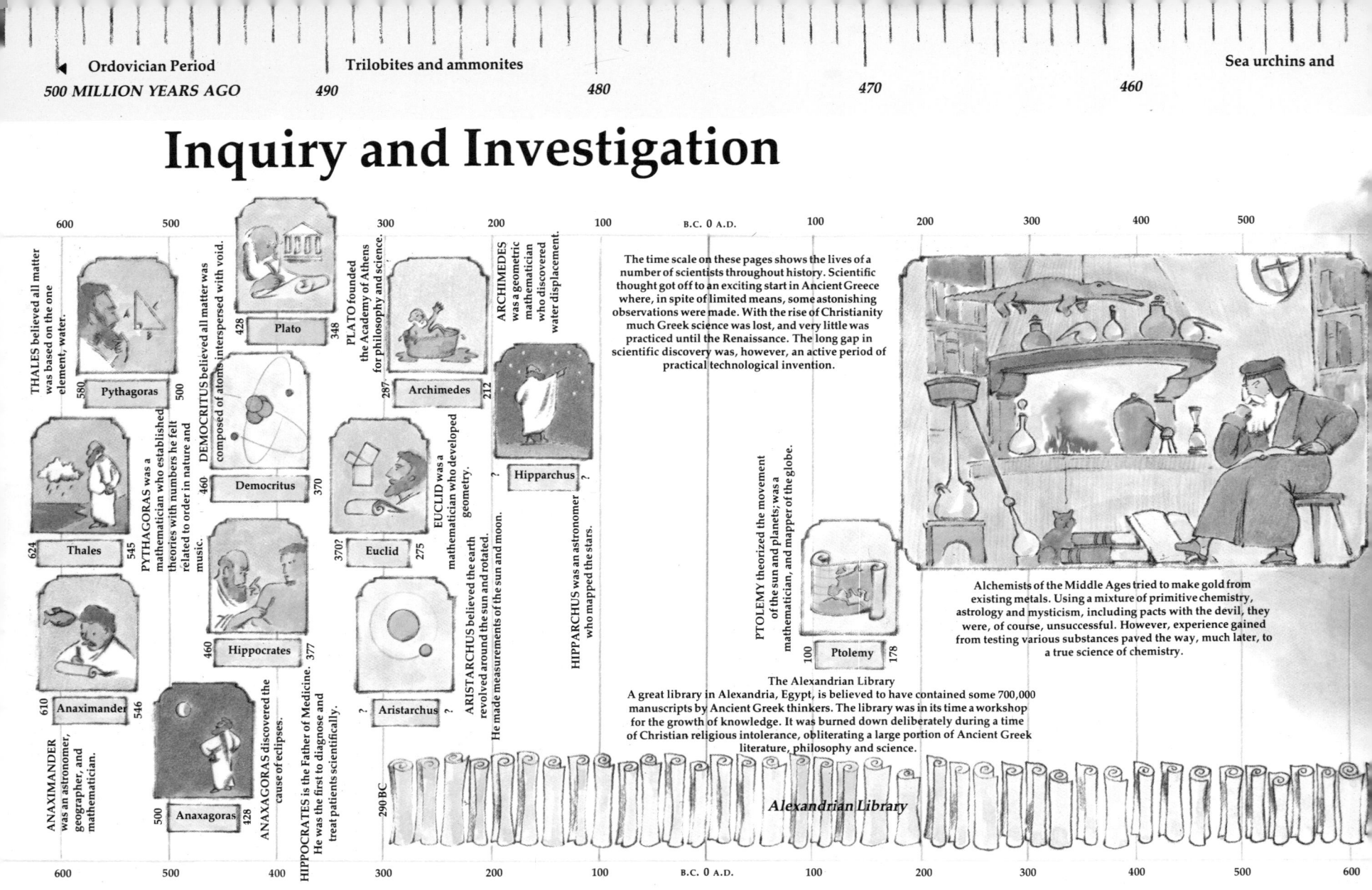

Everyone loves a detective story. We marvel how, presented with some mystery, the detective searches for clues, cross-examines his bits of information to test their validity, and then unravels the whole story to us . . . the mystery brilliantly solved!

The story of our earth is a great and complex one. It is over four and a half billion years old, and the universe far older still. But Homo sapiens arrived only some fifty thousand years ago. Why, he's missed the whole show!

It was never easy for man to understand the earth on which he lived. Some things worked regularly, like the seasons, and others were totally unpredictable, like a rainstorm or an earthquake, so that understanding the earth was impossibly complex. Throughout history man has sought to explain the seemingly dual order and disorder of nature as the work and whimsy of gods. The rising sun was the work of God, and so was a flood. Man lived by mysticism and superstition, but came no closer to finding concrete answers to the mysteries around him.

A few people, however, are born detectives. They need concrete answers, and use concrete means to find them. We call such detectives scientists. Fortunately, nature has

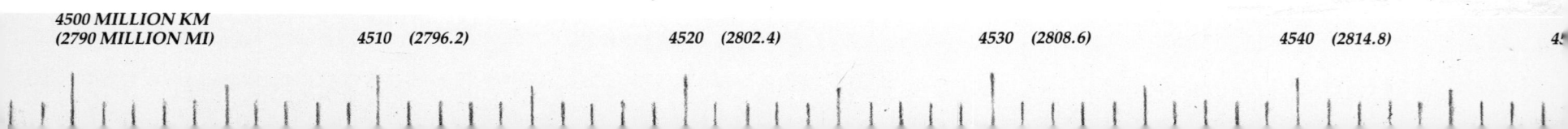

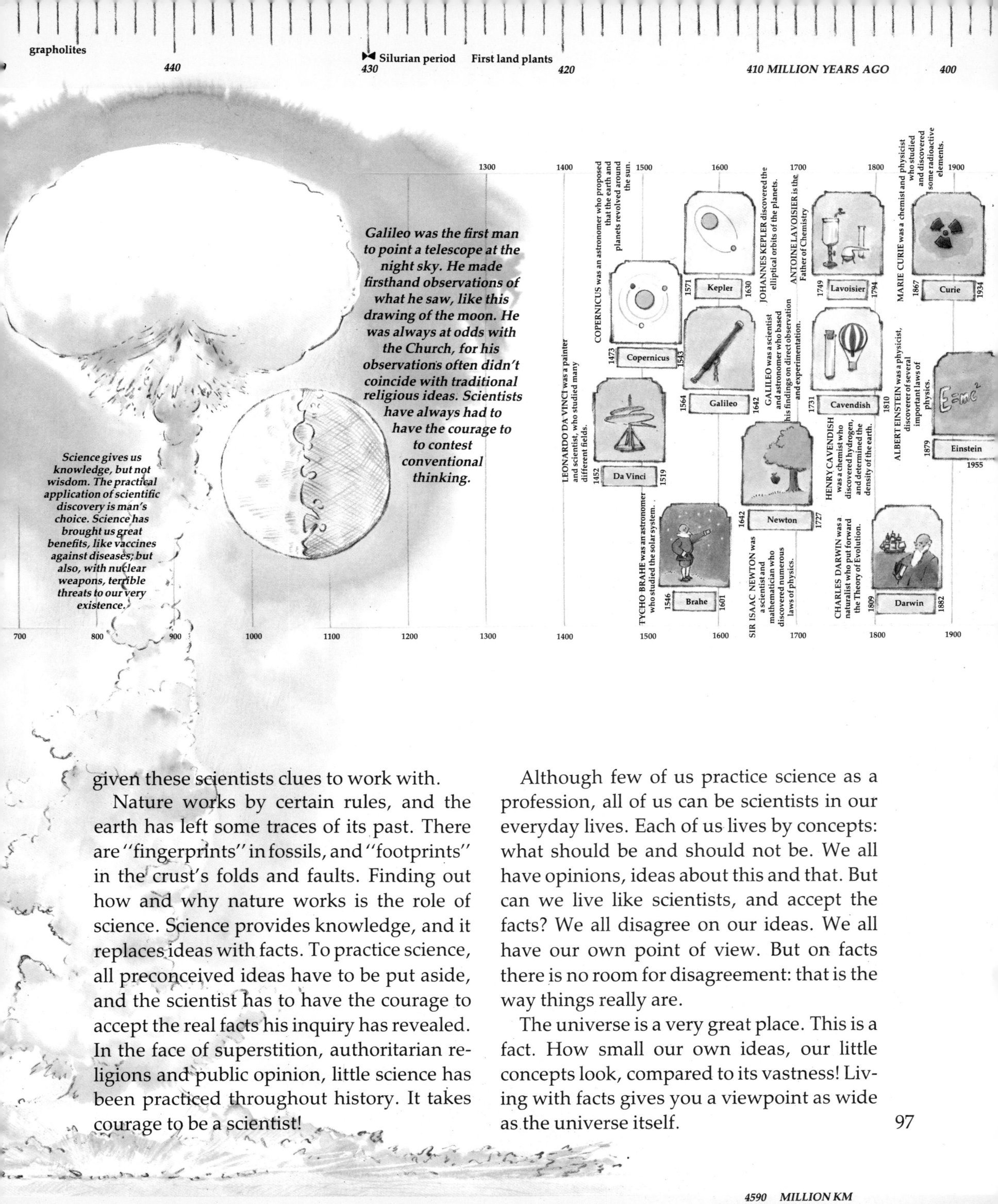

given these scientists clues to work with.

Nature works by certain rules, and the earth has left some traces of its past. There are "fingerprints" in fossils, and "footprints" in the crust's folds and faults. Finding out how and why nature works is the role of science. Science provides knowledge, and it replaces ideas with facts. To practice science, all preconceived ideas have to be put aside, and the scientist has to have the courage to accept the real facts his inquiry has revealed. In the face of superstition, authoritarian religions and public opinion, little science has been practiced throughout history. It takes courage to be a scientist!

Although few of us practice science as a profession, all of us can be scientists in our everyday lives. Each of us lives by concepts: what should be and should not be. We all have opinions, ideas about this and that. But can we live like scientists, and accept the facts? We all disagree on our ideas. We all have our own point of view. But on facts there is no room for disagreement: that is the way things really are.

The universe is a very great place. This is a fact. How small our own ideas, our little concepts look, compared to its vastness! Living with facts gives you a viewpoint as wide as the universe itself.

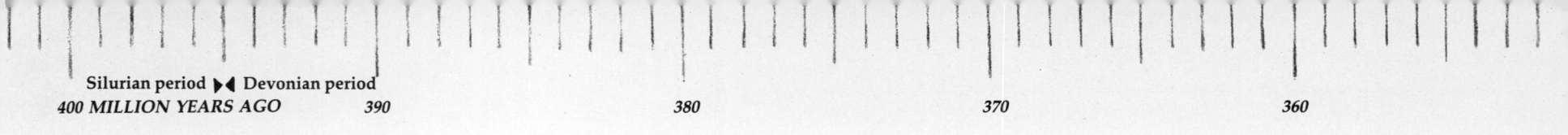

Conclusion

If you're looking for a conclusion, something to round off this book, you won't find it here!

In doing this book I have tried to touch on as many subjects as I could related to our earth – its place in the universe and its past – and about ourselves, its most recent and prolific inhabitants. Of course, the book didn't have the space, and I haven't the energy, to cover every subject. Having drawn my way all through these pages, I should be happy to have arrived at its completion, and write triumphantly "The End." No, arriving here at page 98, we're really only at "The Beginning"! For this is certainly not the best book you'll find about our planet. Indeed, most of the information written here has its source in other books. At your library you'll find shelves of books which deal with the same subject, or go into one field in much more depth. This book strives to be no more than an introduction to the earth, and a personal view about where we live.

If you have looked through all the pages, perhaps you have come upon something you didn't know before, or maybe you have some question. It might be that you don't agree with something I've written. If that's the case, I couldn't be happier! Now it's up to *you* to find out. If I have encouraged you to inquire about just one thing, then all my work has been worthwhile.

Our ancestors lived largely in ignorance of the world around them. In spite of that fact, man felt he held most of the answers. Today, with so much more information at hand, we're not quite so sure any more. In the past, our ancestors were quick to point out our various differences. Today, as communication mixes people from all over the world together, we are becoming aware of our similarities. As photographs of our planet come back to us from outer space, we are becoming aware of our uniqueness. As technology is robbing us of our jobs, and has the power to completely destroy us, we are becoming aware of our preciousness, and our frailty.

At some time or another we have all wished we lived at another time in history. In contrast with so many harsh realities of today, much of the past looks gentle and rosy. Sometimes we forget that for our ancestors, our past was their present, or their future. Doubtless, they found *their* times harsh, and had their own fears about the future.

For my part, I feel that *we* are the luckiest generation. No generation before us has had so much access to so much information, so many facts, so many ideas. No one has ever had such opportunity to learn, or to travel . . . and in some of the world's more open-minded regions, to voice one's views.

Looking and learning is a faculty of prime importance to man. Unlike other animals, he is born without instincts: everything has to be taught! That necessary faculty is also one of his most precious gifts, for there is no limit to what he can take in. His faculty allows him to reflect, and makes him open to change.

Of course, no one should expect a person to know everything; that has no point. But

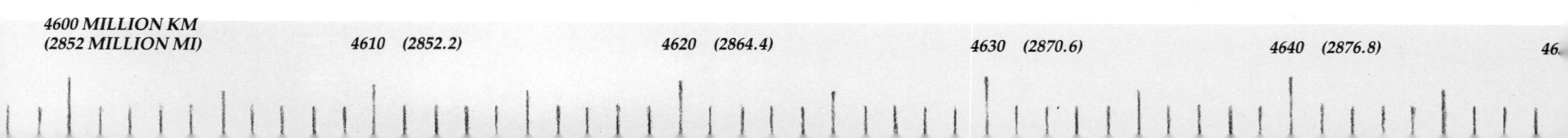

one thing you learn while you're learning, is that the more knowledge you eat up, the more there is to eat!

When I was a little boy, whenever my parents told me something, I would say, "I know, I know!" Today, I see that I really don't know all *that* much after all. Learning is belittling, but that's not so bad – for it leaves still more room for you to expand!

You pick up from here. Good luck to you!

Index

Abu Simbel, 68
Agriculture, 62–3, 65, 66, 69, 70, 72, 73, 74, 93, 105
Alchemy, 96
Alexandrian Library, 13
Algae, 46
Altamira, 57
Ammonites, 47, 48, 96
Amphibians, 47
Anaxagoras, 96
Anaximander, 97
Animals, 42, 46, 48, 50, 58
– communication of, 58, 59
– domestication of, 60–1, 62–3, 65, 66
– prehistoric, 48–9, 52–3
Anthropology, 56, 57, 78, 79
Anticline, 33
Apennines, 26
Apes, 47, 50, 51
Archimedes, 96
Architecture, 80, 82
Aristarchus, 96
Arms, modern, 90–1, 97
– prehistoric, *see* weapons, prehistoric
Arts, 80–1, 82–3, 86
Assembly line, 95
Asteroids, 24, 25
Asthenosphere, 31, 37
Astrolabe, 77
Astrology, 96
Astronauts, 92, 105
Atmosphere, 22, 27, 30, 31, 34, 40–1, 42, 43, 46
Atomic numbers, 18, 19
Atoms, 18–19; *see also* Nucleus of atom
Aurorae, 22
Australopithecus, 49, 51, 55
Aswan, 68
Aztecs, 76

Babylonia, 66, 68, 86
Bacteria, 43, 46
Ballet, 82
Barley, 63, 74
Barter, 70, 71
Bear, 52
Bees, 58, 59
Benz, Karl, 105
Beringia, 60

Bernini, 81
Big Bang theory, 16
Big Dipper, 20
Binaries, 20
Biosphere, 92
Bivalves, 47
Black holes, 20, 21
Blood groups, 79
Boar, 52
Bombs, 90–1, 105
Botticelli, Sandro, 80
Brachiopods, 47
Brahe, Tycho, 97
Brain, 53, 54–5
Bronze, 69
Bronze Age, 49, 51
Buddhism, 84, 85
Building materials, 64, 65, 69
Burial, of the dead, 51, 56, 68
– of bears' skulls, 56, 57, 61, 105

Cabot, John, 76
Caesar, Julius, 73
Calendar, 72–3
Calligraphy, 80
Cambrian system, 47, 48, 50, 94
Cao, Diogo, 76
Carbon dioxide, 40
Carboniferous system, 46, 47, 48 , 50, 99, 100
Carpets, 80
Carrack, 75
Cartier, Jacques, 76
Cave painting, 56, 57, 61, 66, 105
Cavendish, Henry, 97
Cells, 36, 44–5, 55
– membrane of, 44
Cenozoic era, 46, 47, 49, 51
Centipedes, 47
Centrifugal force, 28
Cereals, 62, 63, 74
Cerebellum, 55
Cerebrum, 55
Champollion, Jean-François, 67
Chemistry, 96
Cheng Chou, 69
Child labor, 95
China, 62, 69, 77
Chloroplast, 45
Christianity, 84, 85, 96
Christmas, 23
Chromosomes, 44
Chromosphere, 22
Church, the, 13, 80–1, 97
Cinema, 82, 83
Clay, *see* pottery
Clocks, 28–9, 72, 74, 105
Clouds, 35, 40
Club mosses, 46
Coal, 32, 92
Colonization, 76–7, 78–9
Columbus, Christopher, 12–13, 76, 77, 105
Comets, 24, 25
Compass, 75
Compounds (chemical), 18–19
Computer, 105
Conifers, 46
Constellations, 24, 72
Continental rise, 43
Continental shelf, 36–7, 43
Continental slope, 43
Continents, 9, 30–1, 36, 37, 42, 43, 46, 102
Copernicus, Nicholas, 13, 24, 97, 105
Copernican system, 13, 97, 105
Coral, 47
Corona, 22
Corpus callosum, 55
Cotton gin, 94
Craters, 26, 27
Cretaceous period, 46, 47, 48, 50, 103, 104
Cross staff, 77
Crust (earth's), 19, 31, 32–3, 36–7, 43, 49
Crustal plates, 32–3, 36–7, 43
Crustaceans, 47
Curie, Marie, 97
Currents, atmospheric, 41
– in the earth's mantle, 36, 37
– of the ocean, 43
Cycads, 46

Da Gama, Vasco, 76, 77
Dance, *see* ballet
Darby, Abraham, 105
Darwin, Charles, 46, 47, 50, 97, 105
Da Verrazzano, Giovanni, 76
Da Vinci, Leonardo, 97, 105
Days, 28–9, 73; *see also* time
Death, *see* burial
De Covilham, Pedro, 76
Democritus, 18, 96
Deuterium, 18
Devonian system, 46, 47, 48, 50, 98
Dias, Bartholomeu, 76
Dinosaurs, 15, 48, 104
Distance, 14–15
DNA, 44, 45
Dolphins, 59
Domestication, 61, 62, 65
Doppler Effect, 17

Earth, 15, 16, 23, 24, 27, 31–1, 32, 36–7, 38–9, 106
– age of, 14, 16, 96
– circumference of, 13
– composition of, 19
– distance from the moon of, 13
– distance from the sun of, 13
– formation of, 14, 19
– magnetic field of, 22, 31
– revolution of, 25, 28–9
– rotation of, 25, 26, 28–9, 30, 31, 40, 41, 43
– sphericalness of, 12, 13, 76
Earth-moon system, 26–7, 28–9
Earthquakes, 31, 33, 37, 96
Echinoderms, 47
Edison, Thomas, 83
Egyptians, 12, 23, 29, 67, 69, 71, 74, 80, 84, 105
Einstein, Albert, 97
Electrons, 18, 22
– orbit of, 19, 56
Elements, 18–19
Endoplasmic reticulum, 44
Energy, 92, 93
Eocene system, 48, 50
Epicycles, 12
Equinoxes, 23, 28–9
Eratosthenes, 13
Ericson, Leif, 104
Erosion, 32–3, 34–5, 48, 62
Euclid, 96
Euphrates, 62, 68
Evolution, 42, 45, 46–7, 48, 50, 51, 78, 97
Exchange (money), 71
Exosphere, 31, 40

Exploration (geographical), 65, 75, 76–7, 78, 79, 105

Faults, 33, 97
Ferns, 46
Fire, discovery of, 60, 104
Fishing, 43, 47, 58, 60, 61
Flatworms, 47
Folds (mountain), 33, 34
Ford, Henry, 95
Fossils, 32, 48, 49, 50, 51, 78, 97
Franklin, Benjamin, 105
Friction, 27, 40
Fuel, 92
Fungi, 46
Fusion, of metals, 65
– nuclear, 20, 22

Galaxies, 15, 16–17, 21
Galileo, 13, 97, 105
Gas, 32, 92
Geb (god), 12
Genes, 44, 45
Globe Theater, 83
Golgi, 44
Government, 88–9, 90, 91
Gravity, 21, 22, 25, 26, 28, 30, 35, 40
Greeks, 12, 13, 18, 24, 71, 74, 83, 88, 89, 96
Günz, 53
Gutenberg, Johannes, 82, 105

Hammurabi, 68, 86
Harappa, 69
Hecataeus, 12
Helium, 18, 20, 22, 23
Henry the Navigator, 76, 77, 105
Hinduism, 85
Hipparchus, 96
Hippocrates, 96
Hiroshima, 90
Holocene system, 49, 51, 105
Homo erectus, 49, 51, 55, 56, 60
Homo sapiens, 51, 53, 55, 57, 61, 78, 96
Horses, 74, 75
Horsetails, 46, 48
Horus (god), 84
Houses, 61, 65, 68
Hunting, 51, 60–1, 68
Huygens, Christiaan, 105
Hydrogen, 18, 20, 22–3, 30, 41, 43, 97
– nuclear fusion of, 20
– *see also* deuterium

Ice Ages, 34, 52, 60, 105
Insects, 47, 48
Instruments, musical, 83
– nautical, 77
Invertebrates, 47
Ionosphere, 40
Ions, 18
Iron Age, 49, 51, 105
Irrigation, 29, 64, 65, 68, 93
Islam, 80, 85
Isotopes, 18

Jellyfish, 47, 48
Judaism, 84
Jupiter, 12, 13, 21, 24, 25, 73, 105
Jurassic period, 46, 47, 48, 50, 102, 103

Karnak, 68
Kepler, Johannes, 25

Laccoliths, 32
Lampreys, 47
Languages, 58–9
Lava, 26, 32, 33, 37
Lavoisier, Antoine, 97
Lemur, 50
Lichens, 46
Light, 20–1
– of the stars, 15, 16
– of the sun, 30, 41
– speed of, 14, 15, 16
– waves, 14, 17, 85
Light-years, 15, 16, 17
Literature, 82
Lithosphere, 31
Lobes (of the brain), 55
Lothal, 69
Louis XIV of France, 23, 82
Luxor, 68
Lysosome, 49

Magellan, Ferdinand, 76, 105
Magma, 31, 32, 33, 37, 42, 43
Mammals, 47, 50
Mammoth, 53, 60
Man, 14, 15, 48, 50–1, 52–3, 54–5, 56–7, 60–1, 62–3, 78–9, 104, 105
– Cro-Magnon, 51, 53, 57, 61, 105
– Neanderthal, 51, 53, 61, 104
see also Homo erectus; Homo sapiens
Mantle (earth's), 31, 32, 33, 36, 37
Mars, 10, 12, 13, 24, 25, 73
Mayans, 76
Medulla, 55
Mercury, 7, 12, 13, 15, 23, 24, 25, 73
Mesolithic Age, 49, 51
Mesopause, 40
Mesopotamia, 62, 68, 69, 71
Mesosphere, 31, 40, 68
Mesozoic era, 46, 47, 48, 50
Metals, 19, 65, 70
Meteors and meteorites, 24, 26, 27, 40
Microbes, 47
Micro-organisms, 42
Middle Ages, 71, 74–5, 76, 81, 96
Milky Way galaxy, 15, 16, 17, 21, 22
Millet, 63
Millipedes, 47
Mindel, 53
Miocene system, 48, 50, 105
Missiles, 91
Mitochondrion, 44, 45
Mohenjo Daro, 69
Molecules, 18–19
– ionised, 40
Mollusks, 47
Money, 70, 71
Months, 28–9, 72, 73
see also time
Moon, 8–9, 12–13, 15, 25, 26–7, 28–9, 34, 72, 73, 97, 105, 106
– phases of, 27, 29, 73
Moore, Henry, 80
Moses, 86
Mosses, 46
Moldboard, 74
Mountains, 33, 34–5, 36
– erosion of, 34
– formation of, 32, 33, 37, 49
Music, 82, 83
Mutations, 45, 47

Natural selection, 45
Navigation, 61, 64, 65, 68, 74–5, 77
Neolithic Age, 49, 51, 57, 60, 61, 66, 68, 69, 70, 94, 105
Neptune, 15, 24, 25, 95
Neutrons, 18, 105
Newcomen, Thomas, 94
Newton, Isaac, 16, 97, 105
Nile, 29, 62, 68
Nitrogen, 40
Nuclear power, 90–1
Nucleus, of atom, 18, 22, 57
– of cell, 44–5, 55
Nut (god), 12

Observatory, 73
Oceans, 30–1, 36–7, 38–9, 42–3, 46, 49, 102, 103
Oil, 32, 92
Oligocene system, 48, 50, 105
Orbits, 24, 25, 28
Orchestra, 83
Ordovician system, 47, 48, 50, 96
Oxen, 65, 75
Oxygen, 19, 22, 30, 40, 42, 43
Ozone, 40

Painting, 80, 82
– cave, 56, 57, 61, 66, 105
Paleocene system, 48, 50, 104
Paleolithic Age, 49, 51, 56, 61, 64
Paleontology, 47, 48, 50
Paleozoic era, 46, 47, 48, 50
Pangea, 37, 102
Paper making, 82
Pasteur, Louis, 105
Peneplain, 34
Penicillin, 105
Periodic Table, 19
Permian system, 46, 47, 48, 50, 100
Phonograph, 83
Photography, 105
Photosynthesis, 22, 42, 43
Piccard, Jacques, 43
Pioneer, 10, 67
Pituitary gland, 55
Planets, 15, 24, 25
see also individual planets
Plato, 96
Pleistocene system, 49, 51, 105
Pliocene system, 49, 51, 105
Plowing, 65, 74, 104
Pluto, 15, 24, 25, 105
Poetry, 82
Pottery, 64, 65, 68, 69
Pre-Cambrian system, 14, 48, 50, 94
Primates, 50, 51, 104
Printing press, 82
Proconsul, 51
Proto-fish, 47
Proteins, 44
Protons, 18–19, 22
Ptolemy, 12, 96
Ptolemaic system, 12, 13, 25
Pyramids, 81
Pythagoras, 96

Quartz, 18
Quarternary period, 46, 47, 49, 51, 105

Ra (god), 23

Races, 78–9
Racism, 78
Radio source, 16–17
Radio transmission, 40, 105
Rays, of the sun, 22, 40, 42
– infrared, 40
– X, 105
Red Cross, 7
Red giant, 20–1, 23
Red shift, 16
Reformation, the, 105
Reindeer, 60
Relativity, theory of, 97, 105
Religion, 56, 57, 84–5, 86
Renaissance, the, 13, 96
Reptiles, 47
Revolution, Agricultural, 94, 95
– Copernican, 24
– Industrial, 94–5, 105
– of the planets, 25
Rice, 63
Ridges (ocean), 37, 38–9, 43
Riss, 53
Rocks, 32, 33, 34–5, 48
Rocky Belt, 25
Rolls-Royce, 81
Romans and Rome, 71, 73, 74, 80, 105
Rosetta Stone, 67
Rotation of crops, 74
Rudders, 75

Salt, 32, 43
Satellites, 24, 25, 26, 27, 105
Saturn, 12, 13, 24, 25, 34, 73
Scorpions, 47
Sculpture, 80, 82
Sea farming, 43
Sea squirts, 47
Seasons, 23, 28, 34, 96; *see also* time
Seismic waves, 31
Senses, 54, 55, 58
Shaduf, 64
Shakespeare, William, 83
Shamash (god), 86
Ships, *see* navigation
Shu (god), 12
Silks, 75, 77
Silurian system, 47, 48, 50, 97, 98

Slavery, 71, 74
Smilodon, 53
Solar system, 13, 15, 22–3, 24–5, 26, 27, 30, 105
Solstices, 13, 23, 29, 73
Sonar, 59
Sound, 14
Sound recording, 83
Sound waves, 14
Space probe, 67
Spectrum and spectroscope, 16
Speed limits, 14
Sphere (navigational), 76
Spices, 75, 77
Spiders, 47
Sponges, 47
Squids, 47
Stars, 15, 16–17, 19, 20–1, 22, 23, 24
Steam engines, 92, 94, 105
Stonehenge, 73
Stratopause, 40
Stratosphere, 31, 40
Sun, 3, 6, 12–13, 15, 16, 19, 20–1, 22–3, 24, 25, 28, 29, 30, 35, 40, 72, 73, 106
– god, 23
Sunspots, 23
Supernova, 20, 21
Susa, 68
Syene, 13
Syncline, 33

Tarsier, 50
Telegraph, 105
Telescopes, 13, 15, 16, 17, 24, 97, 105
Tertiary period, 46, 47, 48, 50, 104, 105
Thalamus, 55
Thales, 96
Theater, 82, 83
Thebes, 68
Thermopause, 40
Thermosphere, 31
Tides, 26–7, 28
Tigris, 62, 68
Time, 14–15, 16, 26, 27, 28–9, 72–3
Time scale, 14
Tools, 51, 52–3, 57, 60, 61, 62, 64–5, 80, 104, 105
Tordesillas, Treaty of, 76
Trade, 66, 67, 69, 77, 94
Tree shrew, 50
Trench (ocean), 32, 33, 37, 43
Triassic period, 46, 47, 48, 50, 101, 102
Trilobites, 47, 48, 96

Tropopause, 40
Troposphere, 31

United Nations, 7, 59, 91
Universe, 12, 16, 17, 20–1
Ur, 68, 69
Uranus, 24, 25, 63
Uruk, 68

Vaccination, 97, 105
Vacuole, 45
Van Allen Belt, 22
Variables, 20
Venus (planet), 8, 12, 13, 15, 23, 24, 25, 73
– (goddess), 57
Volcanoes, 31, 32–3, 37, 96

Wages, 95
Walsh, Donald, 43
Water, 23, 27, 30, 34, 35, 43
– cycle, 35, 40, 62
see also erosion
Watermills, 74, 75
Watt, James, 94, 105
Waves, 35, 43
– light, 14, 17, 85
– radio, 16, 40
– seismic, 31
– sound, 14
Weapons, prehistoric, 52, 53, 54, 55
Weaving, 64
Whale, 59
Wheat, 63, 74
Wheel, hydraulic, 74
– invention of, 64, 65, 69
White dwarf, 20, 21, 23
Whitney, Eli, 94
Wind, 41, 43
– solar, 22
Windmills, 74, 75
Wool, 61
Woolly rhino, 53
Working conditions, 95
Worms, 47
Wright, Orville and Wilbur, 105
Writing, 65, 66–7, 68, 82
Würm, 53

Yang Shao, 69
Year, 14, 15, 28, 29, 72, 73
Yellow River, 62, 63, 69
Yin-Yang, 84

Zodiac, 72

Bibliography

If you want to find out more about something you have read in this book, here are some others which might help you.

Britannica Junior, *edited by staff of Encyclopedia Britannica, Chicago, 1980.*
The World Book Encyclopedia, *World Book-Childcraft International, Chicago, 1980.*
The Illustrated Encyclopedia of Astronomy and Space, *edited by Ian Ridpath, T. Y. Crowell, New York, 1976.*
The Discoverers – An Encyclopedia of Explorers and Exploration, *edited by Helen Delper, McGraw-Hill, New York, 1980.*
The Times Atlas of the World, *Times Books, New York, 1980.*
The Times Atlas of World History, *Hammond Inc., Maplewood, N.J.,1979.*
Cosmos, *by Carl Sagan, Random House, New York, 1980.*
Life on Earth, *by David Attenborough, Little Brown, Boston, 1981.*
The Awakening of Intelligence, *by J. Krishnamurti, Avon Books, New York, 1976.*

Formation of Rocky Mountains (USA)

Extinction of dinosaurs

Primates

The Last Million Years

We have finally reached the end of our time scale.

The pages of this book have covered a period of 5,000 million years. The scale is marked in notches, each of which represents one million years. The five thousandth notch represents the last million years.

It is no more than one shred of the ribbon that has unwound in the course of the earth's history but it is quite different from all the others . . . look how many things it conceals.

1 million years

The last notch in the time scale running right through this book represents the last million years of time on earth. That notch, shown here, may not look like much, but a great many things are contained in it. If we cut along the base and magnified it many times, we would have a more detailed time ribbon, shown to the left. There is not much activity most of the way along it, until about 50,000 years ago, when suddenly there is quite a lot of activity on our planet: men at work! When we get just within 1000 years from today, the planet is so bristling with activity, that we have to magnify our ribbon still further, seen below. Our century, the very last minute shred on the scale, can be seen only through the magnifying glass. Look how much has happened in such a short time! We live a unique and exciting moment in the life of our earth!

1 million years ago

900,000

800,000

700,000

600,000

500,000 Discovery of fire

400,000

300,000

200,000 Flake tools

150,000 years ago

100,000 years ago

Neanderthal man

1000 years ago

Leif Ericson visits North America

900 years ago

Improved plow with moldboard

800 years ago

High Gothic cathedrals

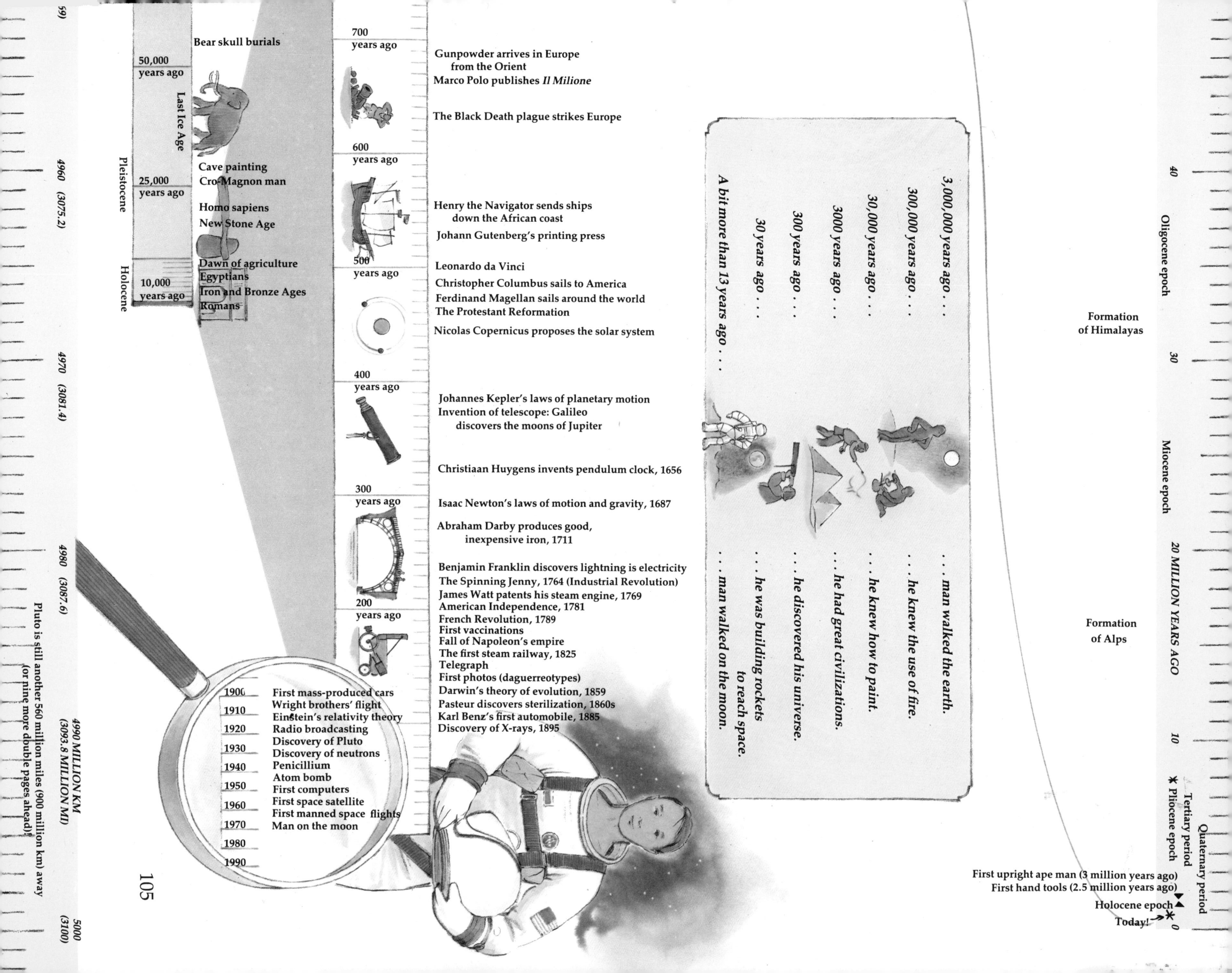
Pleistocene
Holocene
Last Ice Age
50,000 years ago
25,000 years ago
10,000 years ago
Bear skull burials
Cave painting
Cro-Magnon man
Homo sapiens
New Stone Age
Dawn of agriculture
Egyptians
Iron and Bronze Ages
Romans
700 years ago
600 years ago
500 years ago
400 years ago
300 years ago
200 years ago
Gunpowder arrives in Europe from the Orient
Marco Polo publishes Il Milione
The Black Death plague strikes Europe
Henry the Navigator sends ships down the African coast
Johann Gutenberg's printing press
Leonardo da Vinci
Christopher Columbus sails to America
Ferdinand Magellan sails around the world
The Protestant Reformation
Nicolas Copernicus proposes the solar system
Johannes Kepler's laws of planetary motion
Invention of telescope: Galileo discovers the moons of Jupiter
Christiaan Huygens invents pendulum clock, 1656
Isaac Newton's laws of motion and gravity, 1687
Abraham Darby produces good, inexpensive iron, 1711
Benjamin Franklin discovers lightning is electricity
The Spinning Jenny, 1764 (Industrial Revolution)
James Watt patents his steam engine, 1769
American Independence, 1781
French Revolution, 1789
First vaccinations
Fall of Napoleon's empire
The first steam railway, 1825
Telegraph
First photos (daguerreotypes)
Darwin's theory of evolution, 1859
Pasteur discovers sterilization, 1860s
Karl Benz's first automobile, 1885
Discovery of X-rays, 1895
1900 First mass-produced cars
1910 Wright brothers' flight
1920 Einstein's relativity theory
1930 Radio broadcasting
1940 Discovery of Pluto
1950 Discovery of neutrons
1960 Penicillium
1970 Atom bomb
1980 First computers
1990 First space satellite
First manned space flights
Man on the moon
3,000,000 years ago . . .
. . . man walked the earth.
300,000 years ago . . .
. . . he knew the use of fire.
30,000 years ago . . .
. . . he knew how to paint.
3000 years ago . . .
. . . he had great civilizations.
300 years ago . . .
. . . he discovered his universe.
30 years ago . . .
. . . he was building rockets to reach space.
A bit more than 13 years ago . . .
. . . man walked on the moon.
Formation of Himalayas
Formation of Alps
First upright ape man (3 million years ago)
First hand tools (2.5 million years ago)
Holocene epoch
Today!
Quaternary period
Tertiary period
Pliocene epoch
Miocene epoch
Oligocene epoch
40
30
20 MILLION YEARS AGO
10
0
4960 (3075.2)
4970 (3081.4)
4980 (3087.6)
4990 MILLION KM
(3093.8 MILLION MI)
5000
(3100)
Pluto is still another 560 million miles (900 million km) away
(or nine more double pages ahead)!

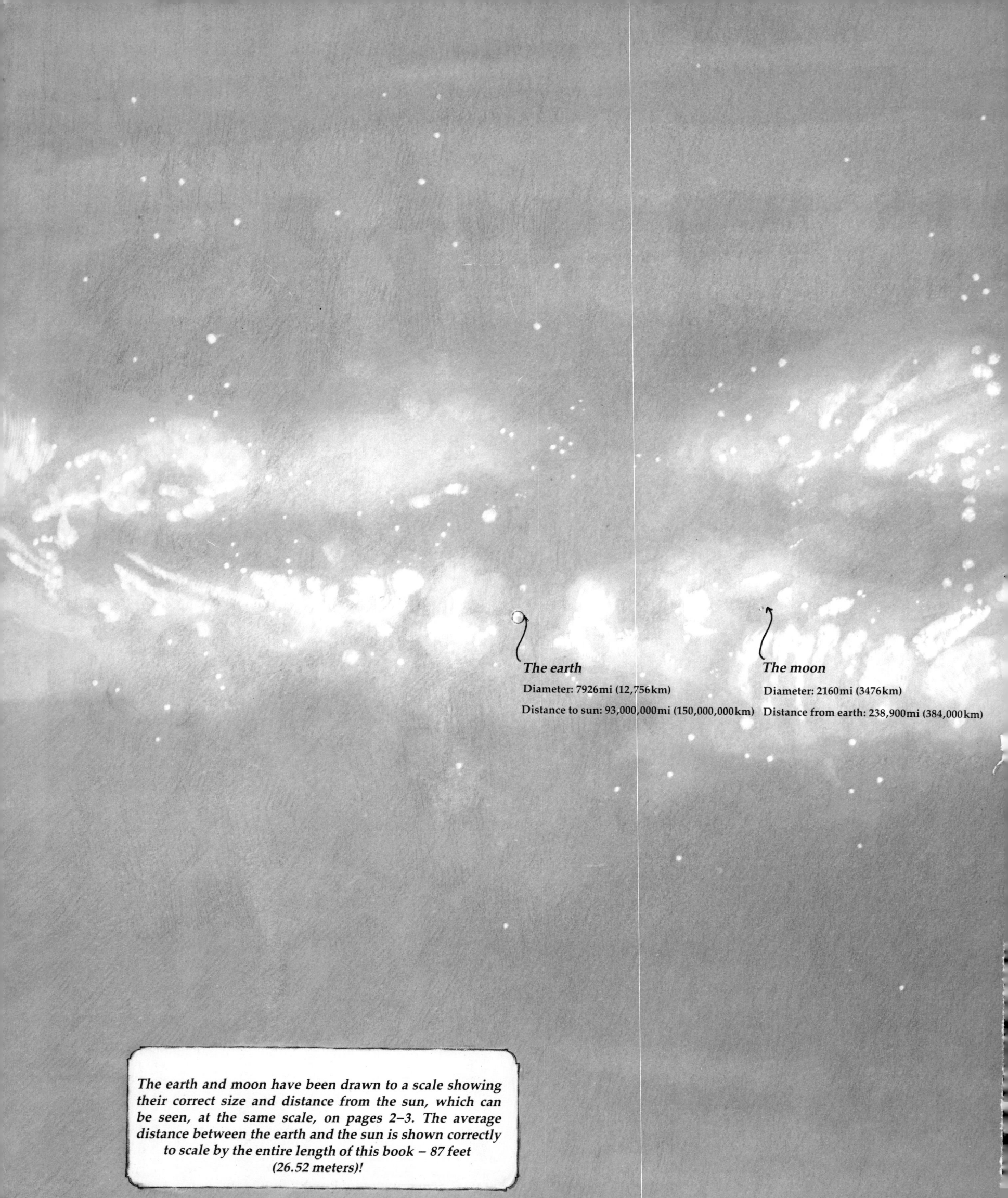

The earth and moon have been drawn to a scale showing their correct size and distance from the sun, which can be seen, at the same scale, on pages 2–3. The average distance between the earth and the sun is shown correctly to scale by the entire length of this book – 87 feet (26.52 meters)!

The sun has been drawn here to the same scale as the earth on the last page. The average distance between the two, some 93,000,000 miles (150,000,000 km), is shown, also to scale, by the entire length of the pages of this book, edge to edge: 87 (26.52 m) feet long!

The sun

Diameter: 865,400 mi (1,392,000 km) Distance from earth: 92,960,000 mi (149,596,000 km)